Denise Pirrotti Hummel, J.D.

SPEAK MILK

BECOMING A GLOBAL CITIZEN

DRINK WINE

FIRST EDITION

Hummel, Denise Pirrotti
    Speak Milk, Drink Wine: Becoming a Global Citizen—1st. ed

    ISBN: 978-1463647346

ATTENTION CORPORATIONS, UNIVERSITIES, COLLEGES, AND PROFESSIONAL ORGANIZATIONS: Quantity discounts are available on bulk purchases of this book for educational, gift purposes. Please contact Denise Pirrotti Hummel, CEO, Universal Consensus, 2890 Corte Morera, Carlsbad, California 92009, U.S.A. or by email at denise@universalconsensus.com for more information.

PRAISE FOR SPEAK MILK. DRINK WINE.

"With more than 10 million frequent flyer miles on one airline alone, I know a little about travel. Denise Pirrotti Hummel's SPEAK MILK. DRINK WINE. has taught this die-hard traveler much about making dreams reality. It's an inspiring tale and a joy to read!"

-Marshall Goldsmith, million-selling author of the New York Times bestsellers, "MOJO" and "What Got You Here Won't Get You There"

"Laughs, love, and learning make this a life-changing read."

-Lyn Middlehurst, Editor-in-Chief, Gallivanters Guide

"We call Denise Pirrotti Hummel a 'recovering attorney.' We were impressed by her savvy, her passion, her humor and her willingness to reinvent herself. She has masterfully set forth in SPEAK MILK. DRINK WINE. the courage to leave behind a life that most would describe as the quintessential American dream, for one that has the potential for true, lasting happiness."

-Michelle Snaddon, Editor-In-Chief, Just the Planet, The Online Luxury Travel Magazine

"People talk about the movement of Peace Through Tourism, but the reality is that unless more people are willing to raise their children in an inclusive environment that is based on the experience of transcending cultures, belief systems, languages, and traditions for more than a day here and there, or even a two-week vacation, we'll never truly understand others, let alone ourselves. Denise Pirrotti Hummel, in SPEAK MILK. DRINK WINE. makes it clear that it is not enough to just travel. One must move about in the world conscious of the opportunity to promote understanding and tolerance."

-John Graff, J.D., Chairman, George Washington University Tourism and Hospitality Management Advisory Council; Member, Board of Directors, International Institute of Peace Through Tourism

"Denise Pirrotti Hummel did what we all long to do, take the leap and head to the great unknown. We never realize how the other half lives until we live it ourselves, and Denise and her family did just that. I couldn't get enough of their encounters, whether it was at the new schools, finding a doctor, celebrating and sharing new holidays, sports and games. Denise writes with wit and knowledge, bridging two cultures in her picturesque tale."
-R.J. Marx, Editor-in-Chief, The Record-Review

"As someone who has had about 300,000 frequent flyer miles in my account, at times I feel like a pretty experienced traveler. Denise's book blows me away with the possibilities that are out there that I've never even heard of much less considered. It's dream candy for anyone who travels."
-Kermit Hummel, Editorial Director, Countryman Press

"Fantasy, arm-chair travel and dreams coincide with reality in this account where taking a risk pays off in ways that money can't measure."
-Jennifer Stahlkrantz, Contributing Editor, Bedford Magazine

"We Americans have spent the past century doing everything within our power to speed up the process of inhaling food at our desks, in our car, and standing at the kitchen counter. The Italians have spent centuries cultivating the art of preparing whole, fresh, unadulterated food for the sole pleasure of consuming it in as long and drawn out a manner as possible. In SPEAK MILK. DRINK WINE., Denise Pirrotti Hummel has captured the essence of why the Italians have raised generations of fit, happy people, while we're running on a perpetual treadmill that burns calories, without ever getting us any closer to a fulfilling life."
-Dr. Susan P. Rubin, HHC, Founder, Better School Food; Founding Member, SLOW FOOD, Westchester County, New York Convivia

"While it may be tempting to categorize SPEAK MILK. DRINK WINE. as the family version of 'Under the Tuscan Sun', the reality is that Italy is merely a succulent backdrop to a memoir that challenges all of us to be who we are meant to be, to shed our fears, and to seize life now and squeeze every drop of *vino bianco* out of it."

-Markus Odermatt, General Manager, Grand Hotel at Villa Feltrinelli, Lake Garda, Italy

"There are clear scientific reasons for rejecting the label ADD when it comes to our children, but if you don't believe them, remove your kids from planet America for awhile and drop them onto another cultural planet, as Denise Pirrotti Hummel has set forth in SPEAK MILK. DRINK WINE. and you may find that the conglomeration of symptoms for which you considered medicating your child, suddenly disappear."

- Michael B. Finkelstein, MD., F.A.C.P, A.B.H.M., Former Chief of Medicine of Westchester County Medical Center, and Founder, Sun Raven New York

To my children, Matthew and Alex,
for reminding me
that I am always home,
if you are.

and *alla famiglia* Stragapede
and *la famiglia* Soru
without whom
this journey may never
have been made.

This story depicts actual events,
however the names of certain characters
have been changed to protect the privacy
of some individuals.

Contents

AUTHOR'S NOTE

A Few Things That Matter

Life is sacred; live on purpose.
Be intoxicated with this world and
astonished with the world you imagine.
Growth is a journey ...
Success doesn't require arrival.
Want what you already hold.
Give no place to public opinion.
Delight in your friends.
Practice the art of doing nothing.
Embrace moments of grace.
Give the child in you a wide sky.
Understand that laughter is prayer.

– Anonymous

I am a recovering attorney and the CEO and Founder of Universal Consensus, a cross-cultural consulting and training firm. My journey to "recovery" and the development of a business that will sustain my professional and personal growth for a lifetime began with a one-year sojourn outside my own culture and comfort zone and into one that delighted and intrigued me.

I have noticed, among some of my dearest friends and colleagues, a correlation between open-mindedness and tolerance of others and the extent to which they have travelled to other countries. My ability to appreciate life has grown with the understanding that others are leading lives so different from my own and yet in the end, as my now 13-year-old son told me recently, we are all "just the same."

By telling this story, I am not trying to compare our journey with the many individuals who have lived, worked and outstretched their arms to the peoples of distant lands where the politics, culture, standard of living, and way of life is so different as to make their experience herculean. There are those who have worked with the Peace Corps, Doctors Without Borders and other organizations, or indeed on their own, selflessly giving of themselves to bring peace and prosperity to others.

Italy is a Western culture and relatively prosperous and "modern" compared to the rest of the world. Their language, traditions, and way of living are diverse from Americans, yet in many ways similar to our country's European roots. What I do want to humbly suggest is that in following our need to experience another culture, by putting ourselves forward as Americans who appreciate and respect other ways of doing things, by absorbing all the good that Italy had to offer us, we were part of a movement that I like to call Peace Through Tourism, Connectivity Through Understanding, or Tolerance Through Immersion.

We were lucky enough to own a home that we could rent out and that provided us with the income to live abroad. Our only act of courage was leaving the security of our privileged lives in order to seek something we were missing, to seek to understand the differences in others, to seek ... period. It was not selfless; quite to the contrary, it was self-seeking, in the broadest sense of the expression. It was the act of transforming our dream into our reality.

Most of this book reflects my own life lessons. In re-reading it between the years I wrote it and when I decided to publish it, I have a certain amount of embarrassment, particularly based on the career path that I have pursued – that of a cross-cultural strategist. Now that I am older and wiser, I read these pages and marvel at my own neuroses – how hard I tried to micromanage and control my environment and how much I thought I could teach my children and the Italians, when in reality, it was I who had so much to learn. To some extent, I have this experience to credit for the humility with which I now approach everything I do. I now at least "know what I don't know" and that makes me more effective in most of what I have taken on in life.

We all have dreams. Sometimes these dreams take the form of things we want to accomplish for ourselves, or experiences we want to share with our children. We let those dreams slip away each time we make decisions based on self-doubt, complacency, or the flawed thinking that we will always have more time to execute them.

It's easy for the sparkling eyes of the child in us to turn dim when faced with the routine, security, and responsibility of the "mature" adult. We live our lives governed by a culture that demands success, and while that success may not yield happiness, we may feel trapped by it. It was from just such an existence that the Hummel family "escaped." We were living the American dream and had it all, except the time to be a family and the time simply to be.

We decided to take a break from the over-achieving lifestyle we had established and immerse ourselves in another culture. At the very least, we felt, it would be interesting to experience life outside the United States. And who knew? Perhaps the change from our familiar existence might give us some perspective about what wasn't working at home.

As discerning adults, we try to calculate our risks: pros and cons; addition and subtraction; downside risk versus upside gain. But in this case, we shunned that analysis and took a leap, with the hope that a net would magically appear. The outcome of our experience exceeded our imagination, and I expect that when our journey on this earth ends we'll be able to look back at our lives and realize that in choosing less, we ended up with more.

I've heard it said that dreams are like the horizon, the longer you walk toward them, the further away they seem. But sometimes, when we embrace a risk, we *become* the horizon, and this voyage was one of those times.

CHAPTER ONE

How to Escape the Take-Out Life

The fact is, that to do anything in the world worth doing, we must not stand back shivering and thinking of the cold and danger, but jump in and scramble through as well as we can.
-Robert Cushing

What exactly is the American dream? To me it has always been an economic model of success and a claim to the unfettered ability to climb that proverbial ladder to the very top, no matter how humble your origins, even if it kills you. And killing me is almost what it did. Maybe not in a literal sense, but with an Ivy League education, a career as a trial litigator and a subway token, I bought myself an ulcer, stock in half the pharmaceutical companies producing depression medication, a flailing marriage, and exclusion from competition for any potential parenting award for which I might have otherwise been eligible.

Is it a cliché to say that money doesn't buy happiness? If so, why is it so hard to detach ourselves from the stressful lifestyle that is so often required to stockpile the cash, and buy the fancy clothes, car and home? I, for one, couldn't reject it. I knew what going after the American dream was doing to my life, my marriage, and my kids, but I couldn't excise myself from it. It took me years to gain a reputation as a lawyer, to obtain the experience, the clients, the lucky breaks. No one walks away from that. It would be insane.

But insanity is a funny thing, and depending on which side of the funny-farm fence you're standing on, your perspective changes. For example, my day often started with screaming toddlers dribbling on my suit and vying for my attention while I was memorizing my closing statement for the jury and passing off the kids to the nanny at arms-length. Is that insanity? I'd go to work and pound on the steering wheel while some old lady took her sweet time crossing the street. How sane is that? I'd come home and negotiate a business call while giving the kids a bath, paying a modicum of attention not to drop the receiver into the tub, potentially electrocuting the children. My discipline for excessive splashing was executed by putting my hand over the receiver and stating, "I will need to cancel my commitment to review the condition of your three-wheeled transportation, if I cannot procure your cooperation until my call is completed." Now, let's be real. In what chapter is that behavior defined in the Diagnostic and Statistical Manual of Mental Disorders?

*   *   *

I still have the drawing that was the impetus to explore whether living in Italy for a while, far from the society that defined me, might help me to see myself and my place in the world, more lucidly. I made it in kindergarten at P.S. 102 in Bay Ridge, Brooklyn. On the left side of the page is a blob that remotely resembles the shape of New York City. It is labeled "Bruklin" in fairly legible handwriting and is surrounded by a sea of blue crayon. On the right side of the page is another blob in the shape of a boot, the same size as the blob on the left. In the approximate location of the Apennine Mountains the word 'Itly' has been laboriously scribed. I was a 5-year-old, and this was my world.

On school days, we lived in Brooklyn. During the summers, we were off to Italy, where my father, the proudest of Italian-Americans, showed us fallen-down rocks called the Roman Forum and more fallen-down rocks, amidst big, fat pillars called the Valley of the Temples. I didn't mind all the run down sights so much because the ice cream was really great. Besides, according to Dad, Rome was the bedrock of all future civilization, the Renaissance was the single most important event in human history, Galileo, DaVinci, Michelangelo and Caruso were the four most important men to have walked the earth, and pasta in its myriad forms was the most important source of sustenance, globally.

In time, my sisters and brother and I became aware that there were other States in America besides New York – in fact, there were entire States where you could not find a *calzone* – and that the world was not comprised solely of the United States and Italy. Nevertheless we nurtured a lasting pride about our Italian-American heritage and a love of the warm and embracing people we met during our vacations. "Travel is the best education," my mother used to say, and I think she was right. Of course, my mom is also the one who said that she could tell that I had advanced analytical abilities by the fact that I could compose a complete list of picnic supplies, including salt and pepper shakers, at the age of 10, so her assessment skills may be a bit subjective, but her point is well taken.

When my ex-husband, Bruce and I met in college – he at Columbia University and me at sister-school, Barnard College – he asked me my goal in life and I told him, "to have as much fun as possible," not then a very trendy goal for a female co-ed. His, at the time, was to get a good job, make money, and although he would not have phrased it this way, to obtain and maintain a strong socio-economic status. In many respects, we could not have been more different, but he had cute legs and made a good running companion in Morningside Park. He, on the other hand, was intrigued by my rather Bohemian style. Somehow, that connection led to love, and love to marriage.

Meanwhile, I went to law school (just to be on the safe side) and Bruce rolled in the snow naked one winter (just to show me he had a wild side) and over time, each influencing the other, I became a little less impulsive, and he, a little more so, until our relationship arrived at the happy median of suburban bliss.

When we married, I convinced him to vacation on the island of *Sardegnia*. Our accommodation was an *agriturismo*, a modest farm, where we met two Italian families who were fated to change our lives. Giampiero and Susanna Soru were vacationing with their two beautiful boys, Tommaso, aged 4 and Vanni, aged 2. The Sorus were accompanied by their friends, Laura and Domenico Stragapede.

Rarely in my life have I been envious of others. I know enough to realize that the slice of life I observe is often only a surface glance and that there might be demons beneath which would make my own life glow by comparison. But this was different. These people had something I wanted. They weren't thinner or prettier. They didn't have more money or a more glamorous job. Their marriage wasn't better than mine.

They did, however, have a certain something that I now characterize as 'extra.' The definition of this 'extra' is not easy to put into words. They clearly were not wealthy people; by their own description, they lived a modest existence. Yet, they appeared to have everything they wanted – everything worth having in life – and the 'extra' was just spilling over the side. It was spilling onto me, onto Bruce, onto the owners of the *agriturismo*, onto complete strangers.

I'm not speaking of extra *things*, although sometimes it seemed that way when Laura brought back extra bread from the bakery just so Bruce and I could try it, or Susanna gave me the last of the sunscreen squeezed from an already overly squeezed tube. It was their availability to discuss things spontaneously, without weighing the utility of a conversational diversion that was not on a list of things to be accomplished that day. It was the way they gave of themselves to others in a way that didn't seem to burden them or take away from their stockpile of emotional resources. It was a stark contrast to my own life, where I never felt that I had enough time left over to sit still, let alone to take the few extra minutes to do more than was actually required of me.

I can't say that it was a type of generosity, although that clearly was part of it. It was more a capacity to share that came from deep inside. It was the extra time that Domenico took away from his vacation to accompany Bruce to the mechanic to fix our car, waiting with him for hours in the hot, sweltering sun in case he needed a translator. It was the extra minutes it took to try to understand our halting Italian. It was the extra thought it took for Giampiero to map out with meticulous detail a route we could take when returning to the ferry so that we would see more of the beauty of *Sardinia*. And every act of kindness was performed in a way that we never had the sense that it was an imposition of any kind. Quite to the contrary, it seemed to bring them joy.

Careful observation throughout our time on *Sardinia* led me to believe that this way of being was not unique to the Sorus and the Stragapedes. Many of the people we met in Italy had that 'extra.' I wondered if it was something about being Italian or living in Italy that brought it out. They were so tuned in to the things that matter – listening to Grandma's stories about the old times as if it were the first time hearing them, treating every grandchild as if they were the first in the family to arrive, or drinking wine as if it were a fourth food group.

At the same time, they had such clear perspective about the things that don't matter much at all.

"The *agriturismo's* website said they had air-conditioning!!!" I complained to Susanna indignantly, with sweat dribbling down my face.

"*Pazienza* (Patience)!" she told me.

"Why don't the toilets flush after 10 p.m.?" Bruce grouched to Giampiero, with a discernable air of entitlement.

"*Pazienza,*" he responded.

"I understand there are certain staples in the *Sardinian* diet," I announced one morning while the rest of the table ate with delight, "but I draw the line at eggplant for breakfast."

Laura smiled and at once passed across her plate of *prosciutto* and melon; her own patience gentle and generous.

Pazienza, pazienza, pazienza. It must be the most utilized word in the Italian language and it is a patience that endures through just about anything beyond the risk of imminent death.

With genuine tears of sadness and promises to keep in touch and see each other again, we said goodbye to our new friends, and returned to our lives as young American professionals. But the experience was to linger. I spent a lot of time after that looking for that 'extra,' but my search took the form of scrambling up the ladder to secure my piece of the American dream. I was looking for the 'extra' in the form of a high salary, a big house, and a fast car. In the end, what I had was a lot of extra space for all of our extra things. What I didn't have was time, or any sense that my human spirit was full enough to spill 'extra' onto others.

When our son Matthew was born, joined two years later by his baby brother, Alex, Bruce and I created spreadsheets to manage everything from whose turn it was to pick up diapers and baby food, to whose turn it was to put the kids to bed, but even Excel couldn't keep up with us. The best laid plans still left us jockeying for position in our own home.

"Hon, don't forget you'll need to leave Tracy money for Matthew's baby-bop gymnastics class tomorrow."

"What are you talking about? I'm taking the last flight out to L.A. tonight."

"Are you kidding me, I have the Anderson case next week. I'll be at the office from dawn to dusk."

"You'll have to figure it out; I emailed you the dates I'd be gone."

"I faxed you the whole trial schedule last month."

But there was no point in being right because it was all wrong. Our life together, that had started with such exuberance and promise, was teetering on the edge and functioned only when we managed to optimize every second of the day in the most efficient and accurate manner possible. There was no margin for error.

In desperation, I turned in my litigation briefcase, for a stay-at-home-mom Lego carry case and Playschool medical kit complete with actual working stethoscope. But far from being different than my life as a lawyer, my days as *just* a mom were *just* as packed; the only difference was that no one was paying me. I drove the kids to school, to the grocery store, to their playdates, and after-school activities. I was always stuck in traffic between trips from Baby Gap to Gymboree, and overbooking myself such that I was a presence in my kids' lives without really 'being' there.

"What's that incessant chatter in the background?" a colleague asked.

"That's the Barney song," I responded. "Let him just finish loving you and me and the chorus will be over. Listen, can I call you back? Alex looks like he's about to fall off the trampoline."

I continually cancelled the yoga class which I specifically joined in a desperate attempt to do something for myself. Then, if I managed to get to class, afterward I took my sweet, spiritual self over to the nearest roasted-chicken chain and sometimes even managed to put the char-browned fowl in a roasting pan for that genuine home-cooked look.

"This is quite the improvement over Chinese food, right Bruce?"

"You betcha; I was thinking that we should go for the flash-frozen biscuits on the side next time."

Life did not improve as a result of the fact that I left my job, because despite the change to my day-to-day routine, my way of approaching each day did not change one iota. By the time the children entered elementary school our lives were a harried mess. I was an expert at blaming Bruce for the downward direction our privileged lives had taken, but this kind of expertise only served to create more distance.

"I did not sign onto this relationship to be alone day after day and raise these kids as a single parent."

"What would you have me do? Want to send a note to my supervisor excusing me from tomorrow's presentation?"

"I can't live like this. We've got the money for a vacation and you're more likely to get time off to get a triple bypass."

Bruce was powerless to make a career change that might be less stressful but would be construed as a step down, and the fact that I was no longer working as a lawyer only meant that he was under more pressure to maintain the lifestyle we had established. The only way the 'extra' green in our bank accounts was likely to benefit us was to provide an excellent divorce attorney for each of us.

As the kids grew, I was there to help them with their homework. They rarely were in the mood (OK, they were never in the mood). Tired after a full day of school followed by after-school activities, their fatigue made them cranky. I was just as tired as they were – perhaps crankier – unable to reap the rewards of my "job change," which was supposed to have the fringe benefit of quality time with my children.

"No Rachel," I said, in one particularly iconic conversation with the mom of one of Matthew's friends, "He's got baseball on Tuesday and drum lessons on Thursday ... No, that won't work ...

Oh, Jimmy's got chess team on Wednesday. I see. Well, let's try next week ..."

Bruce usually returned home late, missing both dinner and seeing the kids, who were already in bed. If we did have a moment to talk, it was usually about how much he hated his job – the rigid atmosphere, the cut-throat mentality of life as a management consultant in a large firm, the futility of creating something that to him was nothing more than hundreds of words and graphs that would take up space on a client's shelf.

He had chosen engineering over his great love, photography. He knew that a photographer's life, even that of a person who could combine artistry with technical precision, was likely to be one economic struggle after the next. But his choice had exacted an enormous toll. For many years, I saw him experience the depression of a man watching his life slip by. We fought a lot. I didn't want to live day after day with a man who hated his life, and he didn't want to live with a woman who wasn't supportive of his choices, or at least quietly grateful for the life he was providing us.

More often than not, he had an early meeting in the morning. He would take a plate of re-heated chicken carcass (or some other delicacy) up the stairs to his office. An hour or two later, exhausted myself from another endless day, and too tired to climb the stairs to Bruce's office, I shouted upstairs that I was going to bed.

"Good night," he shouted back, and that was often the end of our daily connection.

The love we had for each other had grown in depth year after year, but the wall we were building between us was growing equally high and wide, and seemed to take on a life of its own.

One night, during one of our many marathon discussions about our life, the state of the world, our children's futures, and our fears related to our struggling marriage, I asked Bruce whether he felt it was time to step back from our lives for a while. I suggested that we take a year off and spend it in another country. We might begin to change all those things about our lives that weren't working. We could have the time and space to re-examine our dreams, our beliefs, and our values. The kids would have the opportunity to meet people different from themselves, and to be positive ambassadors of our country. I'd always been fascinated by cultural differences and could finally have a first-hand ability to observe what happens when two cultures collide. We could shake up our lives a bit and see what would fall out.

I could not believe it when Bruce looked at me with calm, serious eyes, and nodded his head, yes. Perhaps the idea was palatable to him because it might provide a brief respite from his unfulfilling life, but he clearly would be risking more than the rest of us if we went, and Bruce was not a risk-taker.

I was so thrown by his casual agreement to my suggestion that I began blathering like a 4-year-old in the throws of chocolate overdose, "Can it work? Where could we go? Could we take the kids out of their school for a year? What about the house? What about your job? Do you think we can take the dog? Will we have to spend many expensive weeks at a hotel before we find a place to live? Would we even get approved for a visa? Could the kids go to public school in another country, even if they don't speak the language? Would there be an international school? Should we home-school?" I asked him, with very few breaths in between.

"Too many questions for one night," Bruce yawned. "It's just the first step. We're not leaving tomorrow." He was half asleep when he kissed me gently and turned over.

I have never been able to understand how he does it – how he turns the "thought switch" to the off position and just falls asleep. I lay awake for a long time that night, watching him sleep, his chest raising and lowering in calm rhythm. He had a sweet expression on his face that resembled the Bruce I knew in college when he was spending every spare second behind the lens of a camera and I was spending every moment scrawling the latest opus for my literary professor. We were so young, so passionate, not a thought in the world about paying a mortgage, career growth, annuities, or developing anything more than our grades and our sex life.

His head was shaved now, in deference to his receding hairline, but with his high cheekbones and square jaw line, he could pull it off. Grades hadn't mattered for a long time, and our sex life, sadly, had taken a back seat to a never-ending to-do list. The snoring serenade started, followed by the leg-twitching show, leaving me alone with our epiphany, his snarfling, and a pillow wedged between us to protect me from the stray thought that wandered down and was being processed by his right foot.

CHAPTER TWO

There's No Time Like the Present

Men spend their lives in anticipations–in determining to be vastly happy at some period when they have time. But the present time has one advantage over every other–it is our own. Past opportunities are gone, future have not come. We may lay in a stock of pleasures, as we would lay in a stock of wine; but if we defer the tasting of them too long, we shall find that both are soured by age.
-Charles Caleb Colton

"We're going to spend a year in Italy," we told the kids, when we finally decided where to spend our year away, "Won't that be exciting?" I cringed, waiting for the response. I was determined to make the idea work and I hoped that gushing with optimism would be enough to get them to accept it. I scanned their faces. Looking at 10-year-old Matthew with his huge brown eyes and thick brown hair was often like looking in the mirror. But his temperament was so much more cautious than mine that I often felt like he was a satirical blend of Bruce on the inside and me on the outside. His stare was puzzled, his eyebrows furrowed with concern.

"Why Italy?" Alex asked.

I started to tell them about Leonardo and Michelangelo. Then I took out some old postcards of the ruins of the Roman Forum and the Temples of Agrigento.

"It's broken," said Matthew, his big eyes tearing up.

"I don't get why you'd want to take us to a place where everything's already ruined," Alex added. At 8 years old, his approach to things was often steeped in logic. Peas were best utilized as weapons because they were shaped like BB-gun pellets. Chocolate ice cream was functional as paint and cheaper too. And apparently there was no point in going across an ocean to a place where they couldn't even keep a few temples from falling apart.

"We're going to *Varese*," we explained, but the kids left the room, signaling that for now the conversation was over.

They knew nothing of *Varese*, its perfect international location, not far from the borders of France, Switzerland, Austria and Slovenia. They had no context to know how beautiful it was. It had no famous works of art or world-renown cathedrals, but it was surrounded by emerald lakes and rolling hills that had somehow escaped the notice of the average tourist. Their hasty departure from the room meant that I didn't have time to explain the most important aspect of the location. It was the town where the Sorus and the Stragapedes lived, the two couples who captivated us years before they were born.

For a decade and a half, Bruce and I kept in touch with them through phone calls, letters, photos and occasional visits. Through this intermittent contact, we saw Tommaso and Vanni Soru develop from tender toddlers to young men; they watched Matthew and Alex grow through our stories, Little League photos, and Christmas cards.

Our relationship, at this point, was defined more by our time apart than our time together. But even if a bit of what I remembered about them was true, their influence could have an incredibly positive influence on our experience. I had to hope that the composite of snapshots we had experienced would, in reality, match the complete portrait formed in our minds. Only time would tell.

"I guess it's going to take them some time to adjust to the idea," Bruce said to me. "It'll work out. I'll look into seeing if there's an Italian course for the kids and you look into seeing if we can get Italian cable television."

It was a start. For the next several months, the kids went to an Italian course once a week on Saturday. Judging by their level of resistance, I think they would have rather been making their beds, helping with the laundry, or eating spinach. Bruce figured he'd learn the language through osmosis by watching the Italian cable channel. Personally, I thought he was doing it to watch the Italian models prance around the game-show stage.

"Listening to this is making me depressed," he told me, clearly a ruse to get me off the case of the large-bosomed announcer, who left half her clothes in the dressing room and was rattling on about winning a cappuccino maker that doubled as a vacuum, or some such thing. "I feel like there is no way I'll ever catch on."

"Lay off the game shows," I told him, patting him on the back. "They're just as incomprehensible in English." But he was clearly rattled. I wondered if I'd come home one day and find out that he changed his mind.

I, on the other hand, heard my grandparents speak Italian through my entire childhood. What's more, I had seen more fallen rocks and eaten more *gelato* than most. If I studied diligently, I felt sure that I could get my family through the initial phase of the transition. I pulled out the "Da Capo, A Review of Grammar" by Graziano Lazzarino, and began to read:

> When using impersonal expressions which take the subjunctive, if the verb of the dependent clause has an expressed subject, the subjunctive is used. But if no subject is expressed, the infinitive is used.

"Are they kidding?" I murmured to myself. "What's to compare? I don't even understand what they're saying in English."

> Note the change from "i" to "e" when the indirect forms combine with lo, la, li, le, ne, as in me lo, te ne, etc. gli (to him) and le (to her, to you) becomes glie- and form one word (glielo gliela, glieli, gliele, gliene). In the combined forms there is no distinction between to him, to her, to you.

My confidence began to dwindle.

To complicate things further, preparing to speak the language wasn't the only issue challenging us. Matthew was very shy and experienced transition difficulties at every stage of his young life. For years, he also seemed to be struggling at school, despite the fact that he was so bright. The few times that I observed him in the classroom, he was unengaged, his eyes turning toward the window where a bird was gathering leaves and twigs in the courtyard, then to the hallway as the janitor clattered by with a mop and bucket. The other children were usually intent on their assignment, while Matthew's page was often blank. Within weeks of our decision to go to Italy, his teacher suggested that we hire an educational expert to administer a full battery of educational testing.

I was despondent when he was diagnosed with Attention Deficit Disorder (ADD) and even more distraught when medication was prescribed.

"You need to rethink your decision to go," my mother-in-law, who had been a teacher for 30 years, told me shortly after the visit. "Alex is the kind of child you can drop anywhere and he'll land on his feet. But the last thing a child with ADD needs is to be uprooted and put in an unfamiliar educational environment."

"I know," I acknowledged. "I'm worried too. But kids are resilient. And besides, it's not like he's thriving in the American classroom." Then I smiled, turned, and went into the bathroom to be sick.

Everyone copes with risks in their own way. I've found that the majority fall into two categories of risk. Category One are the kind of people who embrace new ideas, make flight reservations, pack a few suitcases, throw old sheets on the furniture, and lock the door on the way to the airport. Category Two risk-takers cringe at the thought of life outside the normal routine. There is, however, a Third Category, never before studied by scientists because I believe I am its only member, which is the combination 'Adventurer-Neurotic-Type A Category.' This is the person who wants to experience new things, but only if she can control 90 percent of the outstanding variables. That's me.

Our newfound knowledge related to Matthew's situation, helped that personality trait to – shall we say – blossom. After many sleepless nights of agonizing over the "what-if" scenarios that played themselves out in elaborate nightly dreams, Bruce suggested that I go to *Varese* to take the guesswork out of some of those "variables" before I imploded.

*   *   *

When it was time to board a flight to *Varese*, I did so armed with a single-spaced to-do list of pre-move objectives. I held tight to that list like a Bible; it gave me comfort and security, two things I was sorely lacking at this juncture. On the plane my mind oscillated frantically between excitement and fear, my body reorganizing itself in my seat after each disjointed thought as if there were mosquitoes swarming in the seat cushion. The lady in the seat next to me cast me a glance periodically as if to say, "kindly get a grip and sit still."

Outside baggage claim, I looked through the sea of faces for Giampiero. A stunning olive-skinned young man, waiting with a bouquet of flowers that was wrapped in a swath of organza, embraced his beloved. An elderly woman wobbling with the support of her cane quickened her pace to shouts of, *"Nonna!!"* – her grandchildren almost knocking her over with their greeting. *"Che grande che siete! Che belli!* (How big you are! How beautiful!)" The terminal pulsed with the energy of friends and family reunited.

Then, in back of them, not much taller than the oldest grandchild, I saw Giampiero. Blue eyes, his most striking feature, smiled at me as if we had seen each other just last week, though unlike our beach days, his mustache was full and the top of his head was bare. The tension in my body melted with his warm hug and kiss on both cheeks. Maybe everything would be all right.

I took a flying leap into speaking my best "Da Capo" Italian. *"Mi non sono cambiato tu,"* I told him. That's roughly, "I haven't changed myself you," and he nodded sympathetically, probably at my inability to conjugate the simplest of verbs.

"Shall we stop for a coffee before heading into town?" he asked with a voice that said, "We'll be stopping for coffee, *got it?*"

Leaning against the bar sipping *espresso*, the rich, sweet scent alone shook me from my jet-lagged stupor and pulled me into my new surroundings of waving arms and sing-song discussion. Every conversation around me, be it about soup or a recent homicide at a soccer match, was fueled by earnest expressions and passionate gesturing. Giampiero and I took out our wallets to compare photos of our kids.

"They're not babies anymore, are they?" I noted looking at the pictures of Tommaso and Vanni, one playing the electric guitar, the other in the midst of a drum solo.

Giampiero shook his head and smiled thoughtfully. "Time has a way of not standing still," he said in Italian, and I understood perfectly.

"We'll be going to Laura's parents' apartment," he continued. "You'll have the place to yourself; her parents are in Rome." I nodded, both happy at the thought of having occasional privacy and anxious about being alone with my thoughts.

Vespas whisked past the window on either side of the car, hugging us like a motorcycle sandwich. One of the men, who looked to be about 60, winked at me coyly as he swerved, shaving 20 years off my life, both at the thought of the attention and with the fact that he almost careened into the rear passenger door to make his point.

When we arrived, Giampiero made me another cup of *espresso* and then left me to settle in. "Laura will be by to collect you in a few hours," he told me, kissing me again on both cheeks, and he was off, leaving me with a flurry of converging thoughts and the sound of the television urgently informing me of something beyond my comprehension, while I unpacked my small suitcase.

Laura's parents had stocked the house with the essentials *Espresso, biscotti, vino rosso, linquini, cavatelli* and *penne* were on the counter, and in the refrigerator, a liter of milk, some *prosciutto*, *fontina*, *asiago* and fresh tomatoes. A loaf of bread, wrapped in cloth was in the cupboard. The doorbell rang before I could consider whether I could make an argument either in this time zone or Eastern Standard Time, that the hour was appropriate to sample the *vino*. It was Laura, looking exactly as she had the last time I saw her, with the addition of a few laugh lines. Her auburn hair and green eyes gave her a certain movie star quality and her pregnant tummy made her look 10 years younger than her actual age. We hugged for a long time without words. I felt strangely like crying, and when we released each other, her face was, in fact, wet with tears. She wanted to take me for a stroll, but I was keen to get started on the list I had safely tucked into my pocket. Laura, smiled, shaking her head at my linear efficiency, but she put her arm in mine and led me to the car.

We wandered toward the police station, to ask about the visa requirements for a one-year visit. My footing felt awkward on the cobblestoned streets as if to remind me that I was out of my element. Shopkeepers were wiping fingerprints off their display windows, sweeping up, and getting ready for lunch. Women were pointing to pieces of *focaccia* and *pane* to accompany the pasta they were preparing at home. The energy of the *piazza* was that of earnest preparation for the mid-meal table. By the time we arrived, it was 1 p.m., half an hour after the time the public is permitted to ask questions. Nevertheless, we were able to ascertain that THIS particular police station could not answer the question. We needed to go to another type of police station across town.

"You see," explained the officer, as he began to lock up, "they do the same thing we do, but not really. *Capisci* (Understand)?"

No, I didn't '*capisci*' one single bit. In fact, it seemed a bit inefficient to have two "types" of police stations.

"OK. Well, can you tell us the requirements to bring a dog into Italy?" I asked politely.

"It depends on the dog," he answered.

"It's a pug," I said.

"What's a pug?" he asked, and then continued without waiting for a response. "Well, anyway, you must show that the dog is healthy."

"How do we show that the dog is healthy?" I asked. Laura could see I was growing impatient.

"*Pazienza,*" she said in a stage-door whisper.

"You need a certificate of health."

"How do you get this certificate of health?"

He looked at me as if I had a slight mental impairment. "You can get it if the dog is healthy."

I'm not the one talking in more circles than a motorcycle racetrack, I wanted to say, but didn't.

Laura suggested we telephone the American Consulate in Milan, the closest city with a consulate. I dialed and waited. A recording clicked on: *If you are an American in the midst of an emergency, please hang up and dial 111 22 33333. If you are an Italian planning a trip to America, press 1. If you are a foreign national planning a trip to America, press 2. If you are a dog, planning a trip to Buenos Aires, press ...* Apart from my attempt at humor, it seriously looked like if our dog, Buster, was going to come, he'd have to sprout wings.

Laura took the list from my hand and put it gently in her purse. It was only the first day and it was already showing considerable wear, torn at the edges, with a cappuccino stain over the section entitled, 'documents to investigate.'

"We need to have some lunch and catch up," she said, and before I could summon the energy to argue, we were munching an *insalta caprese, mozzarella* the texture of velvet, tomatoes as sweet as a peach, and basil leaves more pungent than an entire herb garden. We talked and talked, filling in the gaps between the letters and postcards. Laura rubbed the tummy that represented her unborn child. She already knew it would be a girl and had named her Chiara. She was expected at about the time we would arrive this summer, and I knew I'd be able to mark our time in *Varese* by the milestones of her development.

By day two, I knew I had to give poor Laura a rest from my "Tour de *Varese*," which was beginning to look about as circuitous as the famed Tour de France, but without the cash prize at the end. Susanna took some time off from work to help me.

"*Ciao, amore*," she said greeting me with a hug and a kiss, first on the left cheek, then on the right. She was as tiny and thin as a sparrow, but the way her arms enveloped me, she seemed more like a mother eagle, and even her simple greeting made me feel loved and protected.

"How are the kids; how are my little baseball angels?" she cooed and extolled their virtues as if my children were her own. Each block we walked closed the gap of 16 years, as if we were walking a timeline through the alleys, under the *portici* (covered walkways) through the *piazzas* to our present day experience. By the time we arrived at *Piazza Carducci*, it was as if we had never been apart.

She took out my crumpled list from her purse. My worries were being shouldered first by one of our friends, then another, as I made my way through the labyrinth of prerequisites to a one-year Italian life.

"Let's go to the bank," she said, pointing to the *vino rosso* stain in the middle of my list. "But first, we need to go to the tax office. A bank account cannot be opened without a *codice fiscale* (tax code)."

Parking was an exercise in defying physics, and after about 15 gyrations, Susanna managed to maneuver the front end of the car into a legal spot near the tax office to the right of the colossal brass door, between two red *Vespas*. We entered the building and waited. When number 101 was called, Susanna rose and explained to the woman what we wanted.

"But she doesn't have a residence," the woman replied.

Susanna responded softly and sweetly, "Yes, but she's looking for one and if she doesn't get the tax code, she can't open a bank account, and if she can't open a bank account, then she can't get an apartment. So, you can put my address. By the way, that's a beautiful scarf you're wearing. Where did you get that? Surely not in *Varese*."

Ten minutes later, we had the tax code and were off to the bank, having been informed by expert demonstration, the importance of bait and switch when dealing with Italian bureaucracy.

Susanna introduced me to her banker. He had four kids and six grandchildren. His wife, apparently, had a cold but was recovering well, he told us while the stamp in his hand smacked the stamp pad and a check booklet 10 times. Then he handed me the booklet, "*Auguri per la tua avventura,*" he said. Good luck on your adventure.

"Are these my temporary checks?" I asked.

"No, *signora*, they're permanent," he responded.

"When will the others arrive?" I asked.

"They don't arrive, *signora*," he explained. "When you run out of these 10, come in, wait in line, and I'll stamp you another 10."

As I left the bank, the security guard with his chubby cheeks and thick handle-bar mustache tipped his hat to me in a gesture of elegance unknown to me on the streets of New York. It occurred to me at that moment that I'd be seeing a lot of him, in fact I might be spending fully one-half of my daylight hours in Italy in one administrative office or another.

Jetlag was finally catching up by the third day of my odyssey, which I was regulating by the infusion of *espresso* and *vino* in alternating doses. When Bruce and I had discussed the public school option, it seemed that it might be a good idea to investigate the school where Francesca, Laura and Domenico's daughter, attended. Francesca was in the same grade as Alex and we reasoned that the companionship might be helpful to him. Similarly, the fact that Laura could introduce me to some of the moms at school might be an advantage socially. It would give her the opportunity to assist me when questions arose throughout the school year, which I could only assume would arise regularly, in all likelihood, every five to 10 minutes. For this reason, I began corresponding with the school before leaving the United States for this fact-finding mission.

When we arrived at *Ugo Foscolo Elementare*, Laura introduced me to the *direttore* and the two teachers who would be the primary teachers in Matthew and Alex's classrooms should we decide to enroll them. We all sat together around a kid-sized table. The teachers were dressed in crisply ironed skirts and blouses, their wrists and earlobes accessorized just so, their hair neatly coiffured. The school was a somber cinderblock construction. It was a stark contrast to the medieval historic center of *Varese*, with its stone *portici*, mosaic-lined shop entrances and piazzas strewn with café tables and umbrellas. A crucifix took the place of the usual colorful artwork, maps or school projects on the walls of our elementary school at home. There in front of me, I could see that the teacher had printed out the emails I sent her, including the photos of me, Bruce, Matthew, Alex and Buster. Next to each photo, she had written our names with an arrow pointing to our image. There were other words and other arrows pointing to each of us. I hoped that they didn't signify "ugly foreigner," "myopic, controlling philistine," or "right-wing capitalist," as she apparently structured one of the English lessons around the possibility of Matthew and Alex joining the class in September.

In halting Italian I asked many of my questions, apologizing profusely for my inability to speak the language well. They insisted that my Italian was "perfect" and encouraged me to keep trying.

"How big is the class size?" (13 in Matthew's class and 16 in Alex's.)

"Do the teachers speak any English?" (Yes, without a doubt.)

"Is there an aide or teacher who can assist in translation of instruction while the children are learning the language?" (Absolutely, they planned for the English teacher to do that.)

So far ... so good.

"There is a 60-minute lunch, consisting of three courses, pasta, meat and dessert, followed by a 45-minute recess," the principal explained, and I knew I had something tangible to take back to the kids. The kids' New York schedule allowed only 15 minutes to eat and 20 minutes for recess. *Ugo Foscolo Elementare* – 1; Pound Ridge, our hometown elementary – 0. With a little more spin, I might be able to make the Italian school system sound like Disneyland.

The teachers planned to continue a correspondence between the students and Matthew and Alex. If we enrolled them, each boy would be assigned two student buddies whose "job" it would be to teach Matthew and Alex Italian. The *direttore* also said that *Le Settimane Pinocchio* (literally translated, "The Pinocchio Weeks") – the adjustment period that marks the first two weeks of school, would include as a theme, something to do with America (hopefully something more docile than an exposé on the Iraq war), to coincide with Matthew and Alex's arrival. On Laura's advice, I didn't tell them about Matthew's ADD.

"There's no point," she explained. "It's not a recognized diagnosis here and they'll just think you're a neurotic American. Take one day at a time and see how it goes."

Given that I was probably more neurotic than the average American, I realized that her point was well taken. It did not, however, leave me with the warm, fuzzy feeling that Matthew's teachers would be ready with the latest techniques for battling an attention disorder. "Is it time for a glass of wine yet," I asked, but she just told me to have *pazienza.*

I was able to take a video of the children in the Italian classroom, while asking them questions like, "*Chi vuole aiutare Matteo e Alessandro ad imparare la lingua Italiana* (Who wants to help teach Matthew and Alex Italian)?" to which all the children yelled, "Me, I do. I will!!!" They clamored excitely, each pushing the other out of the way, one finishing the sentence of the other, in a playful mash of exuberant sounds and flamboyant expressions.

Their enthusiasm convinced me that we could at least try the Italian school and hope that the adjustment for Matthew and Alex would not be too stressful. What was the point of coming all this way just to insulate them at a private school in an English-speaking classroom? It was a fortunate revelation, as I was informed later that day by the *Scuola Europea*, the private international school, that neither the third nor the fourth grades would have room for any other students in the fall. It's startling how these things just fall into place, if you just wait for someone to make the decision for you.

*   *   *

In the days that followed, Laura and I met with a real estate agent. *Signora* Michelle Caball who just emigrated from France, but "specialized" in international relocation and spoke French, Italian and English. Her false eyelashes and mannequin-like makeup indicated to me that our taste might be slightly different. Confirming this preconception, the first apartment she showed us was small and dismal, surrounded on two sides by a stucco wall.

"*Oui. Oui.*" She said enthusiastically as if I had asked a question. "It's a very safe place, because next door — there is a prison," she said.

I was a bit put off. "Yes," I asked, "but is it good to live near a prison?"

"*Assolutamente, perché i prigionieri sono dentro* (Absolutely, because the prisoners are inside)," she said, breaking into Italian.

"I see," I said, shooting a glance at Laura, but her face betrayed nothing out of the ordinary. "I was hoping for something with a bit more light."

We moved on to the next apartment building with great expectations, but it was entirely covered with scaffolding. Inside, workers with hardhats were knocking down walls and re-routing plumbing. I stood in front of a gaping hole in one of the bedrooms; an abundance of light was streaming through.

"This is a wonderful place," she told me, "because it's new."

"I'm sort of looking to commit to something with a minimum of four complete walls," I told her, not wanting to risk having to explain to Bruce and the kids why there was a unique European form of air-conditioning in one of the bedrooms.

"There's one last apartment I can show you," said Mrs. Caball, her rouged cheeks glowing with optimism. "A very quaint three-bedroom apartment with a small garden."

Laura read the description, "Furnished apartment in prime, central location." I nodded hopefully. Given the fact that our stay was limited to a year, this could be ideal.

When we parked, I realized that we were back in the prison neighborhood – a coveted venue according to those in the know. But when we arrived, the apartment was empty.

"Didn't the advertisement say that it was furnished?" I asked.

"You've been looking at furnished apartments all along," Laura said.

That's when I learned that the term 'furnished,' in Italy, means that the four walls in each room are up, though not necessarily painted, and that the kitchen appliances are in place. It also means there is a toilet, shower and electrical receptacles. What 'furnished' does not mean is 'with furniture.'

We met the landlords, *Signor* and *Signora* Gallo, who lived in Lugano, Switzerland. They seemed an ornery sort, but the apartment had it's own little private garden, beyond which was a park-like setting, surrounded by green space and trees, practically in the pedestrian center of town. There were three small bedrooms. If the kids shared a room, Bruce and I could use the third bedroom as a little office. I didn't think Matthew and Alex would relish the idea of living next to a prison, but Laura explained that it was a minimum-security facility.

"You know, the small-time prisoners who are just practicing for the big time," she joked.

"OK, when the kids arrive, we'll tell them it's a practice prison," I said, "You know – a place where prison guards learn how to care for prisoners," I continued staring hopefully at Laura's puzzled face. The prison was across the street from an elementary school, after all ... how bad could it be?

"We'll take it," I told her. Mrs. Caball batted her eyelashes with glee and Mrs. Gallo turned toward me with such velocity that she appeared to have pulled out the two-page contract from the bra of her ample bosom. I was reluctant to touch it, let alone sign it.

It may be that I should have predicted the confusion that would result from such an eclectic collective of participants. The French agent, *Signora* Caball, spoke Italian reasonably well but with a drippy French accent. Laura was primarily speaking Italian, interspersed with English when necessary for my edification. I was speaking Italian in the present tense only, with an American accent. *Signora* Gallo, her large, square Russian form towering over her diminutive husband, spoke halting Italian with a Russian accent. And *Signor* Gallo, who was dressed in a suit and tie so large for him that he looked like a child trying on his father's clothes, spoke nothing at all in deference to his wife, the know-it-all.

"You may bring a собака," Mrs. Gallo sniffed, reading paragraph five. "But not one that is annoying."

"A who?" I asked. Please don't tell me we're now going to add the Russian language to the mix!

"A dog."

"I've never thought of Buster as being annoying," I offered, "But ..."

"And the cot in the second bedroom stays," she said, pointing to a folding bed that looked as if it had been manufactured prior to World War II and slept in by veterans recovering from their wounds.

Mr. Gallo got up silently, and without expression, sauntered out to the garden for a cigarette. When he finished, he returned quietly to the table where the conversation continued with such a lack of progression, that it was as if it was being held in suspended animation in order to allow for his smoking diversion.

"I am not removing that lamp," Mrs. Gallo was saying.

"*Vous êtes déraisonnable,*" said Mrs. Caball.

"Unreasonable," Laura whispered.

"Mrs. Gallo, the kids need to sleep in that room. If you keep that huge thing in there, all we'll be able to do is play bridge."

By this point, Mr. Gallo was appreciating the interaction as some sort of bizarre entertainment and started smoking at the table rather than removing himself to the garden. The room began to take on the odor and visibility of a pool hall.

The smell of smoke reawakened my years of nicotine addiction, and I mused that if I asked for a cigarette, the affiliation between me and *Signor* Gallo, as well as the pulsing of nicotine through my veins, might improve the negotiations somehow. Then jolted back to reality, I realized that I had enough problems right now and didn't need to add a re-activated nicotine addiction to the list.

So I retreated (without a cigarette) into the small garden, lined with terracotta pots of geraniums and rosemary bushes, and tried to imagine how pleasant it would be sitting out there reading a book to Matthew and Alex or sipping a glass of *vino bianco* with Bruce after putting the children to bed, reveling in my accomplishment of having found such a beautiful oasis in the midst of a small city. Then I rejoined the pool hall.

"Can you paint the apartment?" I asked her. "It's badly in need of refreshing."

"No," she told me. "It's not necessary. Anyway, if I paint, you will have to return it painted after the end of the lease."

"Well why don't we share the cost of the painting and do it once," I suggested.

"Is it your house?!" she exploded, leaning over the table in a manner she had to have inherited from czarist lineage. "No, it's mine. I like it the way it is – it gives the apartment character. If you want to paint it – you paint." The cigarette hanging from Mr. Gallo's lower lip fell onto the plastic tablecloth melting a hole which Mrs. Gallo promptly smacked to a cold cinder without skipping a beat.

Every 'take-no-prisoners' litigator should know when she's defeated, "OK, OK, *signora*. If you insist, I will paint at my expense."

"Fine," she answered, "but I pick the color."

When I thought we were finally at the end of a long road, she explained that she preferred that our check for three months rent in advance be filled out without a date and made to the order of no one, but if not, then made out to them and not to their son, even though their son was apparently the lawful owner of the apartment.

I nodded obediently and signed in the three places she indicated.

"*Piacere, signora* (It's been a pleasure)," Laura said as we stood to leave.

And the scary part was, I knew she was being genuine.

*   *   *

At home, Matthew, Alex and Bruce waited patiently for news. I spoke to the kids one at a time, Alex first.

"I found an apartment that's only a five-minute walk from the nearest *gelateria*," I told him.

No response.

"Alex? Alex?"

Bruce got on the phone. "He fell on the floor," he said. "I think he's supposed to be fainting with joy."

"I'm back, Mom."

"Do you miss me?"

"Yes, I guess I do."

"What do you miss?"

"I miss your head."

"Why my head?"

"Well, that's the part that talks."

What a pragmatist. Why pine for the body parts that don't have substantial utility?

"Sweetie, can you put Matthew on?"

"Hi Mom," came Matthew's soft voice.

"Hey buddy, I found us an apartment near a *gelateria*."

Silence. I speculated that rather than fainting with joy, Matthew was absorbing the fact that the reality that we would be going to Italy was made more certain by the success of finding an apartment.

"Dad said it's next to a practice prison," he said. "What the heck is that?"

Apparently my spin on that particular issue was not going as well as my attempt to market the public school's extended lunch and recess hour.

"We'll talk more about it when I get home. I have a cool video of some kids who are already waiting to meet you and I'll take some photos of the apartment too," I told him, but I suspected he wasn't listening.

"I think he's just tired," Bruce told me when he got back on the phone. "By the way, how did it go finding a car?"

"It was a no-brainer," I said, sharing the futile details of my five hour quest to buy a car. "I learned that it would be too difficult to bring our car over, so I bought a Nissan Almera."

"Why a Nissan?" he asked.

"Well ... I did go to other car dealers," I explained to him, "but they're the only ones who had the paperwork to sell to a foreigner."

"I'm sorry I asked," Bruce told me. His voice trailed off and I suddenly felt very far away in every sense. For myself, I had taken some of the guesswork out of what life might be like when we arrived as a family. Matthew, Alex and Bruce were still very much in the dark about what awaited them.

But if they could have experienced what I did in those days, their hearts would have been lighter. Every day, five months pregnant, Laura collecting me by car to work down my list of objectives. Her calm presence at the contract signing, interjecting a few statements here and there to prevent a collision course between me, the formidable *Signora* Gallo, and *Signora* Caball. Susanna's ballet at the tax office. Giampiero's reassuring smile. They were – each of them – the incredible spirits we met so many years ago, open hearts, expecting nothing in return, as if it was a completely normal, daily event to give so much of yourself to a friend you have seen only a few times in 16 years.

Every evening we had a sumptuous meal at Giampiero and Susanna's apartment in the company of long-haired Tommaso and scruffy-faced Vanni, whose dazzling eyes were the only physical characteristic that linked them in my memory to the little boys I knew in *Sardegnia*. The scent of basil, garlic and oregano emanating from Susanna's kitchen was tonic to my anxious soul.

On one such night when we were all together at the Sorus, Laura's husband, Domenico, a creative director in an advertising firm, telephoned one of the commercial photographers with whom he worked closely to see whether Bruce might intern at his photography studio in Milan when we arrived this summer. He paced back and forth the length of the tiny 80-square-meter apartment, smoking a cigarette and rubbing his beard as he spoke, giving me an excellent image of what he'd be like in the delivery room. He emerged with a smile of satisfaction telling me that it looked like it would work out.

Eight-year-old Francesca then sat on Domenico's lap, her long, thick curly hair almost completely obscuring Domenico's face, and regaled me with her ability to count to 20 and name all the domestic animals in English, then she turned to Domenico, "If her name is Bruce-e-Denise," she asked her dad, after hearing us referred to collectively as 'Bruce and Denise' throughout my visit, "what's her husband's name?"

Giampiero smiled, looking up from the map he excised from one of many over-stuffed drawers in the hallway to show me one of the first outings we could take in the Dolomites when we arrived. Vanni made *espresso* and Tommaso offered to get on the Internet to try to get me an Italian email address.

As I looked around the table at the smiling faces of our friends, it was evident to me that it was worth the trip just to have the confirmation of the beauty of their friendship. Already, through their actions, they were challenging me to be a better person, to give with a more open heart, to extend myself, to see beyond my own personal needs and those of my family. I felt the 'extra' building up inside me and I wanted to go home and let it spill over onto Bruce and the kids.

Speak Milk. Drink Wine.

CHAPTER THREE

Flexibility is the Key to Adapting to Any Given Situation

Problems are only opportunities in work clothes.
-Henry J. Kaiser

At home, the reaction was somewhat of a mixed bag. Bruce was very relieved that I accomplished so much that would reduce the difficulty of our transition in July. He was, however, concerned by the financial investment I made prior to obtaining a few fairly important things. For instance, we had not yet obtained an actual visa, nor had we found a tenant to rent our house, a big part of the practical side of our plan. The inverted timing of these events made Bruce very nervous and pushed up against all his instincts to do what was fiscally sound for his family. It was, in fact, a difficult leap of faith for both of us, but we could not change the order of events by willing it that way.

The kids, for their part, were excited about all I reported, but frightened about the growing reality that we would be leaving all that was familiar to go to a strange place where people spoke a language that they recognized only as it related to the food groups *pizza, pasta* and *gelato.* I showed the kids the video of the school, their prospective teachers welcoming them in Italian and a little English, and the Italian children vying for the role to teach them the language.

Alex remained completely silent. Matthew's tears rolled down his round, olive-skinned face.

It was not quite the reaction I hoped for.

I let the videotape play and motioned for Matthew and Alex to sit in my lap. "It's really scary to try something new, isn't it?" I asked Matthew.

A tearful, "yes," was his response.

"And it's really sad to leave friends behind, isn't it?" I asked, turning to Alex.

Another tearful, "yes."

"I'm only asking you to keep an open mind. Think about what it will be like to go to that school, the kind of people you will meet, what you will learn, how you will feel about yourself if you face your fear. In a few weeks, let me know what you decide."

A final tearful, "OK" from each of them.

The following morning, Matthew came to me and said, "I've decided to try it."

"Try what?" I asked him.

"Try the school," said Matthew. "But only because I can't stand the thought of their crying faces when I don't show up."

"Well, I'm not trying it," added Alex, my daredevil, who retreated back down the stairs to his room.

I revisited how to pitch this adventure to Alex. Already I had a feeling there might be bribery involved.

*   *   *

Ever true to my position on the Adventure-Neurotic-Type-A spectrum, I began frantically preparing for the possibility that we might have to homeschool the kids, or at least supplement their education to keep them at grade level. I scoured my bookshelves and pulled from them any book I had purchased related to their curriculum. I searched the Internet for educational websites, software and DVDs. If all else failed, I would be prepared to teach them math at the grocery store, science in the kitchen and art history in the museums.

I was a poster child for the 'prepare-for-every-contingency' model. Bruce was working, so I did what any self-respecting, over-achieving American wife and mother would do. While he was at work, I made flyers to market our house, planned a small going away party, made stationery and envelopes printed with our *Varese* address and airmail stamps for each child attending the party, videoed all our paintings and other wall hangings while they were still on the wall so we would remember how to re-hang them when we returned, performed Q-tip-BandAid surgery on a half-dead chipmunk Alex found on the road, got a quote for movers in case our tenant wanted the house unfurnished – that is with the sink, toilets, etc., but without the furniture. I rented a Dumpster, re-invented the wheel, had the septic pumped and the chimney cleaned, called for annual maintenance on the air conditioner and furnace, discovered a cure for cancer, scheduled Buster for the vet and the kids for their annual check-up, made a list of contractors and telephone numbers for the property manager we had not yet hired who would look after the renters we did not yet have, and ultimately had a small, but tasteful funeral for the chipmunk.

When it came time to go to the Italian Consulate in New York City, only Buster's presence was not required. The rest of us waited in line for hours for *Signor* Martino, who explained that there were categories for going to Italy to study at a university, to work for a specific company, for religious purposes, and for sponsored artistic purposes. There was, however, no "going-to-Italy-for-a-year-for-the-hell-of-it" category, nor was there a "want-to-gain-some-perspective" category. The only category that allowed us to do something along the lines of what we were proposing, said *Signor* Martino, was retirement. Thankfully, Bruce and I discussed the fact that we might have to be flexible in our approach at the Consulate and adapt our goals to the circumstances. I shot Bruce a furtive look before saying to Signor Martini, "We are retired."

After all, as far as I was concerned, we <u>were</u> retired, at least temporarily. I was a stay-at-home mom and Bruce was leaving his job without any definite prospect of another one.

Signor Martino gave me a look of incredulity. "But ... I mean by that, that you must demonstrate that you have enough money in which to live, without working — and not for a year — forever. You know ... retired."

"Yes, well, here are our financial documents," I said with a plastered polite smile on my face, passing a large plastic box of documents to him through the window.

"That's a lot of documents," said *Signor* Martino. "I will have to examine them and I will call you in about a week."

Bruce was perspiring profusely when we left. "What the heck are you doing?" he asked me through scarcely parted lips.

"I don't know," I responded, looking equally as if my jaws were wired together. "It's just that those financial statements are a blur of numbers that I can't make sense of, and I'm sort of hoping that he won't either."

"Great strategy," he replied. "That's not entirely what I meant by being 'flexible' and 'adapting' to the situation."

"Well I didn't see a 'going to Italy to teach your children to be citizens of the world' category on his list," I answered plaintively. "Let's just hope for the best."

At home, every day we straightened up, made the beds, put the toys away, and fluffed the couch pillows for a showing to potential renters. Then it was the kids' job to take Legos out of the toy closet, make a tent on the couch, and fix themselves crackers with peanut butter, without so much as a napkin or paper plate underneath. By and large, the people to whom we showed the house did not seem bothered by the messy playroom and the occasional sticky door handle. We did, however, have one showing that went a bit awry.

We showed the house for the third time to the same couple. We crossed our fingers and, even though it was broad daylight, put the lights on in each room for that light and airy glow. We made the beds, cleaned the kitchen, did the cushion-fluffing routine, swept the driveway and gave Buster a shampoo, cream rinse and permanent wave. Despite a difficult morning that culminated in the suspension of computer game privileges, we even made chocolate chip cookies and coffee so the house had a welcome scent. Bruce corralled the kids into the car and I did one last check of the house. Then, at the last minute, Matthew said he needed to go to the bathroom and ran back into the house one final time. I did experience a momentary pang of stress about whether he flushed the toilet, but he insisted that he did and I let it go.

When we got back, I saw the realtor's card. They had eaten some of the chocolate chip cookies, but didn't seem to have touched the coffee. I started to get the kids ready for bed. On my way downstairs, barking my usual litany – "Get into your pajamas and brush your teeth" – I saw it. In Matthew's handwriting, a big sign on his door read, "I HATE MY MOM AND DAD."

"Matthew," I said in a voice so casually shrill that it immediately signaled him to hide under his bed, "When did you put this sign on your door?"

"When I went in to go to the bathroom right before we left," he replied from behind four stuffed animals and five plastic super-heroes. "I was really mad about you guys taking away video games from us."

"I see," I said softly, teetering precariously between laughter and tears.

"I guess everyone hates me now, right?" said Matthew.

"No, we don't hate you, Matthew. We're just really embarrassed."

"Why?" he asked.

"Well," I explained, "It's because some strange people were in our house and they don't know if we're good parents, or bad ones, or mean or nice, and they read this sign, and ..." Matthew found a way to express himself, despite his shyness. The fear and anger about leaving his home had found a voice on a scribbled piece of paper on his door. It was definitely time for bed.

Despite Matthew's literary outburst, the people to whom the house was shown decided to rent the house and I slept through the night for the first time in weeks. The peace, however, was short-lived. Laura called to tell me that the Italian post office was threatening to send the boxes back since they arrived at the new apartment before we did and there was no one there to receive them and pay the customs duties. I put down the phone and started scanning my brain for uplifting quotes regarding "seizing the moment" to help me "weather this storm." One such quote from Shakespeare kept rattling around in my head:

There is a tide in the affairs of mankind which,
Taken at the flood, leads on to fortune.
Omitted, all the voyage of their life is bound
In shallows and in miseries.

On such a full sea are we now afloat,
And we must take the current when it serves
Or lose our ventures.
–Shakespeare

Just as I was thinking, "F--k Shakespeare. I bet he's never even been on a boat," I heard my computer announcing, "You've got mail." It was Laura:

Dear Denise,

Today they assembled the beds and the sofas you bought from IKEA. They look great. Also, I found an everything-do boy who will cut the grass too. I must tell you that in your new garden, there is not simple grass but stinging nettles. Is any one of you allergic? I can ask him to put some weed-killer to make it die, and then you'll put some new seeds of grass. You will have mud for a while. At this point the "Laura office" is closing to prepare dinner.
Love, Laura

An "everything-do" boy. I've always wanted one of those.

E-mails from Laura continued to arrive daily. She found a few summer camps for the kids near *Varese* that were sports oriented. Bruce and I, in close consultation with the boys, chose the one that had *pallanuoto* ("nuoto" is swimming and "palla" is ball, so *pallanuoto*, we surmised, had to have something to do with a ball and swimming ... maybe water polo), minivolley (volleyball?), minibasket (basketball for short people?), *calcetto* (*calcio* is soccer, so *calcetto* must mean soccer played with a little ball, or by little people?), *monopattino* (pattinare means to skate, so perhaps *monopattino* was skating on one foot?) Anyway, it sounded sporty, and as far as the kids were concerned, sports were a major priority.

Matthew's Little League baseball team (the Red Sox), which was in second place in the league, was scheduled to play the Astros, the team in first place in the league. We dreaded it, as we knew that if Matthew's team lost, life in the Hummel household would be like the aftermath of a grave plague. But that evening, after the championship game, although the Red Sox were still in second place and the Astros were still in first place, the climate of our house remained fairly status quo. Over dinner, Matthew blithely explained that the Red Sox had an off day, pitching-wise, and that the Astros hit better because their team consisted of mostly fourth graders. Having just read a study that claimed that children who blame bad outcomes on things outside their control have a more intact self-esteem, I nodded in agreement and ate another forkful of salad. I still haven't mentioned there probably aren't any baseball teams in Italy ...

*   *   *

On July 4 – a day that will go down in infamy more for the fact that we actually made it out the door, than the mere fact that American revolutionaries were able to stage a successful rebellion against the British – we piled into the car to the airport. We finally had the exact requirements for taking Buster overseas and he was safely ensconced in his all but bullet-proof crate, doped up on every vaccine known to veterinary medicine. Tearfully we said goodbye to Bruce's parents and mine. My father was clearly proud that we were setting off to the only other country of worth in the universe, but sad at the prospect that we would be so far away. Bruce's mother's face was twisted with doubt and discomfort. All four of them already missing their grandchildren.

We shuffled through security at JFK, bags bulging with crayons and pretzels, books, and cameras. Once seated in the plane, the kids asked me to tell them more about *Varese* between pressing every conceivable button on their armrests.

"Is everything there broken?" Alex asked. Apparently, I had left them with the impression that Italy was a falling down mess.

"Not at all," I responded. "We're near Milan where two of Italy's most important modern day structures exist: *San Siro* stadium for soccer and *La Scala* for opera."

After Alex clarified that *La Scala* was not technically a modern day structure because they built it a heck of a long time ago, "like in the B.C.s probably," Bruce and I each ordered a $5 twist-off bottle of wine from the flight attendant and toasted each other.

In the months prior to leaving, we heard every conceivable reaction to our pending journey. We were extolled for our courage, as if we were the Pilgrims heading off on the Mayflower and, alternatively, criticized as acting selfishly, disregarding the well-being of our children. We comforted our parents' tears and those of our children, and hid ours from them whenever possible. We were cautioned about the schools being advanced, or, alternately, "behind." But the most memorable reaction for me was that of one of the kids' friends who put his arm around Matthew and said, "We'll be here when you get back."

It didn't surprise me that it would take a kid to crystallize the optimum way to look at our absence from home. The people who reveled in, or were at least fascinated by our choice, would more than likely be there for us when we got back ... unless they were out and about on an adventure of their own.

CHAPTER FOUR

Play Soccer and a Foreign Language Will be at Your Feet

Language is the close-fitting dress of thought.
R. C. Trench

Benvenuti a casa.

I recognized Laura's handwriting on the sign taped to our door welcoming us to our new apartment. My heart raced as I turned the key and opened the door slowly, unsure of what we would find. Laura had told me not to worry, that everything was going fine. I had been reluctant to ask details about the progress of what we had started together months earlier, fearful of imposing on her more than I already had. Matthew and Alex peeked around me, and Bruce could see over the top of my head. I could tell they were looking for telltale signs of the issues I had described related to *Signora* Gallo's intractability. Matthew, in particular, was looking around to see if there were any signs of practice prisoners lurking. Even I entered tentatively, observing every gesture of my family, trying to read their feelings as they entered their new, temporary home.

The apartment smelled of fresh paint, an uncontroversial shade of white gleamed with a brightness that had been lacking during my earlier viewing. A simple welcome basket of *limone, pesche* and *menta* (lemons, peaches and mint) was on the table along with a hand-drawn card left by artistic Vanni on behalf of the Soru and Stragapede families. The couches that Laura and I purchased had arrived, and the blue-pinstripe accented the neutral walls. In the kids' bedroom, the lamp and World War II cot had magically disappeared. The bunk beds I ordered had been assembled by

Vanni and Tommaso, and Laura and Susanna had made the beds with crisp bright red sheets and duvet covers. The matrimonial bedroom was smaller than I remembered it, but brighter, and the third bedroom was large enough to fit one desk, two chairs, and side-by-side laptops, a cozy, if slightly claustrophobic work environment.

The two small bathrooms, one with washer (but no dryer), were clean, as was the rest of the house. Laura had seen to that. The "everything-do" boy had obviously exterminated the stinging nettles, leaving a few strands of grass and lots of mud, but the small covered terrace leading to the soggy mess was dry, and we swung open the French doors allowing in a warm breeze. Roses were blooming that I hadn't even noticed during my negotiations with the Gallos, and small, butter colored flowers were peeping through under the shade of the pine tree in the corner. Over the hedge, the green courtyard and towering chestnut trees signaled the promise of our outdoor surroundings as soon as the seeds of grass took hold.

Seven of the 13 boxes I sent two months earlier had arrived and were lining the hallway. They now were joined by our eight suitcases. The other boxes, at least for the moment, were lost in the incredible void of the Italian postal system. As I looked around, I was torn between the sensation that we had packed too much for a "vacation," but too little for a "life." I took a deep breath. This was it: home for the next 12 months.

The Sorus and Stragapedes arrived after work and suggested that we have dinner at a local pizzeria.

"*Che belli che sono; sono altissimi* (How handsome they are; they're so tall)!" they cooed, Matthew and Alex surreptitiously wiping off each kiss as the next one followed.

Soon we were all savoring crusty round pizzas served on individual plates: *pizza margherita* (cheese pizza), *pizza marinara* (with sauce only) *pizza con rucola* (with arugola) and *pizza con melanzane e peperoni* (with eggplant and peppers) were the front-runners. Garlic and parmesan, the principle scents in the candle-lit pizzeria wafted through the air as steaming plates of pizza, whisked from the brick oven passed periodically from one table to the next. Afterward, I casually lead us to the local *gelateria* I had been bragging to the kids about for the past several months. Every conceivable flavor awaited through the plate glass. The young girl serving us, smiled and asking us what we wanted, dipping her rounded spatula into the creaminess, massaging it before lifting it into the cup so that the texture would be just so. Alex was all smiles as he ordered *limone* (lemon gelato), though he didn't faint. Matthew wasn't smiling, but he had a peaceful look on his face that seemed to be different from the previous expressions of resignation I had been seeing over the past few months, or perhaps it was just fatigue eased into contentment by the sweet *stracciatella* flavor of vanilla and tiny chocolate bits.

"Just one ice cream per night, I'm warning you," Giampiero jibed as they bid good bye.

"*Buon riposo* (Have a good rest)."

"*Sogni d'oro* (Dreams of gold)."

We went to bed early that night, restless with jet lag, but relieved to have finally arrived, pleased that our new surroundings happened to be in the land of scrumptious *pizza* and *gelato*, and cozy to be surrounded by friends so far from home.

"I want the top bunk," Matthew said to me, as I followed him into the boys' bedroom.

There was no contest, as Alex was already asleep on the bottom. He had managed to extract his special blanket from a suitcase, but hadn't managed to remove his shoes.

*   *   *

The sound of church bells woke me at 7 a.m. The rest of the family slept through the eight resonate chimes of the bell tower of *San Vittore*, so I decided to give Buster a walk around the neighborhood. I planned to stop at a local bar for a coffee and was trying to remember the recent coffee etiquette and nominative lesson given to me by Susanna: *cappuccino* (*espresso* with lots of foamed milk), *espresso* (a thimble of coffee straight up), *caffè macchiato* (a thimble of coffee, marked by a little hot milk), and *caffè latte* (milk marked with coffee). Most importantly, I now knew not to drink *cappuccino* the way Americans do.

"*Cappuccino* is a morning drink, consumed when the stomach is empty and primed to receive a large cup of warm milk complemented by a dash of caffeine," she explained. "If you don't want to stand out as a foreigner, the acceptable cut off for *cappuccino* is at about 11:30 a.m. when the salted and savory tidbits of the first *aperitivo* (aperitif) hour of the day start appearing on bar counters. And NEVER, let me repeat, NEVER, after lunch or dinner when the stomach is already full to the brim with food."

I checked my watch. I was well within acceptable *cappuccino* limits. With this in mind, and wearing a rose-colored shirt that matched my shoes exactly (this color matching thing was also apparently critical to fitting in), I ventured out to make my most important decision since we landed: which bar would be "our" local bar. Domenico explained to me that this decision could have political as well as social implications that I'd have to figure out for myself.

Shopkeepers were already out scrubbing the sidewalks in front of their stores, polishing the door handles and wiping fingerprints off the large plate glass windows. Every storefront summoned me to eat something. Hunks of *parmigiano* of various sizes were laid out like little cheese villages. Huge legs of *prosciutto* and whole *salami* hung above plates overflowing with olives at the *salumeria*. Dairy trucks were double parked in front of the *alimentare* while men brought in crates of milk and cream. An old man was cutting the tops off of broccoli in front of the *fruttivendolo*.

The first bar I passed was filled with scruffy men reading *La Gazzetta Dello Sport*, the country's primary sports newspaper, and drinking *cappuccino* with a shot of something that looked suspiciously like alcohol – a scene that definitely fell outside the realm of my *cappuccino* education and had dubious social implications. The second was filled with young people, also disproportionately comprised of men, who seemed inordinately interested in the rear end of the *barista*. This had the potential of being the wrong choice both politically and socially. The third bar was brightly lit and the pastry case had a dazzling array of *brioche*, cakes and cookies. Although *La Gazzetta dello Sport*, replete with soccer scores, was clearly the most sought-after reading material, the *Corriere Della Sera*, a general newspaper out of Milan, as well as *Varese*'s own *Prealpina* were suitably represented. The barista was wearing a bow tie and the sign centered above the bar read:

E poi Dio creo' il pallone.
Lo getto' su San Siro
E disse a Rivera:
"Vai per il mondo
e insegna a giocare"

Then God created the soccer ball.
He threw it down to San Siro stadium
And said to Rivera
"Go forth and teach the world how to play."

In combination with the presence of diverse reading material, it seemed about as politically correct as I was going to find. Pending family approval that I had good reason to believe would be forthcoming, this was to be the Hummel family bar. I ate my *brioche*, a less fatty version of the French croissant, and Buster scoured for *briciole* (crumbs) while charming the locals. The ladies, in particular, could not get enough of him. *"Che carino questo Carlino; che bello che sei* (What a cute pug; how beautiful you are)!" cooed an exquisite brunette, with ample cleavage and matching fuchsia shoes, handbag and watchband. As an after-thought, she added,"*Buon giorno, signora.*" (At this point, I made a mental note that it might be prudent for me to walk the dog, rather than Bruce.)

Buster and I scanned the scene. My objective was to get more acquainted with our new environment. Buster's sole objective was to snarf up any and all crumbs, if possible before they hit the ground. I could have chosen cafè-like seating, as every table was bare; the clientele preferred to crowd around the bar counter which was a tangle of cups, spoons, sugar crystals and *brioche* crumbs. Some were chattering, others had their noses deeply entrenched in the bar's complimentary newspapers. I chose a variety of *brioche* for Bruce and the kids: one plain, one filled with cream, and one chocolate.

"To take away, *signora*?" asked the *barista,* borrowing a form of the English expression.

"*Si, grazie,*" I nodded and then proceeded to request a *cappuccino* to 'take away' as well. This was not as easy to pull off.

"To take away?" he puzzled, as if he had never heard the words he had so clearly articulated seconds prior.

"*Si,*" I told him.

The *barista* went through a door behind the counter and I heard a lot of banging, cabinets opening and shutting, muttering, and then he reappeared. Carefully, he poured a shot of *espresso* into a plastic, disposable cup, topped it with hot foamed milk and gingerly placed a piece of tinfoil on top.

When Buster finished cajoling an actual corner of a *brioche* from an eager toddler, we wandered out to the *Edicola* (newsstand) to see whether I might be able to special order a daily copy of the International Herald Tribune in English.

"*Le faccio sapere* (I'll let you know)," the elderly man told me. Then he patted Buster and started talking to me about the weather. I was going to give him my usual polite response to small talk and take my leave, but something made me stop.

"*Si, fa caldissimo. È sempre cosi?* (Yes, it's really hot. Is it always like this?)" I asked. Then I shook his hand. *Mi Chiamo Denise. Sono Americana. Non sono parente di Presidente Bush però.* (My name is Denise. I'm American. No relation to President Bush though.)" I chuckled. Recent European press related to our international policy was very unfavorable, and I was quick to create distance between my views and that of our current administration. No sense in making enemies before he had good reason to dislike me on my own merits.

He picked up one of my hands and held them in two of his own.

"You don't have to be ashamed of your nationality, ma'am. The Americans liberated us from fascism. Your soldiers gave my family the first food we had eaten in the week prior when they came. The people of a nation are not comprised of their government, where the players change, but the game remains the same. To the contrary, the people are individuals who are the heart of their country ... and beautiful women like you."

Our conversation continued for some time, moving forward from the initial banality of the weather, to a conversation that stayed with me long after I said goodbye, because, for a change, I gave it the space to happen. Maybe the *brioche* here was sprinkled with magic or maybe they put something 'extra' in the *cappuccino*. Whatever it was, I already felt different than I had 24 hours ago.

I picked up an Italian comic book for the kids and arrived back at home to an apartment as quiet as I had left it. I arranged the *brioche* on a paper plate and put it on the table in the dining area and left the disposable – and now virtually empty cup – in the kitchen, most of the coffee having spilled on my hand. I learned my first lesson of Italian culture — coffee is not to be taken away, but rather drunk hot at the bar counter or made at home. I hoped my future lessons would be as painless.

Matthew and Alex fought over the chocolate *brioche* (I should have known to get two of anything chocolate). "How does this move the world forward?" I asked them, my well-worn response to their nonsensical fighting.

Alex pushed the *brioche* toward Matthew and rolled his eyes. Matthew inhaled the *brioche* almost as quickly as Buster had dealt with the takings at the bar, lest Alex change his mind about moving the world forward, or at least about moving the *brioche* to Matthew's side of the table. Bruce drank what was left of the cold thimble of coffee and deflated foam, and together we ventured out to fill our tiny, but decidedly empty refrigerator.

At the *macelleria*, whole rabbits hung in the window as a declaration that the meat for sale was the freshest one could expect. Inside it seemed that half the town was vying for the butcher's attention. People shouting out their orders simultaneously, meat being cut, weighed, packaged in white paper and handed over the counter to a sea of waiting hands. When the crowd thinned out, we pointed to familiar-looking cuts of meat and for quantity, simply said, "*quattro*," gesturing to the four of us. At the *fruttivendolo*, the old man I had seen earlier was settled into place behind his scale. Clients pointed (no touching!) while he chose each piece, lightly squeezing it, turning it to examine for bruises, before placing it on the scale. Every purchase took three times as long since an update regarding the health of a particular family member of the vendor or customer took precedence over the transaction. We requested eight spectacular peaches, the size of small cantaloupes. He lifted each one, turned it, and offered it up to us for a sniff. "It will be a slice of heaven," he assured us.

At the *panificio*, we bought our bread for the day. Nuns from a convent near *Sacro Monte* dropped by to pick up their daily donation of day-old bread from the back room. On the way home, the kids trailed behind us on the narrow sidewalk carrying their share of the packages and nibbling on the *biscotti* the proprietor of the *pasticceria* gave them to welcome the kids to the neighborhood. Suddenly we heard loud kissing noises behind us. We turned to see the back of someone kissing Matthew all over his head.

"Friendly country," Bruce murmured, a moment before realizing that it was Giampiero.

"*Sono il malefico baciatore* (I'm the mad kisser)," he told Matthew.

We were laughing so hard, it hurt. Where else in the world could your child be attacked by a mad kisser without a police record?

After wedging our groceries into our tiny refrigerator, we considered going out again to buy an iron, a lamp, two cell phones, one land-line phone, a toaster oven, four stools, one butter dish, one pepper mill, one printer, a table cloth, two fans, a broom, an outdoor table with four chairs and a tea pot. I hadn't had to buy so many household accoutrements since graduating from college. Back in the States, we probably would have eaten a sandwich in the car and purchased everything in one shopping mall in the amount of time the kids were at baseball practice. In Italy, however, the stores were closed for the *pausa* (pause, or lunch break) between 12:30 and 3:30 p.m. They were also closed on Sunday and all morning on Monday, except for establishments selling food, which are open in the morning on Monday, but not in the afternoon, and *parrucchieri* (hairdressers) and *gioiellerie* (jewelry stores) which arc closed all day Monday. I needed to learn to slow down and embrace the Italian pace of life or go mad.

Unable to finish our shopping, I decided that in order to use these "frozen hours" in the most efficient manner possible, it was time to try my hand at doing laundry Italian style, which in addition to the usual monotony associated with the chore in America, now included the task of hanging all clothes, as well as sheets and table cloths to dry. After two loads, our small apartment looked like a laundromat. Every square inch, including the backs of chairs, three radiators and one lamp, was covered with something wet. If I was a "real" Italian wife, I would have proceeded to iron everything from my family's underwear and socks to the sheets and towels.

"*Ma, dimmi la verità ... davvero non stiri le calze* (But tell me the truth ... you really don't iron the socks)?" Susanna asked me one day when the Sorus arrived during the laundry folding process.

"Trust me," I responded. "I don't iron anything that isn't visible to the general public, and only then if it looks like it's been slept in."

Giampiero just shook his head in disbelief as if to say, 'these American women were obviously not versed in the art of keeping a proper home.' Then he smiled and winked. "I'm sure you have other redeeming virtues," he jibed.

There was so much more to those first weeks than wet clothes and grocery shopping. Exploring our beautiful surroundings offset the hustle and bustle of transitioning to our new home. Laura was nine months pregnant at this point, and clearly conserving her energy, but Giampiero and Susanna had a knack for calling us at just the moment that we were fed up with unpacking or running errands. Fifteen minutes later, we'd be walking to the *centro* (the historic center of town), or to the park, or packing up a quick picnic and heading for the shores of *Lago Maggiore*. Tommaso and Vanni, now 18 and 20, often joined us, chatting with Matthew and Alex about sports seamlessly as if they were all the same age.

Varese's town center, an *area pedonale* (pedestrian center) just minutes from our front door, was built for the most part from the Middle Ages to the Renaissance and provided a beautiful and tranquil nexus from which we explored the narrow alleys, cobblestoned streets, flower-draped balconies, and *portici* which led off the main square. *Piazza Monte Grappa,* in particular, was perfect for the kids to bicycle, skateboard or scooter around the fountain like a race track, while Bruce and I calmly watched the cascading water and chatted with the Sorus.

On the first and third Sunday of the month, there was a *mercatino* (food market) in town. The experience was the antithesis of the crowded supermarket drudgery at home. Up and down historic *Corso Matteoti,* we'd sample *prosciutto,* buy the local cheese – *taleggio* from *Lombardia, asiago* from the *Veneto* or *fontina* from *Val D'Aosta* – and bread carved from loaves that were so long they looked like they were baked in ovens as deep as the width of the entire bakery. The energy of the experience was intoxicating. There were discussions between husband and wife about what produce to buy for Sunday dinner or whether to spring for the more expensive aged *Parmeseano* or the younger, less pungent variety. Gray-haired women held the arm of their younger daughter or grandaughter, as they negotiated the crowds in front of the fruit vender. Dogs pulled at the leashes of their owners, and pawed at a stray crumb of *biscotti* fallen between the cracks of the cobblestone.

Off we went to the table selling wine from the vineyards of *Lombardia.* My favorite was a *Terre di Franciacorta* from the vineyards near *Brescia.* Giampiero headed for the tables carrying bottles from *Valtellina,* from the vineyards near *Grumello* and *Valgella.* Vanni and Tommaso followed closely behind to help us with the weight of our packages.

"You'll never be fully integrated into *Lombardia* society until you embrace more wine than *vino bianco fermo* (still white wine)," Giampiero teased me as I always avoided the more bubbly variety popular in the region.

Then we made ourselves a picnic on the bench in front of the World War II memorial in the central *piazza*, or took our purchases back to our garden to eat there. The peaches were sweeter, the *vino* more intoxicating when eaten *al aperto* (in the open air).

A minute or so outside the center was *Varese*'s *Giardini Estensi,* lovely formal gardens with a beautiful fountain, piped-in classical music, and soft lighting after dark. During the day, a short hike under the trestles covered with wisteria, brought us to an area up the hill, hidden from the general view. There a young man ran a small car track with mini electrical cars for the kids, while his father drove a tiny steam train for the younger set. There was a bar nearby with outdoor seating for us to have a coffee while the kids enjoyed their entertainment. Children and adults seem to fit so neatly together, the needs of the older and younger fitting together like the pieces of a puzzle.

The nearby towns surrounding *Lago Maggiore*, not far from the Swiss border and no more than 25 minutes from our front door, were also a constant source of relaxation. If we woke up on a weekend and the sky was a deep blue, we could expect a phone call from Giampiero by 11 a.m. informing us of the *programma* he made for the day. We gave Giampiero the nickname 'GP', short for Giampiero Soru but also for "Global Positioning Satellite," as his ability to navigate the tiny streets and towns of *Lago Maggiore* and beyond was nothing short of magic. We nicknamed his outings, and any subsequent experiences with or without him that satisfied his requisite criteria, "GP Moments." The key ingredients included a blue sky and at least two out of these three elements: a beautiful view, a coffee or *aperitivo* in an outdoor cafè, and a scenic walk in a natural or charming setting. All GP Moments started out the same way. A simple high-five from Tommaso and Vanni to Matthew and Alex, then:

"Da' un bacino a Zia Susanna e Zio Giampiero (Give a kiss to Aunt Susanna and Uncle Giampiero)," he and Susanna said to the kids, leaning in to kiss each of their cheeks.

"Today's adventure will be the islands of *Lago Maggiore*," Giampiero told us, his blue eyes dancing and fuzzy mustache twitching with anticipation. "We'll see the botanical gardens of *Isola Madre* because they don't predict cloud cover until late morning and the gardens are best appreciated against a blue sky. Then, the *Borromeo Villa* of *Isola Bella*, followed by a fish lunch at *Isola dei Pescatori* ..."

Susanna took Alex by the hand and Giampiero put his arm around Matthew (or vice versa) and off we'd go. This scene was repeated throughout our time in *Varese* on more occasions than I could possibly recall, and the site of my children walking hand in hand with two adults, not their parents, who loved and cared for them, will always be a vision I can summon to melt my heart on the coldest winter day.

"I don't mind the holding hands," Matthew told me many months later, "but the kissing ... Yuck !!!"

Our outings during the week while the Sorus were at work, included exploring the other lakes surrounding *Varese*. In addition to *Varese*'s own lake, *Lago di Varese*, and nearby *Lago Maggiore*, we were only about 40 kilometers from *Lago Lugano* in Switzerland, 35 kilometers from *Lago di Como* and 100 kilometers from *Lago di Garda*. The entire area was surrounded by "Pre-Alp" mountains, the Alps looming up behind them, offering protection from the wind and the beauty of their snow-capped peaks. There was always the opportunity for a cool hike in the forest or a chair-lift ride to a peak towering over one of the lakes for lunch and a spectacular view. It was difficult to complain about the rigors of settling in, when we could constantly distract ourselves with untold beauty. We were never at a loss of things to do, most of them nearby, without the necessity of much preparation, and often free of cost: A parent's nirvana.

*   *   *

We were invited to the *oratorio* of *San Michele Arcangelo,* near *Ugo Foscolo* Elementary School to celebrate the end of the school year and the beginning of summer. A church's *oratorio* is generally a large room or rooms with an outdoor courtyard for kids to gather and play and families to connect. It's like an extended spare room and backyard. You may live in a small apartment, but have 20 kids to a birthday party simply by calling the local priest and reserving the *oratorio*. This particular oratorio was a single, large room with tables and chairs, a foosball table and a bar with a statue of the Virgin Mary behind the counter. Outside was a courtyard with more tables, a barbecue, and the scent of roasting sausages and peppers. The far corner was a makeshift soccer field, kids laughing and yelling as they played. As we entered, Matthew stood behind me. He literally was holding on to my pant leg. I looked at Alex who seemed fairly tranquil. His dark blond hair and light skin stood out though among the dark-haired, olive-skinned children. Francesca was over in the corner of the courtyard practicing a dance she had learned with four other 8-year-old girls. The Italian boys came over casually, obviously curious to size up "the Americans." Between bites of pasta and pork sausages, a group of kids came over and said, "*Vuoi giocare* (Do you want to play)?" and because it's a phrase that I taught Matthew and Alex before coming to Italy, they understood and went off to play soccer.

When it came time to discuss game strategy, our kids smiled and shrugged, and when the game started, they kicked the ball in the right direction. Intermittently, we could hear the Italian kids encouraging our kids, "*Vai, vai, va*i (Go, go, go)!" and simultaneously our kids added one word to their vocabulary, through a combination of context and osmosis.

Bruce and I sat with the other parents, sipping *vino*. Laura looked as if she could be rushed to the delivery room at any second, and Domenico introduced us to many of Matthew and Alex's future classmates and their families. I expected that physically, I would blend in fine with my brown eyes, curly brown hair, olive skin, and rounded hips. Instead, and in contrast, the Italian women looked liked they walked off a Gucci ad, as smooth and sleek as I had been in college. I felt like a chubby American, and a frumpy one at that.

"It's 90 degrees," I said to Domenico, "Why isn't there one woman wearing shorts?"

"We're not at the beach," he responded. Then seeing my expression, he shrugged apologetically, "It's just not done."

"Huh," I responded, wondering how I would function when nine-tenths of my summer wardrobe was unacceptable in polite society.

A well-groomed, accessory-matching, non-shorts-wearing woman idled toward me. "Tell me again why you moved here for a year," said Catia, the mother of one of the children who would be in Alex's class in the fall.

"We wanted an opportunity for some perspective," I answered, unsure I was capturing the right Italian words.

"So you left your job and your house in the United States and came here ... for just one year?" she asked me, looking up at her husband out of the right side of her face with a look that said, "the chubby *Americana* with the shorted-pant garment has a few screws loose." By now a crowd was gathering. Catia was apparently not the only one who was confused about why we were here.

Bruce nodded politely when he was addressed, and I translated when I could. From the look on his face, I wondered if he was feeling even more like a fish out of water than I was. His Italian game-show watching had only taken him so far, and he looked as if he had entered the live version of the bombarding sounds and accents he had been listening to on television before leaving the States. I envied the children's ability to use play as a method of communication. It was so obviously a tool that transcended cultural and language differences and I fantasized that we might find a grown-up equivalent that would help me overcome my adult self-consciousness. I was struggling with my own lack of ability to communicate, which although not as significant an obstacle as Bruce was facing, included a lack of familiarity with the nuances and subtleties of language I took for granted when I spoke in my mother tongue. Would I ever be able to explain the philosophical basis for our journey here or would I have to be satisfied with the possibility that the way we lived our lives and interacted with others might somehow transmit our intention?

*   *   *

Bruce and I debated whether to wait a week or even whether to skip camp altogether, but after observing them at play in the *oratorio* we decided that the boys' interaction with other children was probably more important to their language development than any by-the-book studying we could do at home.

On the first day of camp, both kids practically needed to be surgically extracted from bed. After a discussion in which both appeared to be on the brink of tears, they reluctantly agreed to go for a half-day. I watched them leave looking as if they had been drafted into the army against their will. Matthew was looking at his toes and shaking his head, silently chastising me for putting him through yet another challenge. Alex annoyed that there wasn't just a little more *gelato* and a little less of trying something new.

When we picked them up at the end of the day, though, they seemed no worse for the wear.

"Pallanuoto is water polo," Alex informed me.

"What about *minivolley* and *minibasket*?" I asked.

"Dai, Mamma (Come on, Mom)," Matthew said, using the Italian expression he picked up that day. "It's volleyball and basketball." Picking on your mother must be an international concept.

"Yea," added Alex, "and *calcetto* is foosball, which I'm really good at. You have to have really fast wrists. And *monopattino* is rollerblading."

Needless to say, baseball was not one of the selections.

The second day, we asked them to try a whole day, including the offered *pranzo* (lunch) of three courses: pasta, meat and dessert – a far cry from our grilled cheese and chicken nugget days. Still, 9 a.m. to 4 p.m. is a long day when you don't speak the same language as your peers. I wondered if we were pushing it, but upon their return they seemed triumphant.

"I tried this new pasta dish, Mom," said Alex proudly, who had up until now not ventured much beyond pizza marinara and spaghetti with butter. "It's called *gnocchi.*"

"I had *scalloppine* with mushrooms for my second course, but Alex didn't try it," Matthew said, with a look meant to assure me that Alex's culinary transformation was not complete.

"I made a friend named Giacomo," Alex told us. "And Matthew's best friend is Davide."

"Wow," I said, "a best friend after two days. That's got to be a record."

When they went to sleep that night, they asked us if they could go to this same camp next summer. I could only marvel at how their emotions rocketed from trepidation to joy in such a short time. One friend, one warm meal, and sports – the universal language of boys – were the ingredients to instant success.

Our plan for augmenting the boys' Italian, beyond attendance at summer camp, was limited to playing an alphabet game while waiting for food in restaurants. We went from person to person around the table, identifying Italian words that start with A, B, C, and so on. Any resistance in this regard fell subject to a secret weapon Bruce and I developed through exhaustive research into behavior modification. Any child who whined, argued, talked-back, or was otherwise annoying was sentenced to a *gelato*-free evening; remarkably successful, really.

Positive reinforcement also helped. We put a sheet of paper on the refrigerator and added, day by day, any new Italian word we heard them use. Then, while pondering the fact that Alex was, in general, still refusing to try most foods other than spaghetti with butter, lemon *gelato* or pizza, added another sheet entitled "new foods." The boys got to go to the toy store for a token prize for every 20 new foods and for every 100 new words. *Figurine di calcio* cards relating to the various Italian soccer players, much like baseball cards at home, became the favored toy store prize. Matthew and Alex seamlessly transferred their childhood obsession from American style to *stile Italiano,* while I continued to search in vain for my favorite American hair products and brand of ibuprofen.

There was no question, though, that our efforts to teach the boys needed some assistance. I called Barbara Heinkel, a tutor I was introduced to during my May visit. Though German, she married an Italian, Fiorenzo Pennati, and settled down in *Varese*. Not only did she speak German, Italian, English, French and Dutch, which she taught at the *Scuola Europea*, she was a gifted artist, and played the piano, saxophone, and cello as well. If the kids didn't learn Italian, they'd surely learn something. She greeted us at the door with the youthful exuberance of a teenager, tussled the kids' hair, and sent me on my way for a one-hour walk by *Lago di Varese*.

"They've learned the most important words in the Italian language," Barbara informed me when I returned.

"Really?" I asked, "What are they?"

"*Centrocampista, attaccante, difensore, portiere* (centerfield, attack, defense and goalie)," Alex informed me.

"*Calcio di punizione, fuori gioco e gol* (penalty kick, off sides and goal)," Matthew chimed in exuberantly and with an Italian accent not discernibly different from the local children.

I thought they'd be conjugating verbs and learning about when to use "impersonal expressions which take the subjunctive, if the verb of the dependent clause has an expressed subject ..." *alla* "Da Capo Grammar Review", but Barbara had other ideas.

"These are the most important words in the Italian language?" I asked as politely as possible.

"Certainly," Barbara answered matter-of-factly. "If they know enough to play with the other children, the rest of the language will be at their feet."

"At their feet – get it Mom?" said Alex, and Barbara laughed.

When I picked them up from their second lesson, they were beaming and holding a *crostata*, a warm cake topped with *marmellata* (jam). They learned the terms for flour, sugar, eggs and most kitchen utensils, and converted oven temperature from Fahrenheit to Celsius.

"No verbs?" I asked.

"No verbs," she responded. "But would you like to come to dinner on Saturday?"

"Can we?" asked Matthew, looking at me expectedly.

"Sure," I said. "That would be great."

On the way home, Matthew and Alex chattered to each other about who made the most substantial contribution to the *crostata*. I realized we had just made our first non-Stragapede, non-Soru friend. It made me feel more powerful, more independent, more at-home, somehow.

*　　　*　　　*

The *barista* at our local bar was no longer asking me what kind of coffee I would have in the morning. He just greeted Buster and me and set about making my *cappuccino*. Just for fun, we began to teach Buster his obedience commands in Italian. Soon the locals at the bar were even more enamored with him.

"*Seduto!*" they'd say, and Buster sat.

"*Stai li!*" they commanded, and Buster stayed.

"Vieni!" they encouraged him, and Buster would prance over, his tail wagging.

"Che bello!!!" said a man with a black cap and foam-stained mustache peering over his newspaper.

"Che carino!!" said an elderly woman sneaking Buster a fair portion of her *brioche*.

Buster would be in for a shock when he returned to a country where coffee bars like Starbucks didn't appreciate his vacuum-cleaner talents. He'd have to settle for the clandestine pieces of pancake passed to him under the kitchen table at home.

CHAPTER FIVE

It's Never Too Early for a Glass of Wine

Wine ... moderately drunken
It doth quicken a man's wits,
It doth comfort the heart.
-Andrew Boorde, 1562, "Dyetary of Health"

In a short time, we accomplished a great deal. Nevertheless there were times during those first few weeks when I looked at my watch and asked myself whether it was too early to have a glass of *vino bianco* before lunch. Fortunately for me, *aperitivo* hour in Italy comes twice a day, once at about 11:30 a.m. or noon, before lunch, and once again at about 6:30 or 7 p.m., before dinner. I will admit there were several times I took advantage of this cultural tradition as soon as the first of the olives and *bruschette* hit the bar counter, signaling the acceptability of imbibing.

Bruce and I made several trips to the *questura* to obtain a document called the *Permesso di Soggiorno*, a document that was our official "Permission to Stay" in Italy for more than the three months allotted to the average tourist. It was a prerequisite to many steps of our transition, including the ability to pick up the car I ordered months ago. Every visit to the *questura* to obtain the document involved waiting for hours in the sweltering non-air-conditioned office, squeezing through the door into the small over-crowded room, where the only semblance of order was a sweaty, survival-of-the-fittest pushing contest. Each trip presented a new obstacle. On what we thought was going to be our third and last visit, I presented the clerk with our visa, our financial documents, a copy of our lease, four photographs, and everything else listed on the data sheet given to us on our second visit.

"Where are your stamps?" the gentleman behind the glass asked.

"What stamps?"

"Go to the *tabacchi* and ask for the stamps for immigration. Then come back."

My *pazienza* for the entire process had just about come to an end; nevertheless, I proceeded to the *tabacchi*.

"Can I have the stamps for immigration?" I asked

"No, you have to go to the post office," I was informed.

At the post office I received the all-important stamp (which looked exactly like a postage stamp) for 10 euros each. Back to the *questura* I tramped, where the agent prepared the document. I could see it. I could smell the ink on the page. I could practically touch it. After reviewing our lease, financial documents, and spending half an hour filling out forms, he handed us two pieces of paper.

"*Devi prendere il timbro digitale,*" he said.

"What?" I despaired.

"*Digitale,*" he said, pressing his thumb on the paper to mimic a fingerprint, "but they're closed today. You have to get them and return on August 20."

I was hot, tired, thirsty, fed-up, and fighting back tears. August 20 was a month away. No *Permesso di Soggiorno* for one month meant that we couldn't pick up our new car for one month. Desperate, I resorted to the world-renowned, Italians-love-children ploy.

"If we return on August 20," I pleaded, trying to use the soft, sweet tones Susanna used at the tax office, "we will have to tell our children that they will be unable to explore this lovely region of *Lombardia* before school starts because we won't have the documents we need to pick up our new car."

After several awkward moments of stare-down, he finally relented. "OK," he said, "get the fingerprints and come back tomorrow. But bring the children."

I was truly overwhelmed by the degree of effort it took to do things here. Yet, had not all the stores been closed by the time we exited the *Questura*, Bruce and I, in true American fashion, would have gone directly to the next item on our multi-paged 'to do' list. Instead, we strolled through the light mist to a bar and took a table under the *portici* where we were able to sit outside without getting wet. We ordered two *piadine* (grilled sandwiches) with *mozzarella*, *prosciutto crudo* and *pomodori freschi,* and two glasses of grapefruit juice, hand-squeezed behind the bar. A glass of wine was calling me, but I reasoned that I had to call upon my mental faculties for our post-*pausa* (siesta) errands. Watching the rain fall, we were able to laugh at the day's events. We were beginning to realize that one of the effects of the *pausa* was to wean us from the mind-set that faster was better.

"I get the feeling we should forget about putting in a claim for the excess customs charges or lost boxes," Bruce said.

"Done," I nodded, taking out my pad, and crossing it off the list. Succumbing to the inefficiency of certain processes was so much less stressful than fighting it and it felt, in a strange sense, almost freeing to understand that there were certain situations I just could not control.

But my ability to relinquish control was constantly being tested. I kept thinking that with enough tenacity some things could get done on American time. Whether it was the *questura* or Telecom Italia, I was determined to do things *alla Americana* and the result was alarmingly similar.

"*Signora*, this is the tenth time I've called to ask when we'll have the high-speed connectivity we ordered," I said tersely to the Telecom Italian operator.

"Yes, yes, *signora*," she told me with amazing repetitiveness, "we will get to that *adesso*."

"*Signora*, my Italian is not very good, however, my understanding of the word,' '*adesso*',' is that it means 'now.' Exactly how long does 'now' take?!"

We also needed to find out why our cell phones stopped working shortly after we purchased them.

"You have to 'charge' your phone, *signora*," the clerk explained.

"It is charged!" I retorted, three times.

Then on the fourth call, "No *signora*, not with electricity, with money. You must go to a Bancomat machine, you know, where you get money, and choose the selection to re-charge your phone. Choose the amount of money you want to credit your phone with and just keep making calls until you run out of credit. It's easy!"

"What ever happened to getting a bill once a month with an addressed envelope, inserting a check, attaching a stamp and mailing it?"

"You don't send checks in the mail in Italy, *signora*. Even when your bills arrive for other things, like electricity and gas, you will have to pay them at the post office or at your bank electronically. We don't mail checks in Italy, *signora*. They have a way of getting ... shall we say ... 'lost.'"

There were so many challenges to stumble through and I found myself longing for the days of being a simple tourist on vacation. Touring Italy for a week or two was nothing like living there. On those trips, there were no bills to pay, other than the ones related to my credit cards after returning to the States. As a tourist my biggest challenge had been making rough calculations about the equivalent of what I was spending in dollars when I bought a souvenir. In contrast, living here required dealing with the daily vagaries of a fluctuating rate of exchange, pulling us into an endless game of predicting the best time to convert money. The 'new-to-us' European measures of distance, weight, volume, length and temperature were confounding, ever-present challenges to simple processes like cooking or buying things the right size for the right space. The measure of time, as well, was different. Europeans use a 24-hour clock. Perhaps that shouldn't have been a big deal, but that part of my brain had been dormant for decades and I often found myself counting from 12 silently to myself for afternoon appointments. I was experiencing a unique form of brain-freeze – the human version of having too many computer windows open and not enough RAM to back it up.

Grocery shopping, too, had its perils. There was an inherent danger in relying on the label of supermarket products. It was actually possible to think you were buying something like Uncle Ben's Rice when you were actually buying food for your hamster. One day Domenico arrived with a handy gift.

"I bought you a bottle of dish soap," he told me, "because I noticed you didn't have any."

I wondered what he was talking about.

"It's right here," I said, showing him our dish soap. It was a bottle of liquid that clearly had a picture of brilliantly clean dishes on the front.

"That's a rinse for your dishwasher," he said.

I wondered why the dish soap here was so watery ...

In just a few weeks we also discovered no less than seven styles of toilets in a five block radius from the center of town. Style number one: the handle turned counter clockwise until flushed then manually turned back. Style number two: the flat flush button on the wall behind the toilet. Style number three: the ceiling-pull flush. Number four: the round, rubber foot-flush on the floor. Five: the no seat – just toilet. Six: the very low toilet, no seat (better to remove at least one pant leg, have strong thighs, and good aim). And, finally, style number seven: the no seat or toilet – just foot rests for squatting (better to totally remove pants).

What about electricity? Buy an appliance, plug it in, and turn it on, right? Wrong. Every electrical outlet had a different width and every appliance had a different, seemingly random, plug size. We became regulars at the local electrical supply store because it became an absolute certainty that any appliance we bought had a plug that didn't match the wall socket for its particular location of use in our house. Even the electricity supply was not a "given." Judging by the number of times we were left in total darkness if we dared to run the washing machine at the same time as the dishwasher, I expected to look out into the garden and see Benjamin Franklin, or some Italian equivalent, flying a kite with a key dangling from it waiting for a jolt of lightening.

When the evening finally arrived to have dinner at Barbara's house, we were quite ready for a conversation involving the day-to-day cultural contrasts between our two nations. Barbara was a supportive and sympathetic person – just the shoulder to lean on in the midst of all this turmoil. We met her husband, Fiorenzo, who owned a motorcycle shop in town. He spoke English almost as well as Barbara, which gave all of us a welcome break to communicate in our mother tongue and me a rest from my translating duties.

Barbara's cooking rivaled the best of Italian wives. We ate a savory *spaghetti con frutti di mare* (spaghetti with seafood) followed by a *filetto* (sliced beef) and roasted vegetables. The table's centerpiece was a crystal bowl of water in which rose blooms and candles floated over a coarse white-linen tablecloth, and each napkin ring was personalized with a different dried silk flower. For dessert she prepared a lovely *crostata*, similar to the one she prepared with the kids during a lesson, though looking a bit more "professional." We shared with them our recent challenges while they listened sympathetically.

"The washing-machine flooded the bathroom," I told Barbara.

"Did you clean the filter where the water exits the machine into the pipe after each load?" she asked.

"The pipes under the sink detached," Bruce explained.

"They're plastic pipes in newer construction," Fiorenzo said. "You should have checked to see how old they were before signing the rental contract. They'll need re-gluing."

"There's only a trickle of water that comes out of the showerhead," we mentioned feebly.

"That's due to calcification," they informed us. "You have to buy an *anti-calcare* product and clean the shower head."

They looked at us with a cross between polite compassion and confusion that we could arrive to the ripe age of 43 without having this basic knowledge of plumbing.

I decided after that night to stop pining for our "New World" comforts. After all, each Italian contrast had its advantages: A kitchen big enough for only one person meant there wasn't room for me to help while Bruce made dinner. A refrigerator too small for more than one day's fare meant we had fresh food every day. A smaller living environment meant I didn't have to shout when I needed to call for a child or correct behavior. A shared office desk meant the possibility of renewed intimacy. A shower so narrow that I always knocked the knob from hot to cold meant that I was always VERY awake in the morning. The bidet that I labeled as a useless waste of space made a great library for bathroom reading. A single closet that was only as deep as a hanger meant I didn't have to struggle to find my clothes and didn't spend a lot of money for clothing I couldn't fit into its two-foot width.

Our tiny garden had even more significant advantages. It meant that we got to say hello to our neighbors regularly, since nine times out of 10 the ball the kids were playing with sailed over the hedge into our neighbor's tiny garden. In fact, so many times did I have to slip a note under their door, that I finally just wrote, "*il pallone ancora* (the ball again)" on a yellow sticky Post-It note, so that it could be recycled the next time the ball went missing.

At one point, Matthew and Alex invented a game that they thought might lead to fewer problems. They used two empty plastic water bottles as bats and a rolled up pair of socks as a ball. On the inevitable day that the pair of socks went flying into our neighbor's garden, I told Alex to put a sign on our neighbor's door.

"And what am I going to say?" he asked me. "The socks again???!!!"

It was obvious we were making great strides to see the positive side of confounding experiences. When the car insurance policy arrived for the car that we could not yet pick up without the *Permesso di Soggiorno*, Bruce said,

"I don't understand one word of this policy. I sure hope you do."

"Not really," I responded. "When the agent gave me a choice of policy terms, I couldn't understand her so I just told her to give me *il solito* (the usual) that they give their other customers and this is what she gave me."

"Is that what they mean when they say that only the dentist's family has bad teeth, or some such thing?" Bruce responded, amazed that my law school education had failed me. Then without waiting for an answer, he asked me, "Listen, if we get the car in time to go away for a weekend here and there, what are we going to do with Buster?"

"I didn't want to disturb the Sorus or Stragapedes for that, so I called a kennel recommended by Laura and Domenico's vet," I told him. "But first Buster has to *fare la prova*."

"*Fare la* what?" he asked.

"*La prova*," I explained. "The kennel lady says he has to try out overnight to see if he's a suitable kennel candidate. We have to provide his food."

"He needs to try out for a position at a kennel?" Bruce repeated. But without waiting for an answer, he nodded, and went out to find a store that sold Buster's special food – the kind for little dogs who have the appetite of big dogs, but the waistline of little dogs. He too was learning to take things in stride.

When I picked the kids up on the last day of their first full week of camp, an Italian boy waved goodbye and yelled, "Ciao *Matteo*."

"Ciao," Matthew responded.

I asked him the boy's name and he said, "His name is Flavio. He doesn't like Bush either." I asked Matthew how he knew what Flavio thought of our president. Matthew, at this point, could communicate only basic needs and statements.

"Well, he said, 'blah, blah, blah Bush.' And I said, '*Non mi piace* Bush (I don't like Bush)' and then he gave me a high five and now we're friends." His young mind was engaged in a process that not many adults have perfected. He was finding commonalities in those who were different from him and using them to build social bridges. They could use him at the United Nations.

Of all the events that brought us step by step to a place of ease during our adjustment, two of them rival each other as the hallmark of turning the corner to a place of truly positive perspective: the arrival of the *Permesso di Soggiorno* and the birth of Chiara. Yes, one bright day toward the end of our first month in *Varese* we received the mysterious *Permesso di Soggiorno*, signifying our right of passage into Italian culture. For the entire time period that we were without that document, and therefore without a car, Laura and Domenico, ever true to the concept of 'extra,' allowed us to use the car that Domenico ordinarily took to the train station. He rode his bicycle instead. We owed them so much.

"I really can't find a way to express how thankful I am for your thoughtfulness and the sacrifice to your own convenience," I told them both. "*Perché? È normale ...* (Why? It's normal ...)" Domenico told me.

And in some ways, it was becoming "normal." Each of us, in our own lives, was beginning to give to others with a more open heart. I found myself looking for opportunities to give back or give to others in the way I had been receiving. I was helping the old ladies crossing the street, rather than beeping at them – literally.

"Excuse me that I'm so slow," a woman said to me.

"Slow, are you joking? You're walking faster than Camoranesi (an Italian soccer champion)."

She chuckled so hard, I thought she'd fall over.

One splendid summer day, the kind with a blue sky and a gentle warm breeze, the phone rang.

"*Ci siamo* (It's time)," Laura said breathless.

She was in labor. I was soon to be one of those adults, who although not her parent, would give the Stragapede's new child the feeling of being surrounded by love, just like *Zia* Susanna and *Zio* Giampiero, *Zia* Laura and *Zio* Domenico were to my kids. Outside the delivery room, a poem reminded me of my responsibility as *Zia* Denise:

Dici che sono il futuro;
Non mi cancellare dal presente.
Dici che sono la speranza della pace;
Non mi indurre alla Guerra.
Dici che sono la promessa del bene;
Non mi affidare al male.
Dici che sono la luce dei tuoi occhi;
Non mi abbandonare alle tenebre.

You say I am the future;
Don't erase me from the present
You say I'm the hope of peace;
Don't lead me to war
You say I'm the promise of goodness;
Don't lead me to what is wrong.
You say I'm the light of your eyes;
Don't leave me in darkness

I was in the room when Chiara, the newest member of the Stragapede family, arrived. In the un-air-conditioned delivery room, I held Laura's hand, and pressed a cool towel to her head. I remembered being the one on the bed pushing and groaning so many years ago when my children were born. Watching her, the painful sounds coming from her lips, the joy and relief when Chiara arrived, I felt as if I were a video recorder, imprinting the image so that I could tell her about it when she was old enough to listen.

I certainly underestimated the difficulty of the first month of transition, but I underestimated the joy as well. Joy's definition was the intensity of a smile and a wave from a new friend, the resolution of a seemingly never-ending bureaucratic saga, and the generosity of friends that seemed to have no limits. Last, but by no means least, I had been separated by an ocean from my dear friend for 16 years and I was reunited with her just in time to experience her treasure of new born life.

"I want you to be the *madrina* (godmother)," Laura said softly.

"Nothing would make me happier," I said, and the 'extra' within me welled up in my eyes, resembling tears.

CHAPTER SIX

Speaking Milk Can Be
Dangerous To Your Health

It was a high counsel that I once heard given to a young person,
"Always do what you are afraid to do."
-Ralph Waldo Emerson

The *Permesso di Soggiorno* was the magic key from which many things flowed, not the least of which was the ability to register and pick up our car. Once we finally gained ownership, we were determined to put on some kilometers before school started. Close by we hiked the *Campo dei Fiori* and the 14 chapels of *Sacro Monte*. Further away, we explored the mountainous areas of *Valle D'Aosta* and the stunning valleys of *Ticino* in Switzerland. We were relatively far away from the traditional tourist sites of Florence, Rome or Venice, yet there were treasures to be found all around us that continued to surprise us: The tiny hilltop town of *Arcumegia* had frescoes adorning every other house. *Santa Caterina del Sasso*, an ancient monastery perched on a cliff alongside *Lago Maggiore*. Lunch with a 360-degree view of the Alps and *Lago Maggiore* from the summit of Mt. Laveno, or watching the hang gliders landing in the field below.

I began to see patterns of language acquisition. Back in the States, Matthew and Alex showed a great deal of resistance to learning Italian. In their New York home, attending their American school, and speaking English with their friends, there was little reason in their minds to learn a language they had no use for. But, little by little, after our arrival here, the language crept into the little gaps in their armor of resistance ... mostly based on necessity. To order an ice cream, they needed to know the word for the flavor they liked: *stracciatella* for Matthew and *limone* for Alex. Then, of course, manners dictated that they had to say please, "*stracciatella, per favore*," and thank you, "*grazie.*" If they needed to use the bathroom, it helped to know how to ask where it is, "*Dov'é la toilett?*" so that they didn't have an unfortunate consequence while pantomiming. Once the expression, "*dov'é* (where is)?" crept in, they could find themselves anywhere. And in Italy when the phrase "*posso avere ...?*" is assimilated into a child's vocabulary (can I have ...?), that word plus a smile will get a youngster almost anything he wants.

Barbara's lessons taught the boys all the phrases they needed to play soccer. They learned *vai!, pari, passa, fuori* and *cambia campo*, which meant go!, tie, pass, out and change sides. At camp they learned all the critical curse words, *porca miseria* (miserable pig) *idiota* (idiot), *scemo* (fool) *and stronzo* (shithead) -- all essential to their survival in Italy.

With a vocabulary of about 50 words, 10 of which were *parolacce* (curses), they were getting by. Soon I noticed that they were unconsciously using certain Italian expressions while playing card games such as "Uno" (played in the United States as well as in Italy). I heard, "*tocca a te* (your turn)", "*tocca a me* (my turn)" or the colors and numbers of the cards in Italian. All this before school even started. As the gaps in their resistance grew wider, they become more receptive to the inevitable process of osmosis that children are famous for. The results were exciting.

Meanwhile, truth be told, Bruce's language progress was not as fast paced. Earlier in the summer, the kids asked me to pick them up from camp in the future, instead of Bruce.

"How come?" I asked.

"Well, put it this way," said Alex. "Dad was trying to say, '*Parli lenta* (speak slow)' and instead he said, '*Parlo latte* (I speak milk).'"

"First of all, Dad," added Matthew, "you should have said, *lentamente*, which means slowly, not *lenta*, which means slow, and second of all ..."

"It's OK," Bruce interrupted. "Sometimes I really do feel like I'm speaking milk."

Bruce didn't have the benefit of hearing the Italian language growing up and he was resistant to taking an Italian course for foreigners, feeling that his days of organized schooling were over. This decision had its disadvantages, as there was no telling what would come out of his mouth in any given situation. The night before school, he remarked that he was putting the "*cane sulla griglia,*" which translated as putting the dog, rather than the "*carne* (meat)," on the grill. He then added that he wanted "*troppo vino rosso,*" an announcement that he wanted 'too much' red wine, rather than 'more' wine – perhaps revealing his wish to be inebriated rather than his language deficit.

Once in a while, not speaking Italian as well as the children did, was as dangerous as it was embarrassing. On the same night of the barbecue, Bruce bought fireworks as a treat for the kids in anticipation of their first day of school. He lit the fuse and turned his back to watch their reactions.

The kids began shouting, "*Papà, fuoco! Papà fuoco!*"

Bruce just smiled, seemingly very pleased with himself.

"Dad, fire!!!!" they screamed in unison as a nearby lawn chair burst into flames.

*   *   *

The 7 a.m. bells of the Church of *San Vittore*, are not a mere seven chimes. They are a clanging cacophony, exuberantly exhorting parishioners to find a pew. As such, even if the children of the neighborhood had no intention of going to school, at one minute after seven, they were sure to be awake, ready or not to start their day. But on the first day of school, the Hummel family was far from ready. We were actually, all of us, petrified. We ate breakfast in silence. Then Bruce, speaking milk, and me, armed with a pocket dictionary, prepared to take Matthew and Alex to *Ugo Foscolo*, their Italian public school. I felt truly sick.

"What will they want from me?" Alex asked, referring to his teachers. It was a question I revisited many times throughout the school year, with an answer that varied as time progressed.

"Your only job is to listen and do your best to learn more and more Italian every day. Other than that, your job for now is to enjoy your new friends," I said. "It's going to be OK," I added feebly.

In the car on the way to school, you could cut the tension with a knife. We drove in complete silence until we heard Matthew beginning to distract himself by reciting scenes from various movies. I could vaguely make out scenes from the movie "My Big Fat Greek Wedding" coming from the back seat. "Is he a good boy? I don't know ... Does he come from a good family? ... I don't know ... I don't know ... I don't know" and "Show me a word, any word, and I can show you that the derivation of that word is Greek ..." The silence turned to laughter and then abruptly back to silence as we pulled up to the curb in front of the school.

Kids were milling around outside, excitedly chattering about their summer, girls showing off their new shoes or backpacks, boys chasing each other around the four pillars in the entrance courtyard. Mothers greeted each other after the long summer break, talking about how fast time was flying, just as I had done each year in the States. We saw a few children that I had met during my initial visit, and that Matthew and Alex also met at the *oratorio* at the beginning of the summer. Many waved hello. It was nice to be recognized.

Domenico arrived with Francesca and I chatted with them nervously about whether Chiara was sleeping through the night. When the bell rang, Matthew and Alex went in the front door and before I knew it each was standing with their respective classes. I'm not sure how that happened or how they knew with which class to stand. Maybe the heavens equip kids with some sort of homing device to accompany their osmosis programming.

I hurriedly introduced myself to one of Matthew's teachers whom I hadn't met in May. She apparently was replacing the teacher I had met. Much to my dismay, she spoke no English. Another teacher, also new, introduced herself to me as Lella. She spoke a few English words, haltingly. Matthew shot me a glance as if to say, "I thought you told me ..."

"We're a little worried about their ability to communicate," I said to her.

"*Non ti preoccupare* (don't worry)," she said to us and gave Matthew a big kiss, that made Matthew smile for a second.

"You can come up with them for a few minutes if you like," she told me.

Matthew shook his head "no" and I surmised that he was at the age where having your "mommy" come into class was not good form. Alex however, looked relieved and took my hand.

In the third grade classroom, Alex's principle classroom, *Maestra* Alma (teacher Alma) introduced herself. She was absent the day I visited in May, but I was told she spoke some English.

"I'm Denise, Alex's mother," I said in English.

"*Sono Alma*," she told me. I heard no English from her that day, or any day after. She had all the kids introduce themselves one at a time and say one thing each about themselves.

"*Mi chiamo Giorgio. Ho otto anni.* (I am George. I am 8 years old.)"

"*Mi chiamo Anna. Sono stata in Sardegna per la vacanza.* (I am Anna. I spent my vacation in *Sardinia*.)"

"*Mi chiama Nico. Ho fatto a botte con mio fratello per le vacanze.* (My name is Nico. For my vacation, I fought with my brother.)"

In fact, three of the boys, in addition to Nico, said that for their summer vacation, they fought with their brother. I translated this important point for Alex and he smiled.

Francesca explained that this summer she got a new baby sister. When it was Alex's turn, he said bravely,

"*Mi chiamo Alex. Vengo da New York.* (My name is Alex. I come from New York.)"

Then the children asked Alex questions, to which he seemingly randomly answered, "*Si.*" Fortunately, it was the appropriate response for the question.

"Do you like *Varese*?"

"*Si*"

"Do you like New York?"

"*Si.*"

At the end of this discourse, Alex leaned over towards me

soulfully and said,

"Is the whole day going to be like this?"

Before leaving, I looked in on Matthew. He was slumped in his chair, but he was holding it together. I had no choice but to wait until 1 p.m. to see how they did. I anticipated many meltdowns during the next few weeks. The only outstanding question was who was going to melt down more ... them or me. I spent most of the day walking Buster all around the city of *Varese*, or in the toy store buying presents to assuage my helpless pangs of guilt. I didn't realize until that day how cavalier I had been about enrolling them in a school system where they didn't speak the language. I oscillated between congratulating myself for my courage (and theirs) and thoughts of rushing back to school, grabbing them by the hand, thanking their teachers, and explaining that we made a mistake.

Bruce, on the other hand, was cool as a cucumber. When I went into the office (where his papers were decidedly strewn on my side of the desk) he was calmly flipping through the dictionary, writing down a few choice translations.

"Are you for real?" I screeched. "Aren't you freaking out?"

"About what?" he asked.

"The kids ... in school ... not speaking Italian. Aren't you wondering if they're surviving?"

"I have no doubt they're surviving," he said calmly. "Besides, we'll find out in 15 minutes."

How do men do that? They are so damn logical, and Bruce is the most logical of all of them. While I sometimes chastised him for his linear thinking, so true to his engineering background, this is the kind of scenario where that personality trait shined. As far as Bruce was concerned, they'd go, the day would progress, and they would live to tell the tale. Instead, I spent the whole day at the cusp of a full-fledged panic attack until we were standing outside *Ugo Foscolo Elementare* with Laura, Domenico and baby Chiara to see the expression on the kids' faces as they exited.

Some kids were running to their parents to share their day, others were dragging their backpacks behind them with the classic look of first-day stupor. But Alex had a rather neutral expression on his face and Matthew even smiled. Francesca bounded out the door to fill us in.

"They had a whole assembly to introduce them," Francesca told us. "They're doing the theme of the United States for the *Settimane Pinocchio* (adjustment weeks) just to welcome them. I saw that Matthew has a new friend named Enea," she continued breathlessly, "and Alex has a friend named Michele."

"My day was awesome," Matthew said simply.

"That's great," said Bruce. "Why's that?"

"Because I made a friend, we didn't have to work, and it wasn't as bad as I thought it would be."

Alex explained that he had a great day too because he lost a tooth.

I thought those were two very good reasons to celebrate.

"Do you have a tooth fairy in Italy?" I asked Domenico, as Alex listened anxiously.

"No," he told us, "we have a *topolino*, a little mouse. You don't put the tooth under your pillow, you put it under a cup on the table and he comes and you get money."

"They really should globalize these childhood imaginary personalities," I laughed.

With that, we said our goodbyes and drove home. The kids ran straight to the garden to play a little "sock ball" and Bruce set about preparing an early dinner. Bruce's prediction was fulfilled: we had all survived.

Every day the scents that emanated from the kitchen became more and more profoundly Italian. Bruce often offered to cook, something he really enjoyed, but rarely had time to do in the States. Every new Italian dish was better than the night before. The kids requested *spaghetti alle vongole* for their first day of school dinner and in short order the perfume of clams, garlic, and fresh parsley filled the air. I forgot to eat lunch and suddenly remembered how hungry I was.

"You should patent that recipe," I said.

"It's easy," he told me. Then he started walking me through the recipe, something he did most times I complimented his cooking.

"Rinse the clams under cold water," he said. "Then heat the olive oil over medium heat, sauté the clams in it, adding some red pepper flakes ..."

But the recipe was lost on me. I was too emotionally exhausted to think of anything other than eating and bed, and besides I had no intention of competing with Bruce's developing culinary talents when I could be relegated to taste tester.

"We need to get them to bed early," I said to Bruce after dinner, but the reality was that I needed to get to bed early. I had left most of my energy somewhere between *Piazza Montegrappa* and *Piazza San Vittore.*

"We're really proud of you guys," I said as I tucked them in.

"I guess that means we're going again tomorrow, huh?" Alex replied, smiling.

I gave them each a good night kiss and sighed with relief as I turned off the light. I stood outside the door thinking that a little eavesdropping might give me more insight into their experience. For a while, I heard nothing. Then I heard Alex ...

"I don't get how it could be a fairy at home and a mouse here."

"Well," explained Matthew, "different things happen in different countries. In Africa, it could have been a chicken."

Judging by the ensuing silence, it appeared that answer was acceptable.

CHAPTER SEVEN

Sometimes it Takes a Lifetime to Find the Perfect Cookie

Go confidently in the direction of your dreams.
Live the life you have imagined.
As you simplify your life, the laws of the universe will be simpler.
-Henry David Thoreau

There is an undeniable truth in life. If you repeatedly take the same course of action in response to the same set of facts, the outcome will be remarkably similar. So it was with Bruce and me. We moved from New York to Colorado before the kids were born with the hope that the less frantic pace of life of the Rocky Mountains would inspire us to appreciate life and each other. We moved back to New York after the kids were born, thinking that being around family would ground us. Remarkably, we were unaware when we packed up from New York to Colorado and back again, that we were also packing our problems, carefully transporting them to the next location. In every geographical move, we maintained the same stock-option-fueled lifestyle, and so all it really meant was that Bruce traveled to Dallas, Chicago or wherever, from the humidity of New York or the aridity of Colorado.

But I wasn't employed as a lawyer at the time we left for Italy; I was a stay-at-home mom. So, when our hometown newspaper offered me a monthly column to write about our Italian adventures, it gave me a voice I hadn't known since my college days. Maybe nothing would come of it, but it was an excuse to write. And since every day I was inspired to write about our life in Italy, I was in some small way changing my life by seizing an opportunity to express myself in writing without the phrases, "Party of the First part," Whereas" or "Herein." Finding my passion again after so many years, gave me an energy that I hadn't known for a long time. I leaped out of bed in the morning, eager to begin the day.

The days slid past and the hours the kids spent in school flew. There was always something to do. When I wasn't keeping notes on cultural differences or writing articles, I was dealing with daily events *alla italiana*. Based on Bruce's developing aptitude in the kitchen, we decided that he would do the shopping and the cooking and I would be the one to take care of the things that required a working knowledge of the language, like dealing with teachers, homework, telephone calls, the post office and the bank. I thought I was getting the better end of the deal, but as the days rolled on, I could see that this evaluation was questionable.

Coping with Telecom Italia, alone, was a test of *pazienza* that consistently left me on the losing side. On the day our high-speed Internet was finally activated, albeit two months after we ordered it, I called Telecom Italia. Although they did not activate the service until the second week of September, they billed us for July and August.

"*Buon Giorno, sono Denise Pirrotti Hummel,*" I told the operator.

"*Chi?*"

"Hummel, *con* 'H.'"

"Kummin??"

"No, Hummel, like hotel."

"*Si, OK,* in any case, how can I help you?"

"Well, *signora*," I said, "we received a bill for high speed Internet access for July and August, but it was not activated until this morning."

"I see by your records that you ordered it in July."

"Yes, that's right. We ordered it in July and it was activated today."

"*Signora*, you requested the line in July. You didn't cancel it, did you?"

"No, I didn't cancel it, but it only began today."

"Would you like me to cancel it, *signora*? If I cancel it today, I can credit you as of today."

"No, no ... please don't cancel it. I was just saying ... never mind."

"Is there anything else I can help you with, *signora*?"

"No, thank you. That was it."

"Very well, then, *signora*, thank you for calling Telecom Italia."

And so it went.

With our brand new high-speed access, I sent an email to some friends to let them know the ups and downs of the first day of school. A good friend from Boulder responded:

> Hi D, Small triumphs matter, and I am proud of your boys, and you and Bruce, for knowing that difficult times have a way of making people better identify what is important in life. I'm reading your September 10 email on September 11, a day of reflection for all Americans, and I find myself thinking about my own values, as well as how we humans get ourselves into good and challenging positions (like going to *Varese*) and bad and challenging positions (like terrorism and retaliation). Love to all, Charcie

Due to our over-taxed brain cells, Bruce and I had limited time to philosophize on a global level. We were very much focused on our personal path and were in the process of reflecting upon our own values. We came to *Varese* in an attempt to change our lives, which meant confronting what wasn't working for each of us individually, and in our family life as a whole. We were aware that one of the big problems we needed to face was the fact that we had traded extra time with each other for extra money and extra stuff.

It was pointless to beat ourselves up about it or speculate about what would have happened if he or I had made different choices. Maybe I would have become be a Pulitzer Prize-winning author of cross-cultural theory with several titles to my name, and Bruce would have been photographing semi-nude models for a multi-million-dollar campaign while we happily raised two kids in New York. Alternatively, maybe I would have crashed and burned while writing a revival of Archie comics and Bruce would have had an affair with one of the models and we'd be divorced and living in separate continents. Who knew?

Coming to *Varese* was intended to be something other than just another geographic move. We were going to do something bold. Something that took my breath away even to think about. We decided that Bruce would quit his job. First, because we had no expectations that he could leave for a year, ask his company to put his job on hold, and then drop back in after 365 days. But more importantly, because Bruce struggled so long in a career he despised, we hoped that this year off would represent an invaluable opportunity to "try on" a life that did not include the security of Bruce's comfortable salary. One of the principle features that controlled our thinking was not to have a re-entry plan, despite urging by friends and family. Why? Because it was the only thing we could think of that gave us the mental freedom to grow in whatever way fate would have it.

If we left ourselves the space, without defining in advance who we would be at the end of the experience, perhaps the real us – stripped of our professional titles and social status – might emerge. The idea was a bit lofty, and the possibility that maybe all that would happen in Italy was that we'd gain a few extra pounds from eating great pasta and *gelato* and see some fallen-down ruins loomed in the distance as a possible outcome of our year away. But Bruce and I finally became aware that we were losing the battle against an addiction to the very life that was not working. So, in some intuitive way, it made sense to go cold turkey, and pray that miraculously our time away and our break from the security and extra things that Bruce's income could buy, might actually be replaced by the less tangible 'extra' I saw in our Italian friends.

We had countless discussions about this particular subject before we left the States. I was surprised and gratified that he had the courage to agree that quitting his job was the best way to achieve our long-term objective, despite the short-term insecurity it might produce. When he wavered, I encouraged him to stick with the plan. I blocked out any fear I had about the fact that we were relying on the rental of our New York home for income, or the fact that when we returned there would be no job waiting for him.

But several weeks before we left, Bruce informed his supervisor that we would be going to Italy for some period of time and briefly explained the circumstances of our intended journey. Much to our surprise, they told him that since his position was global in scope, he could continue working from Italy. I remember Bruce saying, "I'll just continue working for a little while to absorb some of the expenses we'll have during our first month there," and I hesitantly agreed.

Two weeks into the school year, Bruce announced to me that he would be calling his boss in New York to quit.

"We're unpacked. The kids are settled into school. I think the worst of the transition is over. It's time," he told me.

I froze. Notwithstanding the fact that I was the one espousing the "leap and the net will appear" theory and the fact that Bruce leaving his job was key to our plan, I secretly was feeling much less anxious because he was still working, still earning. Bruce's continued employment represented a tenuous stability amidst the complete lack of security or sameness that now was ever-present in our lives. Paradoxically, I welcomed it as an important remnant of our former life. We were at the jumping off place – a place where I had prayed we'd be someday – and rather than feeling exhilaration and celebration, I felt fear and despair. What if Bruce quitting his job was just that – the end of a job – with nothing else in the horizon? What if he wasn't able to figure out a career path that gave him a sense of enjoyment and the less hectic lifestyle he was seeking, with an income that wouldn't require a drastic change in our economic circumstances? What if all we accomplished in our year off was a long vacation, without any other answers?

"Are you sure we're doing the right thing?" I heard myself saying as if I were the spineless protagonist of a B-movie.

He looked at me, astonished.

"Denise, we've talked about this a hundred times. Why are you wavering now?"

"Well, you know, the economy isn't what it used to be, and maybe we should be looking at the fact they said you could continue working as a gift. It means we can stay here and still have a cross-cultural experience and all, but at least we won't be risking as much." I wasn't looking at him as I was speaking. I knew I should be embarrassed by what I was saying, but I couldn't stop. We had the kids to think of, saving for college, retirement. What were we thinking? I was shaking. Bruce put his index finger under my chin and pulled up gently so that his gaze met mine.

"Is that what you really want?" he asked me with more tenderness than I had heard in years. Neither of us spoke for a few seconds.

"No," I said, "it's not."

All at once I was crying and Bruce was holding me. Mine were tears of embarrassment, even betrayal. They were tears of relief that we had reaffirmed our convictions. They were tears of faith that everything would be all right. But mostly, they were tears that represented a closeness that I hadn't felt for a long time. Maybe if we kept this up, we would stop blaming each other for the problems in our marriage and start looking for answers together.

In retrospect, I realize how much I had judged him for staying in a job he didn't like instead of moving out boldly. But who was I kidding? I never wanted the career path I chose either; I wanted to be a psychologist or a writer. I just didn't have the guts to make it happen. Lawyers made good money; writers and psychologists didn't always lead a lucrative life. I had been judging Bruce throughout our marriage, without confronting my own self-betrayal. I was the one who had been able to stop working, without confronting what to do next to support my family.

It hit me like a rock that it took so much more courage for him to come to Italy than it had for me. He came not speaking a word of the Italian language, facing feelings of isolation and inadequacy. He gave up the safety and security he had spent a lifetime building. And here he was, finally able to separate Bruce the person from Bruce the breadwinner, and through my own weakness, I was giving him an opportunity to allow his fear to supplant his courage.

Bruce picked up the phone and dialed his boss. "September 30 will be my last day," I heard him say. He looked at me and I nodded my head, 'yes.'

Bruce began interning with Carlo Fontana, the still-life commercial photographer whom Domenico contacted during my initial *Varese* visit. The night before he went, he sat down with his English-Italian dictionary. He was looking up potentially useful words: *ottica, riflettore, filtro* ... (lens, reflector, filter). The next morning, with about 20 photography-related Italian words in his vocabulary, he set off to Milan. Later that evening, he was quiet, but seemed peaceful and content. I imagine it was difficult to be a business executive one day and an intern photography assistant the next. To have a limitless professional vocabulary one day and a vocabulary of 20 words the next. But every day he went, and every day he seemed more at ease.

At night, Bruce regaled us with stories about the day at the studio. A commercial still-life photography studio was very different from the elaborate, but homemade, set-ups he used to construct in the laundry room of his childhood home or the one in our New York garage that he set up but had no time to use. He was assisting in producing complicated shots, using very sophisticated equipment, guessing at many of the technical terms based on the nature of the set-up, hoping he was handing Carlo the right lighting gel or setting the right camera aperture. Ironically, some of the shoots were so technical, that Carlo was grateful to have an assistant with an engineering background. If a product needed to be positioned a certain way or affixed in a manner that required creativity combined with precision, Carlo said, "*Chiedi al ingegnere* (Ask the engineer)" and Bruce found a solution.

His first shot was a cookie for a renowned Italian food-product company that utilized Bruce's engineering exactness along with a full team of food stylists, picking through 45 bags to find the perfect cookie to shoot. Bruce positioned the cookie on the table to match the precise orientation of the artist's mock-up, apparently no small feat considering the height, rotation and angle of the cookie vis-à-vis the camera. Test shots were taken and re-taken. Adjustments were made to the lighting, including an additional light to highlight the bottom-right portion of the cookie. Yellow and orange gel strips were added to the main light to make the cookie look warmer. Then the food stylist added individual grains of course raw sugar onto the cookie so that the crystals stood out like little diamonds. The shot was then taken at various different apertures. After the photograph was reviewed by the food stylist, the agency art director, the creative director, and the account representative, the process was repeated with a second "perfect" cookie, and the shot retaken. Between every shot, a spirited conversation took place between all the players about whether the table should be tilted yet another centimeter, whether the lighting was too yellow, or whether the placement of an individual sugar crystal should be altered. Bruce retained a look of careful concentration, pretending to understand the overlapping Italian opinions flying through the air. He watched calmly as one expert tilted the table in one direction, while the next expert tilted it back, until ultimately it was placed back to the original position. After the final shot was taken, Bruce nicknamed it "*Il Biscotto Perfetto* (the perfect cookie)" and I think it will always hold a warm place in his heart as the first moment he was able to translate his childhood hobby into a professional endeavor.

When Bruce wasn't at his internship, he was at home cooking up a storm in our tiny kitchen, and not just the average pasta with tomato sauce. Instead, he was assimilating into the Italian culture before my eyes. Two courses, every night. *Spaghetti alle cozze* floating in *pomodoro* and garlic, followed by *vitello* smothered in fresh *Portobello* mushrooms from nearby Brinzio ... *Fusilli con salsicce, asparagi e fagioli*, followed by Florentine *porchetta con spinaci*. Maybe when we returned to New York he would become a photographer, put on a television cooking show or open a restaurant.

Or would we just go back to the way things were?

It was a fear that I carried in my head and in my heart. I looked everywhere for signs of stress, wondering if one day soon the reality of what he had done would hit him. Perhaps he'd miss the intensity of racing for a flight and being in multiple time zones in one day. Maybe without the important presentation, critical meeting or paycheck to define him as a man, he'd be just as unhappy as he was when he was working in a job he didn't like.

But day after day passed without any sign that Bruce was yearning for his old life. Every once in a while he'd pick up the phone to check his office voice mail, only to remember he no longer had voice mail. Sometimes in the quiet of the evening, when it was just the two of us, he spoke of his fears of the uncertainty of what would happen when we returned. But for the most part he was taking one day at a time, absorbing his new found liberty, waiting to see what the next day would bring. It turned out that Bruce was the only practice prisoner we had ever known, and now he was free.

Sometimes when we sat at our one office desk with our side by side laptops, we engaged in an elbow contest. Bruce finally got a piece of black electrical tape and put it down the center. I took a photo of him sitting in front of his computer, next to the black line to remind me how little we had to fight about lately. I personally think he cheated a bit and put the tape a few centimeters more on my side, but I planned to let him get away with it. He was my hero and he deserved a little extra space.

As the weeks passed, I began to see with even more depth the metaphorical drama in what my husband had done. After being stuck, literally and figuratively, in a career he hated for so long, he was "free." Not free from the worry of how he would ultimately support his family, perhaps, but free from the constraints of having convinced himself for so many years that there was no other way. The "other way" if we could pull it off, would probably not include a big house or a stylish SUV, but it would include more time for himself and his family, less wear and tear on his body and mind, and more control over his daily life.

Several days a week he walked or rode his bike 10 minutes to the train station for the 45 minute journey into Milan to his internship. He wore no business suit and carried no briefcase. He had no lofty professional status, no high-level business meetings and no executive salary. With his limited vocabulary for verbal expression, at times he had no voice. With his limited comprehension, at times he felt inept. But he was giving himself the time and space to do something he loved and neither the hot train nor the lack of a paycheck or the language gap seemed to matter much.

I will never forget the day Bruce saw the shot of *Il Biscotto Perfetto* bigger than life aloft a huge billboard at the Malpensa airport. He stared at it as if he were seeing an old friend after many years of separation, or as if he had been on another planet for a long, long time and seeing Earth for the first time in many years.

CHAPTER EIGHT

Organic Therapies, Particularly When They Include Chocolate, Are Often Superior to Those Offered by Medical Science

Good Living
is an act of intelligence,
by which we choose things
which have an agreeable taste
rather than those which do not.
-Brillat-Savarin

In the midst of re-inventing our lives, we were called upon to remember that we had two children who almost literally *had* been dropped on another planet. Playing soccer was one thing, but when it came to the school environment we hadn't adequately anticipated what the boys would face.

Matthew's "planet" apparently was the screaming planet. Day after day, he came home with a description of chaos that defied the boundaries of our American imaginations.

"Mom, they just all call out at the same time, whenever they want, and without being called on," he told me, "It's impossible to hear what they're saying."

"Matthew, is it possible that the fact that you don't understand what they're saying makes it seem as if they're all talking at the same time?" I responded, remembering what the ADD specialist in New York told me about Matthew's reaction to sensory overload. Could it be that Bruce's mother was right – that I was asking too much to expect a child with ADD to adapt in a classroom where no one spoke English?

"You're just going to have to see for yourself someday, Mom," he said. "All they do is shout to each other all day long. Then the teacher screams even louder, '*Mario ... basta! Vai Fuori! Dammi questo! Marriiioooooo!!!!* (Mario, stop it. Go out of the room. Give me that! Marrriiiioooo!!) *Basta!!! Basta!!!*'"

"*Baaaaaaaaaasta!!!!,*" Alex screamed in harmony, to help Matthew make the point. I realized then that I needed to cook up some excuse to visit the classroom.

Ironically though, I was more worried about Alex than Matthew. The child that we all believed we could "drop anywhere" and he'd fit in, be happy, and make the best of things, was falling apart. He dissolved into tears at the drop of a hat. His soccer playing in the piazza was akin to gladiatorial combat. Francesca indicated that he was a bit 'rough around the edges' in class as well.

"Mom, one of these days we're going to get beaten up by the teenagers in *Piazza San Vittore*," Matthew told me.

"Why's that?"

"Because when these certain guys show up, I tell Alex that we should just leave, but he won't. And when they steal the ball, he chases them and calls them every *parolacce* in the book. He's gonna get us killed."

In time, he earned himself the family nickname, "the Taz," after the cartoon character, the "Tasmanian Devil." While we knew his behavior was, in all likelihood, related to the challenges of his adjustment, we couldn't get a clear picture of what he was experiencing or how he felt, despite my repeated prodding. If we didn't understand the situation, we were at a loss to help him, and I felt pretty bad about it. I so wanted the kids to remember their time in Italy as happy – to look back on it as a positive milestone in their lives. How was I going to live with myself if all I managed to do was create stress for them?

"Mom, he's gone too far," Matthew told me one day. "When *Padre* Filippo told him to stop kicking the ball against the door of the *Chiesa San Vittore* while mass was in session, Alex told him that he didn't own the church, God did. I swear, Mom, if there is a God, he's gonna strike us down for mouthing off at a priest!"

Every day, I dropped them off at school, the bell rang, and off they went into the entrance and down the corridor until they disappeared into a world I knew very little about. How much or how little of the language did they understand? Was their lack of comprehension in the classroom impacting their self-esteem? Could they distinguish between their lack of comprehension of the language and their own innate intelligence? I couldn't answer any of these questions.

While waiting for the kids to come out from school one day, I held a sleepy Chiara, and spoke to Laura about it.

"*Pazienza*," she told me. "Sometimes I think American mothers over-think things; or maybe it's just you," she said with a playful jab to the ribs, but I wasn't laughing.

"I think I'm going to try to find a child-psychologist who speaks English," I said. But that proposition, in *Varese*, was easier said than done.

"If you decide to do that, I wouldn't talk to the other moms about it," said Laura.

"Why is that?" I asked.

"Well, it's not really something we do unless there's a very extreme problem," she told me.

The afternoon bell rang and the kids came streaming out, a fray of backpacks, untied sneakers, and shouts of, "*Ciao, mamma!!*" I braced myself for another emotional swing, hanging on the kids' every sentence.

"How'd it go?" I asked.

"It was boring," said Matthew casually, "but I like my friends."

"That's very balanced," I winced, carefully choosing my words, cautiously waiting for the other shoe to drop. "Something bad. Something good," I continued cheerfully. "I'm glad you can see the positive as well as the negative. And you, Alex?"

"My day stunk, but I got this," he said happily, holding up a piece of clay about a centimeter in diameter that he had rolled into a ball, and I breathed a sigh of relief.

"Oh, by the way, Mom," said Matthew, all smiles, "my friend Enea has a father who owns a bakery and he made us a cake with chocolate in it that we all ate at school."

Then Enea, himself, came bouncing over with a plastic bag tied at the top.

"*Questo è un regalo per voi due* (This is a present for you two)," he said. "*È un gioco che io non uso più* (It's a game that I don't use anymore)."

Matthew thanked him, and Alex's face lit up. By this point, a crowd of eager onlookers from the third and fourth grades, as well as several of their moms and a local cat, were looking on.

"This is my house, right here," Enea continued, grabbing my hand and leading me toward a gate about 20 meters from the school.

Matthew, Alex, Francesca and the rest of the merry band followed. I let out a loud breath, as if I had been holding it for several minutes. I tried to take in the moment and appreciate the sweetness of it. I wanted the feeling to last a long time so I could remember it when the next emotional swing plagued me.

"We can play at my house some day after school," Enea said to both boys.

Matthew and Alex were beaming as if everything was right with the world. Laura, too, was smiling. "I'll bet you've never read about the Italian chocolate cake therapy in any of those parenting magazines they have back in the States," she said.

I continued to let my emotions bounce me around for several more weeks. Each time I picked the kids up from school, I was in a state of apprehension.

"Hi kiddos. How was your day?" went my usual litany.

The responses varied, but the theme was fairly consistent.

"I listened to, 'Blah, blah, blah, blah … *capito* (understand)? Blaah, blaah, blaah ... *capito*?'" Alex told me. "That's when she's explaining things. When she's mad, she says, 'Ta dada Ta dada Ta da ... *capito*?' while yelling and wagging her finger."

I just nodded, and wait for the next barrage, the downward descent, the guilty feelings augmenting with every sentence I was hearing. Sometimes I felt so dizzy that their words came in drifts; I missed every other word of what was being said.

"At lunch ... they keep trying to get me to eat ... I don't want to eat it. I say, '*non mi piace* (I don't like it)' and they say, '*ma dai!*

Non c'e niente che non puoi mangiare!! (But, come on! There's nothing here you can't eat!!)' Then I say, '*non mi piace*' and they say, '*ma dai*' and it just keeps going like that ... until they give up."

And before I could respond –

"They keep making me read and write and I have no idea what I'm reading and no idea what I'm writing."

"I see," I started, "I wonder ..." but I never got to finish.

"On line, they always push you forward and say, '*Avanti ... mai dai!* (Go on ahead ... come on!)' even if there's only an inch of space ... I mean, what is their problem?!"

"They put a whole bunch of numbers on the board and everyone was writing them down, so I wrote them down too," said Matthew. "But I kept getting it wrong ... supposedly ... so I kept writing it again and kept checking it. They kept saying it was wrong. It ends up that I was supposed to put them in order of smallest to greatest. Why didn't they just say so? Then a kid did something wrong and the teacher wanted to write him up for the bad thing he did and the kid came up to her and was pulling at her and begging, '*No, no ti prego!* (No, no, I beg you!)' We could never get away with that in New York!!!"

My kids were clearly in the deep end of the pool without a life preserver, and I was the one who threw them in.

On one particular Friday, Alex's class was dismissed first. He took the opportunity to bend my ear about his day's strife. Apparently he didn't have computer class (again), and gym consisted of *Maestra* Alma shouting in English, "left-a, right-a, *sinistra, destra, destra,* right-a ..."

"I think it's fun," Francesca offered.

Alex rolled his eyes. "Gym is not gym," he said dejectedly. "It's English class with your feet. By the way, Mom, did I mention that none of the teachers speak English ... I mean, other than 'left, right, left, right, left ...'"

Then suddenly, Enea and Matthew came running over to me. "*La Maestra di matematica ha preso l'orologio di Matteo*!!! (The math teacher took Matthew's watch!!!)," he said, breathlessly. Whereupon, both Enea and Matthew began speaking at the same time in Italian and English, telling a story of woe about how they were only looking to see what time it was and that the watch fell and the math teacher took it and didn't give it back.

"Where is your watch now?" I asked.

"I have no idea," Matthew responded, with downcast eyes.

"She told me to tell you to get it from her so she could tell you why she took it," Enea told me in Italian.

"And where is she now?" I asked, bewildered.

"She already left," said Enea.

It will never cease to amaze me how quickly the Italian teachers depart from school, and at that, through some sort of secret back entrance that for all I know leads to the Bat Cave in Gotham City, because I've never seen them re-emerge in broad daylight after that final bell. The mystery of the missing watch would have to remain unsolved for the weekend. Frustration and powerlessness was written all over Matthew's strained face. I could picture his confusion as the watch was being taken, without understanding exactly why, or whether or when he would get it back. I was so angry that I'd have to wait the whole weekend for answers.

Alex continued his lamenting, mimicking *Maestra* Alma's tortuous, "left-a, right-a, *destra, sinistra, destra, destra,* right-a ..." as we marched over to the car.

"Alex, *pazienza,*" Enea called out wagging his little finger.

As he walked away, I realized how lucky we were to have him in our lives. His chubby cheeks and *Napolitano* accent always put a smile on our faces. He, his baby brother, and his cousin, Gianni, lived together in the same house, and were being raised by Enea's parents. Their life did not seem easy; His father worked all night in their bakery and his mother worked all day. Yet Enea was always *solare*, the epitome of a sunny disposition.

"What is the name of this math teacher," I asked Matthew.

"I have no idea. Everyone just calls her *maestra* (teacher). She never introduced herself."

"I know what you mean," chimed in Alex. "For the first two weeks, I thought my teacher's name was '*stranna* (strange)' because they say it so fast ... It sounds like 'mae stranna' instead of

Maestra Alma."

Alex continued to be presented with challenges that exasperated him. As part of her theory of augmenting the class' reading level, *Maestra* Alma dedicated one period of the day to having the children read a chapter of their history lesson five times successively. Every night, the homework consisted of a similar task. The children were to read and re-read until they memorized the content of the lesson. The next day, there was an *interrogazione* (interrogation) of what they read. The students needed to repeat back to the teacher what they read in the order they read it.

For Francesca, and most of the Italian children, homework took about 30 minutes. For Alex, the task was difficult and frustrating, as he and I spent hours reading and looking up in the dictionary several words in every sentence of every page. Often I wondered who might start crying first, Alex or me. But in the confines of the classroom, the challenge was even greater, as it was impossible for him to finish in the time allotted. He was often still reading, long after the other children moved on to another activity. Humiliation compounded the fatigue of the task.

One day at school, after about a half hour of reading, with all of his classmates finished, Alex stopped reading too, and closed the book.

"Are you finished," *Maestra* Alma asked him.

"No," Alex answered.

"Then open your book and finish," she said.

"I won't," replied Alex.

"Yes you will," said *Maestra* Alma, opening the book.

Alex had no words to reply. He simply slammed the book closed and threw it to the floor. He was forcibly removed from the classroom and sent to the first grade classroom as a punishment, where he kicked, screamed and cried for an hour. I was never called. I found out what happened later that afternoon after seeing his tear-stained, exhausted face and Francesca's hushed explanation of the events. Exhaustion overwhelmed me as well; I had not been there to protect or comfort him.

The reasons for Alex's aggressive behavior in the *piazza* were becoming clearer to me. He was being pushed to the edge. In the States, the "crisis" of Matthew's problems with attention in the classroom had driven me to seek weekly consultations for him. Here, without those resources to readily rely upon, we needed to rely on the 'extra' around us to get us through. At times, it was the usual call to *pazienza* that helped me to realize that this phase would pass. Sometimes it was the kids' ability to bounce back, racing out to play so soon after what seemed to be a major calamity. Often times, it was Enea's counsel and just knowing the kids were under his watchful eye.

"*Signora* Hummel," I remember him telling me, "I keep reminding the teachers ... they have to speak slowly if they want these kids to learn ... they talk like a freight train ... are they crazy ... speaking like that with these American boys in class ... how does she expect them to understand?"

"You're so right Enea," I told him. "And what about you, how are you doing in school?"

"Never mind about me," he said. "I'm Italian, I know what's going on. Did Matthew tell you he needs a *quaderno a quadretti* (graph paper notebook) with bigger squares? The one you got is too small. Maybe they do it like that in America, but here ... you need bigger squares."

"I'll get right on it, Enea," I told him.

"OK, there's plenty of time for that. For now, come across the street to my house, I need to show you something." When we arrived, he lifted the latch of the gate to his family's garden and started handing me vegetables through the wire.

"Take this pepper," he said. "You'll like it. It's really good ... Really fresh. Take this tomato too. It's really good. OK, that's it. Wait. One last thing. What about some basil? You need basil to go with the tomato. Hold on a second. Let me just pick some beans. You know how to make beans? B-E-A-N-S. They have those in America, don't they? Put them in a little salt water, but not too much salt. Boil them. Then you eat them. But drain them first and don't eat them boiling hot. You have to wait. OK, that's it. Oh, one last thing." He bent down to cut a rose then he handed it to me. "Watch out for the thorns."

That day I put the single rose in a vase on the dinner table.

Bruce was serving a first course of *gnocchi alla salvia* with a second course of *vitello con funghi* and a bizarre medley of vegetables on the side that included one pepper, a handful of beans, and one tomato. It was garnished with basil and prepared with such care that even Enea would have approved. Enea was our honorary 'extra' expert and unofficial family therapist. He used his family's extra vegetables and his dad's chocolate cake as two of his primary tools during professional consultations.

Speak Milk. Drink Wine.

CHAPTER NINE

Learning Takes Place Between the Lines on a Page, Not on Them

It is a miracle that curiosity survives formal education.
-Albert Einstein

I had not lost sight of the fact that there were many profound benefits associated with our decision to enroll the kids in the Italian public school system. After all, they were learning another language, something that many American children never learn to do. Alex's situation was unique to his role as a foreigner struggling to keep up with the others and was likely to improve as he absorbed more and more language. But based on Matthew's description of his classroom, his classmates took the famous Italian educator, Maria Montessori, quite literally when she espoused "leaving children free to learn." They may have understood it to mean, "we'll learn if we feel like it."

Early in October, Bruce and I finally had the opportunity to come to school to participate in a craft event in Matthew's classroom. We were at last in a position to see if Matthew's description of his classroom environment was an exaggeration of the objective facts, based either on the way he was experiencing things through his filter of ADD, or based simply on the language gap.

"Good morning class," said *Maestra* Lella. "Today we have some special guests to help us with our project. *Signor* and *Signora* Hummel, Matthew's mother and father, will be working with us."

Giovanni, one classmate, leapt to his feet excitedly. "I already met them!" he shouted.

"I saw them at the *oratorio*," screamed Mario from the back of the classroom.

"What kind of project?" yelled three of the kids practically simultaneously.

"*ADESSO BASTA!* (Now, that's enough!)" screamed *Maestra* Lella from behind Bruce, scaring him half to death, "*NON C'È UNO DI VOI CHE CAPISCE CHE SIAMO IN UN' AULA E NON IN UNA PALESTRA* (There isn't one of you who understands that we're in a classroom and not a gymnasium)!"

One child was cutting up his class diary into tiny, little pieces and turning them into confetti, while another was making a glue design on the cover of his math notebook. Meanwhile two other children were wandering into the hall and another was climbing on the window sill.

Maestra Lella continued like a motorcycle careening down hill without the brakes. "*VI HO DETTO CHE NON MI SENTO BENE. HO MAL DI DENTI E NON VE NE FREGA.* (I told you that I don't feel well. I have a toothache and no one gives a damn.)"

Apparently Matthew was not exaggerating one bit. The teacher not only had a pair of lungs that gave Pavarotti a run for his money, her use of vocabulary was fairly questionable, and the students continued their conduct oblivious to her tirade, while she ranted about how she had a "damn toothache" and no one "gave a damn." Matthew gave us a look as if to say, "I tried to tell you..."

Later that night, at dinner, I asked him, "How do you deal with it?"

"I just sort of block it out," he told me, and I wondered whether he could selectively block out what didn't work for him, and still absorb some of the language or the content of the lessons.

Alex shared with us his own new coping mechanism for when things went wrong at school.

"Today they separated me from my friends in the lunch room. I was sitting at the third grade table, right next to the second grade table, and at recess they were pointing at me to go with the second graders and I just shook my head, 'no.'"

"Then what?" Bruce asked.

"The teacher's aide shook her head 'yes' and she pointed

'louder' and she yelled at me," he continued.

"And??" Matthew asked. He clearly wanted to know how this story ended.

"She turned around because someone was talking to her and I hid under the table until the second graders left and then I went to recess with my friends," he finished proudly.

Well, I was way too old to be hiding under a table; it was time to confront the situation head on. I asked for a meeting with both Matthew and Alex's teachers. We all sat around in a circle: Laura, *Maestra* Alma, *Maestra* Marta (Matthew's primary teacher), *Maestra* Lella (teaches Matthew's class English and Science and teaches Alex's class Math), *Maestra* Roberta (Matthew's Math teacher), *Maestra* Patrizia (who teaches neither Matthew or Alex's class but is the only teacher in the school who's English is somewhat fluent) and me. The scene brought back memories of my school meeting during my initial *Varese* visit. How naïve I was to think that their integration into the school would be seamless.

I started by asking *Maestra* Roberta why Matthew came home from class this week without his watch. From what I could gather from her explanation, Matthew and Enea were playing with Matthew's watch and she was irritated with the distraction and took it away. I explained to her that it might be helpful to Matthew if she spoke slowly and I asked her if she attempted to explain to Matthew why she took the watch away and when it would be returned. She answered with lightening speed that she did in fact speak slowly, in fact she always speaks slowly, and she never spoke quickly, especially with a foreign child, and moreover it's not her nature to speak quickly anyway, but if she were to speak quickly, she certainly would not speak quickly under these circumstances. Then she took a breath.

Changing the subject, I turned to *Maestra* Alma.

"I think Alex is overwhelmed by having to do some tasks which, although routine to most of the children, seem insurmountable to him," I explained.

"He's a bright boy," she answered me. "You'd be surprised what he is capable of."

"I understand from Alex that he was punished for bad

behavior, separated from his class, and cried hysterically for over an hour. Is that correct?"

"Yes."

"Why didn't you call me?" I asked.

"Why would I do that?" she asked. "It's not my job to worry you unnecessarily. Children have temper tantrums. They only need an adult to set a limit. Alex's upset at school was none of your concern."

I had no words, so I said nothing.

After a pause that seemed like an eternity I said, "I am concerned because when I look at Matthew and Alex's notebooks, they are filled with paragraphs of information in Italian that my children have written, which I know are far too complicated for them to understand. When I ask them what they have written ... or what it means, they respond by telling me that they have no idea and that they copied it from another child's paper. I'm not sure they are learning anything from that, but more importantly, they seem very frustrated by the experience."

"On the contrary," said *Maestra* Alma. "Alex does his own work, but in a group setting. I will explain my method to you so that you will understand, keeping in mind that I have no intentions of changing my method of teaching, only that I will explain it to you. It is my method to teach children in groups. So, it is true that Alex may have learned some of what he wrote from another student."

"My method," interjected *Maestra* Lella, "I must say, is completely the contrary. I work with the children one on one and I have to say that I always ask Matthew, in particular, if he understands and he always says, 'yes.'"

"By the way, Matthew needs another notebook with bigger *quadretti*," said *Maestra* Roberta.

Maestra Marta, Matthew's main classroom teacher and the loudest yeller of all his teachers, said nothing.

"I really think that perhaps the children are putting on a different face in school than they are at home," I responded. "I think at school, they want to fit in and so they claim to understand things that they do not understand and they seem not to be under stress, when in fact they are. I also think they are having trouble understanding because when everyone speaks at the same time it makes the language gap more profound."

"Children just want comforting," replied *Maestra* Alma. "When they complain, you can comfort them briefly and then just be strong. Don't show them you're worried."

"I don't feel I'm showing them that I'm concerned," I said. "I just acknowledge their feelings and I tell them that my only expectations are for them to try to learn the language, to make friends, and to have fun."

"I don't think so," said *Maestra* Roberta. "I think you are upset that they may not get good grades. Americans are always upset about grades. I don't think you should worry about it."

"I'm really not worried about grades," I answered. "I don't even know how you would grade them," I added. "What would you grade them on? They don't speak the language yet."

"Yes, exactly the point," added *Maestra* Alma. "You must be patient."

By this point, I felt like I was on a merry-go-round run amok and that either I couldn't adequately communicate my concerns because of the language deficit or that they were limited by their own viewpoints and lack of experience in dealing with children who do not speak Italian and that nothing was ever going to change.

Then *Maestra* Patrizia began to speak. "My husband and I went abroad to Brazil for two years with our daughter who was 10 years old at the time," she said in a soft, thoughtful voice. "She was put in a classroom where she did not speak a word of the language. She received no support from the teachers and I was permitted no communication with these teachers. It was not like you are experiencing here, *Signora* Hummel, where we are all sitting around talking about Matthew and Alex. At a certain point, my husband told me to pack the bags. 'We are going,' he told me. But it was not to be; we had to stay for his job. For three months my daughter came home and cried every day. For three months I comforted her. Then one day, she came home with a friend from school. When the friend asked her a question, she answered in Portuguese. Just like that – as if she had been speaking it her whole life. The notebooks are not important, *Signora* Hummel; don't look at them. They are nothing more than a pretext. The learning happens from the time they walk through the door and a friend asks them what they did the night before or during the weekend or tells them about a new board game, and it continues through osmosis as long as they have ears to hear. Whether they understand the words in their notebook is not the point. They are doing the exercises like the other children so that they don't feel different ... so that they fit in. The learning is taking place between the lines of the notebook. Not on them."

I started tearing up and trust me, it's really embarrassing to cry in front of a room full of elementary school teachers.

"Go home and don't ask them from now until Christmas anything about school. Don't even ask them how their day was," said *Maestra* Patrizia.

"I can't do that ..." I answered haltingly.

"Just until Christmas," she told me. "Just until Christmas."

When I got home, I could hear Matthew playing the drums. Tommaso Soru had begun to give him weekly drum lessons. *Signor* and *Signora* Talini were fighting about money in the apartment upstairs. Their arguments were so repetitive that sometimes I swore they just flipped on a tape-recorder to save the energy of an actual fight. Their argument was punctuated by the rhythmic beats of Matthew's drums which obscured some of the words, making it seem all the more absurd. Alex and Vanni Soru were hard at work at the kitchen table. He had offered to give Alex art lessons during the same hour that Matthew did his drumming with Tommaso. Alex loved art and Italy, for him, was like one big canvas. Having Vanni, an aspiring artist, just a few blocks away, was the perfect opportunity for him to connect with a big guy and learn new artistic mediums. Whatever Vanni learned at the *liceo artistico* (art high school), Alex learned at the Alex-Vanni Art School. He was learning to sculpt one week, *prospettiva* (perspective) the next, cartooning, shade, and shadow, and even computer "paint" programs.

I used the opportunity for privacy to explain to Bruce what happened during my meeting. He cooked; I recapped the afternoon's events. It was difficult to capture exactly what had transpired, but I tried to synthesize the essence of it.

"They asked us not to even talk to the kids about their day until Christmas," I told him.

"What?" Bruce asked.

"They want us to just let it happen until then."

Bruce said nothing, but nodded his head with a look of ambivalent acquiescence, continuing to stir the savory *fra diavolo* sauce on the stovetop as if it required his intense concentration. I knew that look meant he was processing things internally; he'd take a wait-and-see approach on this one.

After dinner, I put the dog on a leash and set out for an evening walk to clear my head a bit. Matthew asked to join me and although at first I wanted to tell him that I just needed some space and quiet, I agreed that he could come along. We walked along the path of the apartment complex surrounded by the trees and grass in the common areas where the children were not allowed to play because the *portinaia* (groundskeeper) insisted that they would "break the grass." Matthew began speaking to me in Italian in short phrases, interspersed with English.

"*Mi fa ridere che dice che si spacca l'erba* (It makes me laugh that she says we'll break the grass)," he told me, and then in English, "Isn't it silly?"

I was startled to hear him speak a complete sentence in Italian. I responded in Italian as well, and he understood the nature of my response. I could hardly believe it. We strolled along *Corso Matteotti* with its covered *portici* and storefront windows. All the stores were closed, but the Italians dress their windows so beautifully, vicarious shopping is almost as much fun as actual shopping and far more economical. At the end of the pedestrian mall, we curved right to the *Giardini Estensi* where they were showing an outdoor movie. Buster seemed amenable to stopping for a while and curled up under Matthew's seat. Whenever Matthew couldn't catch the gist of what they were saying, doing, or intending, he turned to me and whispered with great interest, "*Cosa?* (What?)" On the way home Matthew wanted a *gelato*. He ordered his usual *stracciatella*, licking it in a counter-clockwise spiral and smiling as if every moment were as easy and blissful as this one.

I held on to these precious moments in time as if the memory of them were as important as my next breath. I needed to remember them when I was confronted with self-doubt. I needed to believe that we were not selfish to take the kids away from their home and that in the end, meeting the challenge of each step of this experience might, contrary to my fears, enhance their sense of self-esteem rather than detract from it.

CHAPTER TEN

It Takes a Village to Raise a Child

It takes a village to raise a child ...
For most of us, though, the village doesn't look like that anymore.
In fact, it's difficult to paint a picture of the modern village,
so frantic and fragmented has much of our culture become.
Extended families rarely live in the same town, let alone the same house.
Where we used to chat with neighbors on stoops and porches,
now we watch videos in our darkened living rooms.
Instead of strolling down Main Street,
we spend hours in automobiles and at anonymous shopping malls ...
It takes a family, it takes teachers, it takes clergy, it takes business people ...
it takes all of us.
Yes, it takes a village.
-Hillary Rodham Clinton

For school-transition stress relief, I activated one of the "prepare for every contingency" models I labored over in New York. Contingency model number one was the "private field trip," overtly intended to augment their cultural experience, but the covert action involved keeping all of us from mental breakdown until things improved at school. One such field trip was to *Villa Della Porta Bozzolo*, not more than 20 minutes from *Varese*. I gave the kids some of the history of the Villa. It was constructed in the 16th century as a country home, and was updated in the 18th century with an imposing garden. The interior was ornately decorated and the stables and wine cellar were still intact. Not wanting to let all my Type A energy go to waste, I prepared a question and answer form for them to complete while they were there. I expected resistance, but instead got absolute cooperation.

Q&A form or not, it represented a welcome reprieve from the rigors of traditional classroom.

"*Maestra* Denise's Worksheet" looked something like this...

Villa Della Porta Bozzolo

Casalzuigno, Varese

Constructed in 1500

Field Trip: September 30

Participants: Matthew, Alex

Instructor: *Maestra* Denise Pirrotti Hummel

1. Before we go, I will read to you something about the history of this villa. When we go, you will see historic sights that remind you of something in present day. You can write those connections here in this space when you get there: (**Example**: This villa is older than Grandpa's dentures.)

2. Second, (before we leave) find Casalzuigno on the map. (**Hint**: It is east of New York and west of Russia.)

3. Villa Bozzolo was originally built as a country house and later became a holiday retreat. What evidence did you find that it was also a farmhouse? (**Warning**: Please don't point to clumps of dirt and tell me that it's fossilized horse excrement, like you did when we visited the Vatican for the changing of the guards.)

4. Gian Angelo della Porta, one of the original owners was very brave in that he went against accepted rules which stated that a garden should be in line with the principle rooms in the house. (He was one crazy dude, huh?) What did he do differently in his garden than we do in ours. (**Hint**: I'm not talking about the fact that they actually weeded theirs.)

5. There is a beautiful little building with a "portico" and a "fresco" depicting Apollo and the Muses.

a. What do you think "portico" means? (No, it has nothing to do with a port.)

---

b. What is a "fresco?" (Yes, it has something to do with something being fresh.)

c. How can you tell which figure is Apollo and which figures are the Muses? (Yes, it does have something to do with breasts – stop pointing.)

6. The Della Porta and Bozzolo families were obsessed with making their property very fancy in the "Baroque" style that was fashionable at the time. They painted almost everything, even a crack in a small half-closed door!!! Can you find the crack?? Where was it? (**Warning**: Don't stand still. Some docent might paint YOU as well!)

7. The library is considered by many historical experts to be the most impressive room in this villa. Why do you think that is? (**Note**: The books with the dusty covers are not "ruined" – they're just a bit "tired" from sitting on the shelves for a few centuries.)

8. If you lived in the 15th century in this particular Villa, describe one day in your life here. (**Note**: You may be shocked to know that didn't have television, computers, or for that matter – light bulbs.)

No complaints. Their answers and exhaustive essay on Medieval sock ball by candlelight showed me they were paying close attention to the lesson. At this point in time, I think both Matthew and Alex were happy to take *Maestra* Denise's worksheets over *Maestra* Alma, Marta, Roberta or Lella's *interrogazione* any day of the week.

Contingency model number two, "Baking With *Maestra* Denise." There is no denying that the only meal I cook well is roast beef with roasted potatoes. I did, however, inherit my grandmother's chocolate chip recipe, a secret weapon whose day had come. The overt objective of the day was to produce some comfort food, but the unanticipated result was the study of language, cultural differences, mathematical calculations and scientific experimentation.

The language part of the lesson was the translation of certain ingredients. After several interviews of local friends and grocers, we learned that the closest product resembling the white all-purpose flour we used in the States was *"farina manitoba."* The closest product to American brown sugar was *"zucchero integrale di canna."* Baking soda was *"bicarbonato di sodio purissimo."* Vanilla extract, *"vaniglia aroma per dolci e creme."* Chocolate chips were *"Gocce di cioccolato fondente."* Walnuts are *"noci senza guscio."* White sugar, butter, salt and eggs were fortunately run of the mill translations that we could at this point tackle without even a glance at the dictionary.

As for the cultural studies part of the lesson, simply discovering how to say chocolate chips and brown sugar in Italian, was just the beginning. To actually find these products meant incorporating the It-Takes-a-Village concept of baking. Most of the ingredients were not Italian staples and, to my knowledge, did not appear in the local market or even the larger supermarkets. Finding chocolate chips and the right kind of brown sugar was the most formidable challenge. First, we visited Tiziana at the *pasticceria*. Since she made cookies for hundreds of clients, we reasoned that she probably knew where to get these key ingredients. Unfortunately, she didn't have a clue.

"Let me know how you make out," she said. Then off we went to the *alimentari* where they sell a lot of gourmet products.

"No, signora, non l'ho mai visto (No, ma'am, I've never seen them)," she told me sympathetically.

Then to the *drogheria*, an all-purpose specialty items store.

"Il zucchero, no signora, ma probabilmente le gocce di cioccolato fondente le posso ordinare (The sugar, no, ma'am, but the chocolate chips I can probably order)."

I called Laura to see if she could shed some light on this cookie caper. I could hear Chiara fussing in the background and Francesca making *cluck cluck* noises at her in an effort to sooth her.

"We found *zucchero integrale di canna* in the market around the corner, but it's granular. What we need is more compact."

"I saw it at the *Esselunga* supermarket," she told me. "It's imported from Ecuador. You'll find it in the specialty foods aisle.

But don't go today. It's Sunday and I don't think they're on the Sunday rotation."

"What do you mean?"

"Check the newspaper. The supermarkets are on a Sunday rotation that changes from month to month. I don't know if *Esselunga* is on the schedule this Sunday as the supermarket that is scheduled to remain open."

"You mean to tell me that every time we run out of milk on Saturday night, we don't have to wait until Monday?"

"*Pazienza.*"

Two weeks and much assistance later, we had collected all our ingredients.

The lesson resumed and we began the mathematical segment: the calibration of the difference between Fahrenheit and Centigrade and the difference in American weights and measures and the European metric system. Easy enough.

As for the scientific experimentation, there was no question that the first few batches consisted of something that resembled the preliminary stages of a science fair project, much more than it did the simple art of baking cookies. For example, 375 degrees Fahrenheit might translate to 190 degrees Centigrade according to the calculator, but after three batches of burnt cookies, we finally settled on 150 degrees Centigrade as the optimal choice of temperature. Likewise, 2 ½ cups of flour might technically be the equivalent of approximately 500 grams, but in "real life" 450 grams worked.

Four batches and 30 cookies later, we "invented" the mathematical and scientific translation of *Biscotti Americani* and by the end of our project, we had nine perfect cookies, which took only slightly less effort than it took Bruce to photograph the Italian version in Milan. We kept four cookies for ourselves, one for each Hummel. Then we went around the neighborhood to give the 'extra' to everyone in the community that helped us. One each for Tiziana from the *pasticceria*, Maria from the *alimentari*, and Veronica from the *drogheria*. Laura's family got two. Grade for the day, "A+" for all participating students.

Contingency Plan Number Three: Play hooky for the day, wait for your friends to get out of school, and go directly to after-school international playdate model. Overt objective — have fun. Covert objective — increase language absorption and cultural assimilation. Who should we choose for the First Hummel International Playdate Initiative? Enea and his cousin Gianni, of course. I picked them up from school and they slid into the back seat.

We entered the apartment complex with cries of, *"Ma, che bello. Che verde.* (How beautiful. How green.)"

Then Buster greeted us at the door. *"Che bel cane* (What a beautiful dog)!" Enea asked me the name of our dog. I told him his name was "Buster."

"Ah, si," he said. *"Anche il nostro cane è un bastardo* (Ah, yes, our dog is a bastard too)."

Bruce had the table all set and served them pasta *al pomodoro* (tomato sauce) and *melone* (melon).

"How did he make this sauce?" Enea asked. "To make sauce the real way, you have to use tomatoes, a little garlic, some oil, some basil. Did he do that? I don't taste any basil." He then proceeded to eat every strand of pasta on his plate.

Alex got up from his seat to play the piano for them. Matthew played the drums. Enea and Gianni chased Buster. Then scooters outside and walkie-talkie-scooter-hide-and-go-seek. Matthew and Alex both had to speak Italian to be understood. I shadowed them a bit to see whether they'd need a translator, but with a few phrases here and there, they got their point across just fine. At one point, while the boys were climbing one of the many trees on the property, the elderly man who lived above us screamed down from his balcony,

"Scendi subito dal albero, se no vengo io e ti tiro giù i pantaloni e ti do un schiaffo sul culo (Get down from that tree immediately or I'll come down and pull your pants down and smack you on your rear-end)."

Enea and Gianni promptly handled the situation *Napolitano* style. "Come down here if you want," Gianni screamed up to him in dialect, "but I'll be the one to pull your pants down and smack your butt."

Matthew and Alex were in hysterics laughing. After enduring countless moments of being told that the green space in the complex was no place for children, they were vindicated.

Enea even helped to bolster Alex's confidence, while teaching Matthew brotherly etiquette. After lunch, while they were playing soccer, Matthew called Alex an *idiota* (idiot).

"Ohhhhhh, *pazienza*!! Why did you call him an idiot?" Enea scolded. "That's not how you play. Either we all play nicely or we don't play at all. I mean, if I kicked this ball and it went into a rose plant and hit a thorn, and the thorn deflated the ball, would you say 'what an idiot!'? No, we go and find another one. *Dai* (come on)!"

When it was time to leave, Enea kissed both my cheeks. "You may want to come over for Christmas. Or maybe New Year's. Yes, New Year's is better. I suggest New Year's, because my father lights fireworks. You can choose Christmas if you like, but I prefer New Years. You decide. The door is always open."

There were so many lessons that first month, it was difficult to take them all in. We did learn that small triumphs, like playdates and making chocolate chip cookies, mattered. The kids did survive the first 30 days of school and Bruce did make his phone call to New York. As for me, all the transition issues I worried about ultimately amounted to minutia, and all the things that never occurred to me to be anxious about, ultimately became life-shaping challenges. This led me to believe that perhaps the whole concept of worrying about moments that had not yet transpired, was best left on the other side of the Atlantic.

Speak Milk. Drink Wine.

CHAPTER ELEVEN

Certain Circumstances Require The Good Judgment to Back Off

If you don't know where you are going,
you'll end up someplace else.
-Yogi Berra

Dear Matthew, regarding baseball cards, can you tell me what players you would like, or do you just want a pack of cards? Here it is a beautiful day and tonight we are going to the opera to see Madame Butterfly which is an opera set in Japan about a Japanese woman who falls in love with an American sea captain who then goes back to America. The music is so beautiful but sadly in the end there is a tragedy and she dies. Of course everyone in the audience is sad and wishes for a happier ending and that the players had made better choices. The opera is kind of a study in life where we can learn from the characters. Sometimes the behavior should be admired and sometimes we have to reject that behavior and make better choices. I suppose it is like watching one of your action movies. There is the 'good people ... bad people' stuff going on. Love, Grandma

*   *   *

Dear Grandma, I would prefer a Catfish Hunter baseball card, but whatever comes easier is fine with me. I hope you liked the opera. I came up with a new idea that would be really helpful for kids (including me) who are really interested in memorizing baseball stats. I don't understand why most operas have to have a sad ending? My dad says that one day he'll take me to see *Figaro*. Well I hope everything is well, and cross your fingers that the Red Sox win today. Love, Matthew

*　　　*　　　*

Dear Matthew, the Red Sox won 6-1. Also the Mets beat Houston. I think the score was 8-1. I will look for a Catfish Hunter card for you. I hope to get to the baseball store within the next few days. We heard you had an awesome practice pitching with Dad last week. Congratulations! What ideas have you devised to memorize stats? Sounds interesting. Do you follow any golf? Tiger Woods won the Masters for the third time I believe. That is very good. Love G.M. Lee

*　　　*　　　*

Dear Grandma, I already heard that the Red Sox won because I go on MLB.com every morning. Tim Wakefield was awesome on the mound, and Doug Mirabelli hit a home run. I also heard that the Mets won. Andy Pettitte stunk and Tom Glavine did good. If you're going to find a Catfish Hunter card you'll have to look in the places that sell old baseball card from the 60's. My idea for kids who are crazy about memorizing stats is that we make a dictionary full of year-by-year leaders in stats. I'm not a big golf fan, but I do know that

Tiger Woods is one of the best. Speaking of golf I read in one of the Almanacs that there was this 14-year-old Chinese woman who became one of the only women in golf history to be nominated to the men's tournament. Well I gotta go. Let's hope that the Red Sox win. Arroyo is pitching. I hope everything is good in New York. Love, Matthew

*   *   *

My mother was never very enamored with sports. I'm not sure she even knew for what city the Red Sox played before Matthew fell in love with the team. He was six when his Little League team donned the name "Red Sox." When the next year, by coincidence, his team again was assigned the name, he put on the jersey and announced that it was a "sign" that this would be his team for life. He wasn't kidding. The fact that the Red Sox had not won a World Series for 86 years was irrelevant. So too was the fact that most of his fellow New York buddies were Yankees and Mets fans. After months of trying to get Matthew to sit down to respond to his Grandma's emails, I gave up. My mother, however, did not. She figured out that if she watched the games, or listened to the news afterward, she had targeted information to engage him. Any email she wrote to him about baseball received a speedy and thorough email in return.

While Alex also loved baseball, he was not as passionate about it as his brother. He chose to root for the Yankees, more because they were rivals to Matthew's Red Sox than for geographical reasons or their statistical status in the league. But for Matthew, next to leaving behind his friends in New York, the single greatest loss to him was the unlikelihood that he would play baseball that season. He insisted that we pack his cleats, old uniform, baseball caps, baseball bat, baseballs and eight extra gloves in case the Italian kids wanted to learn how to play, despite the fact that the average Italian wouldn't know a baseball glove from an oven mitt.

Defying what seemed to be the impossible, the Boston Red Sox "chose" the year we were away from our country to drive themselves into the World Series. As most games took place at least six hours earlier than "*Varese* time," it was often impossible to know the score before he went to bed. Matthew slept restlessly, not knowing the fate of his beloved team. Every night of the 2004 World Series games, he went to bed praying and woke up every morning asking us, before his eyes were even completely open, who won. When the Red Sox won their first World Series in 86 years, Matthew woke up to victory signs Bruce placed all over the house. I mused that had we been in New York, this event would have been just one more moment Bruce missed while traveling to Chicago or Dallas and I could tell by his face that Bruce was thinking the same thing. We went out to celebrate that night and Matthew slept soundly for the first time in several weeks.

Matthew not being able to play baseball was definitely one of the things that pulled at my heartstrings about being away from home. But it wasn't just that. Eight and 10 are such tender ages – years where every birthday with friends and grandparents, every Halloween costume chosen, every tooth left to the tooth fairy counts. Whenever I discussed my feelings with Bruce, he reminded me that with every American tradition or memory they "lost" that year, they were gaining something else. That "something" was sure to be different – perhaps they would celebrate *Carnivale* in February, rather than Halloween in October. They'd have the tooth "*topolino*" rather than the tooth "fairy". They'd risk losing the strength of their ties with old friends, but learn how to make new ones. I agreed with all these premises, or I probably would not have taken them away from American soil. But baseball was different.

"You might want to just let it go for now," Bruce told me. "If he's really a fan, the passion won't diminish. If he really has talent, he'll catch up when he gets back." I know that loss is part of life and that I probably don't do them any favors by constantly trying to protect them from it. Nevertheless, I decided that the best way to handle the situation was to distract them from American baseball by encouraging their interest in Italian soccer. The Italians are so passionate about it, maybe that passion would be the gain that would offset the temporary loss of baseball. I, for one, actually liked soccer. It was fast paced – never a dull moment. And there was a socio-cultural component to it that I really valued. It unified countries and crossed borders in a way that baseball didn't. True there were occasional episodes of hooliganism, trampling and overcrowding in the stadiums. But the European championships and the World Cup have international appeal that rivals the Olympics. There was even the potential for bridging cultural gaps and overturning prejudices. The 2002 Cup had taken place in South Korea and Japan. In less than half a century, South Korea went from prohibiting the Japanese national team to cross its borders for a World Cup qualifier, to co-hosting the tournament. Who knew, over the next 100 years, maybe Israel and Palestine could play each other in the same stadium without any consequence more egregious than the red-card ejection of a player. In soccer, anything seems possible.

I started telling the kids some stories I had read that might pique their interest. They were already collecting *figurine di calcio*, the Italian soccer equivalent of baseball cards, so with a little reinforcement and re-direction, I reasoned that they could channel their baseball energy temporarily into soccer.

"Soccer is a very international sport. It's appreciated worldwide and every culture brings to the game its own traditions," I told them enthusiastically.

No reaction.

"I read that in the African Nations Cup, witch doctors scattered charms on the field and smeared goalposts with magic ointments to keep the ball out of the net. In fact, some of the teams take a bath in magic potions and make wishes into the ear of a pigeon. Isn't that cool?"

Matthew crinkled his nose in disgust.

Still, I had no intention of giving up. In Italy, soccer was all around us in a way that baseball had not been at home. In New York, we knew people who were into baseball and people who were not. We knew people who preferred football or basketball. We knew people who didn't even know where home plate was or what it was for, and people who wouldn't know a goalpost from a basketball hoop. In Italy, you *knew* about soccer. If you wanted to engage in conversation with someone new, break down a social barrier, get someone to trust you, or even like you, you had better know about soccer. And if you missed a game, you might miss a key political event as well, particularly when the prime minister of the country is also the owner of a key team like A.C. Milan. During the *Milan-Livorno* game, *Livorno tifosi* (fans) appeared in Milan with bandages on their heads to belittle the prime minister about his recent hair transplant. Some even attribute that little joke as the beginning of the billionaire's political demise.

Every morning at the bar, you could find a general newspaper – the *Corrierre della Sera* or the *Prealpina* were always available. But you had to skulk around prepared to pounce to find the pink sports pages of the *Gazzetta dello Sport* or risk not being in the know about who scored, what teams won, who was out with injuries, and what the most recent soccer scandal was by the time you finished your last sip of *cappuccino* or *espresso*, which would lead to being socially ostracized at work or on the playground.

The major teams were *A.C. Milan*, out of Milan, and *Juventus*, out of Torino, with *Inter* trailing behind as *A.C. Milan's* rival from the same city. And this was just the tip of the iceberg. There are 132 professional teams in Italy alone (20 of them in *Serie A*, the top league). Then there were of course, the international powerhouses such as Reale Madrid, Manchester United and Lyon. If you were a foreigner and/or a female, knowing just the outcome of the national games that occurred the day before was sufficient, but for the rest of the population, including children over the age of six, a more in-depth knowledge was definitely advisable. If you were a *tifoso* of *A.C. Milan,* you were a *Milanista*. If you were a fan of *Juventus*, you were a *Juventino*. If you were a fan of *Inter*, (one of the only teams that never seemed to be implicated in a betting scandal), you were an *Interista.*

Every morning, Aldo, our local barber came to the bar for coffee. He saw Matthew and asked him if *Juventus* won the night before. Matthew waved his hand, *alla Napolitano*, in a circular gesture that could roughly be recognized as "you know how it is" or "you know how it goes" or something neutral enough that Aldo couldn't be sure if he didn't know or wasn't telling. Then he waited for the first free *Gazzetta dello Sport* (despite his need to know, there was no point paying for a copy across the street at the *Edicola* when our *barista*, Adriano, had them available for free.) Then the banter between Aldo and Adriano began.

"*Avete perso ieri sera, brutto Interista* (You guys lost last night, ugly *Inter* fan)," Aldo might say.

"*Eh si ... siamo abituati a soffrire* (Yea, yea ... we're used to suffering)," Adriano responded.

And so it went for the remainder of breakfast – Matthew and Alex watched and laughed at this entertainment, but remained at the periphery. Surely if I took them to a soccer game and they saw all the enthusiasm, they'd be hooked.

Tommaso explained to me that most of the professional games were sold out for the remainder of the season. He also advised me which games not to see. The tensions between *Milan* and *Inter* for example, rivals from the same city, were too extreme and subject to violence. *Lazio* vs. *Roma*, both from the province of *Lazio* was also a bad choice. So was a game between *Sampdoria* and *Genoa*, *Verona* and *Chievo*, and *Atalanta* and *Brescia*. I decided it might be best just to pick a game between an Italian team and a team from another country entirely during the European championships, and set about the business of procuring tickets to the *A.C. Milan* versus *Barcelona* Champions League game.

When the day of the match arrived, we found the specific gate where we were supposed to enter and climbed the tower to the first tier. I was really psyched to see the kids' expression when they saw the great tickets I scalped; they were practically on the field. Fans wearing red and black *Milan* jerseys were all around, each with the last name of different key players – Pirlo, Gattuso, Schevchenko.

"Why do I see all these T-shirts with the name, 'Schevchenko'?" Bruce asked. "That name doesn't sound very Italian."

"He was recruited from the Ukraine, Dad," Alex answered.

How did he know that?

The entrance to the portal that contained our seats seemed unusually crowded. We arrived 45 minutes before the start of the game and the crowd to get to our seats was huge and unmoving. I asked the man in front of us what was causing the delay for people to get to their seats.

"It's full," he told me.

"Full?" I asked. "But we have tickets."

"So ..."

"So, how can I get up there to talk to the usher?" I responded.

"What usher, *signora*? There's no usher stupid enough to put himself in the middle of that crowd."

"So what do I do with these tickets?" I asked him.

"Keep them as a souvenir," he suggested.

We descended the stairs to the entrance of the stadium. I had definitely seen an usher there.

"We have these tickets," I told him, extending them toward him.

"*Signora*," he looked at me kindly, "I suggest you go into Tower B and go all the way to the top."

"But these are for Tower A, first level," I explained. It was probably his first day on the job.

"I can see that, *signora*," he told me, and then pointing to the kids said, "but there are certain considerations that require your good judgment to take your family to the top of Tower B. I'm sure the seats where these tickets are located are full by now ... and truthfully, that location is no place for children." He put his right index finger to the bottom right corner of his right eye and pulled the skin around his eye down, the Italian gesture for 'keep your eyes open.' "*Occhio* (eyes)" he said, emphasizing the point.

I realized at that moment that Tommaso assumed that even though I didn't know the games to stay away from, I at least had the common sense to know not to sit close to the field at a championship game.

Frustrated, but with a sense that listening to this guy was the right thing to do, we climbed the tower to the helicopter seats. The players looked like little ants chasing a seed across the field. People around us were screaming, chanting wildly and waving flags the size of a small child. From our seats, we watched the tiny dots scurrying across the field.

"*Vaffanculo!*" screamed the guy next to us wearing an *A.C. Milan* shirt. At least it appeared we were in 'friendly,' although perhaps not, 'family' territory. I assumed the kids already learned the Italian equivalent of "f--k you" at camp.

"*Vaffanculo!*" yelled the guy to my left.

Alex leaned over to Matthew. "This is cool," he screamed in his ear so Matthew could hear him over the roaring crowd.

"You bet, Taz," Matthew yelled back.

While the tiny dots ran around the field, I could tell when one of the teams scored by the screams, "Gol, gol, GOOOOOOLLLLLL!!!", simultaneous with people springing into the air, waving their fists, shouting "*Gol!*" or "*Vaffanculo!*", chanting, and the tips of flags swaying in my hair, eyes and mouth. Bruce was running interference with stray flags, waving fists, and people occasionally kissing the top of the kids' heads, while he darted glances at me that could roughly be translated as "and why did you say the kids should see a live soccer game?"

"Ohhh, aaaoooo aaaaooo," Matthew and Alex were chanting with the other *Milanisti*, as if they had been raised with the tune and knew it by heart.

Then the crowd, including Matthew and Alex, began chanting the Italian anthem,

> *Fratelli d'Italia*
> *L'Italia s'è desta*
> *Dell'elmo di Scipio*
> *S'è cinta la testa.*
> *Dove'è la Vittoria?*
> *Le porga la chioma;*
> *Chè schiava di Roma*
> *Iddio la creò.*
> *Stringiamoci a coorte,*
> *Siam pronti alla morte:*
> *Italia chiamò!*

***

> Italian brothers,
> Italy has arisen,
> With Scipio's helmet
> binding her head.
> Where is Victory?
> Let her bow down,
> For God has made her

The slave of Rome.
Let us gather in legions,
Ready to die!
Italy has called!

"I think it's going reasonably well," I shouted to Bruce through occasional gaps in the flag waving between my face and Bruce's head.

"If you don't mind," he responded, "Let's leave here about 20 minutes before the game ends and save the 'angry fans life lesson' for later in life. What do you say?"

The kids weren't happy about our premature exit, but I think they could see the prudence of the decision, because they got up without more than a grimace.

"Can we do that again soon?" Matthew asked.

Soon is a relative term.

On the way home, we called Laura and Domenico to tell them what happened, the tickets we couldn't use, being relegated to helicopter seats, our early departure. They seemed to be waiting for the punch line.

"*È normale*," Domenico told me.

"At least you didn't choose a really contentious game," Laura congratulated me. "Do you remember the television coverage when you came in May? The flares being thrown on the field, the fights, the bottle throwing and the cars lit outside the stadium?" No, I didn't remember that. May was a blur of furnished apartments without furnishings, practice prisoners, and dogs who needed to be healthy to get a health certificate.

"I was hoping to get the kids involved in after-school soccer," I told her, "so I took them to a game to get excited about it. But now I'm not so sure."

"Soccer is serious business here," Domenico said. "Even the parents of little kids at the games are a bit over the top in my opinion. You might want to consider having them play baseball."

"Baseball?" I asked. "I thought there wasn't any baseball in Italy. I didn't even think to ask."

"Oh sure," he told me. "Didn't you see the signs on *Corso Matteotti*? I thought you were just waiting for the kids to settle in, or I would have said something. It's not exactly popular, and you'll have to drive 10 kilometers to *Malnate*, but it might be a little more relaxed than having them play soccer. Every parent of a child who plays soccer expects him to be the next *Del Piero*. You're better off having them watch soccer on television and playing it in the *piazza*, than you are watching it at San Siro or playing on a team."

Sure enough, a baseball team in the small town of *Malnate* did exist. One Saturday, we went to pay them a visit. We saw a lot of kids in very professional-looking uniforms playing baseball! The first, very obvious difference between the *Malnate* team and that of our suburban New York team was that 7-year-olds were practicing on the same team with 16-year-olds. Indeed, in order to get together a complete team of players, every child with an interest in baseball from all over the province was playing on the *Malnate* team.

On this particular day, the *Malnate* Vikings were playing a team from Milan.

"*Vai Aldo!*"

"*Forza Giacomo!*"

The Italians watching sounded every bit as exuberant as the fans at Yankee Stadium in New York, but much more relaxed than those at San Siro Stadium in Milan. When the game was over, we went to speak with the coach.

"We're American," I said. "We're living in *Varese*. Our kids have been playing baseball since they were six. They're just learning Italian, but I don't think it will be a problem."

Matthew and Alex picked up a ball, and began practicing, Matthew his pitching and Alex his catching.

"I don't know," the coach said to me. "You really need a strong command of the language to play on a team. I'm not ... sure ... if ..." his voice trailed off as he became distracted by something.

I looked over and saw that the distraction plaguing him was Matthew and Alex and the sound Matthew's pitches were making when they hit Alex's glove.

"Try a curve ball," Alex yelled. "That (pretend) guy was a lefty. You just pitched a ball, not a strike."

"Taz, your strike zone is ridiculous," Matthew retorted, winding up.

"What are they saying," the coach asked me.

"Uh ... Alex is saying that Matthew's pitches are too hard; they're hurting his hand," I translated, a bit loosely.

"I can see that ..." he said. "That kid can pitch. The little guy is pretty good too ... what's their batting like?"

The conversation soon segued from his concerns regarding Matthew and Alex's abilities to follow instruction in Italian, to discussing the merits of the Malnate team. I think we were being recruited.

The coach informed us that there was a game next weekend.

"When is the practice?" I asked. "I need to organize getting to and from the field this week because I scheduled several appointments."

"Don't worry about the practice," he said. "Just show up for the game. We'll start them practicing the following week."

When we returned for the first game, it was clear that our presence was anticipated favorably.

"*Sono arrivati gli Americani* (The Americans are here)!" the team greeted us.

The kids were looking forward to the first game with great anticipation. But shortly after we arrived, we realized that they intended to separate the older kids from the younger ones. This meant that kids from age 13 up would be playing a baseball team of similarly aged kids from Milan, whereas the younger kids, ours included, would play a softball team of girls. Matthew and Alex were gravely disappointed, but took their positions, Matthew as shortstop and Alex as first baseman, and settled into a mode of concentration that would make David Ortiz proud. From the first hit to the last, Matthew fielded the ball as if his life depended on it. For the first few years of his baseball life, he had an imaginary square painted around his body on the field over which he could not run to catch a ball, taking *literally* the coach's instruction as to the area his position encompassed. On this day in Malnate, he was all over the place and seemed to catch pop flies out of thin air no matter where they were on the field. Alex jumped to catch balls that were thrown several feet over his head. The Americans were hot. People in the stands started shouting, "*Bravi Americani*," and offering us *prosciutto e melone* in the stands. We felt like the parents of Olympic team members, watching their final attempt for the gold medal.

Meanwhile, a 5-year-old girl from the softball team came up to bat.

"*Brava, piccolina* (good job little one)!" both teams began to shout. The Italian parents sounded noise-makers, tambourines and little cymbals. The pitcher threw her about eight strikes and when she finally hit the ball about a meter and a half, both teams cheered, including Matthew and Alex. As we drove home, we were smiling and laughing. The whole experience was priceless.

When we got home, Matthew asked to turn on the television.

"It's a beautiful day," I said. "Why don't you go out and play."

"*Dai, Mamma*," he told me. "*A.C. Milan* is playing *Inter*."

I looked at him dumbfounded before finally responding, "Fine, fine, at least we'll be on top of the conversation at the bar tomorrow morning."

There was something to be said for cultural assimilation and something to be said for maintaining our cultural traditions. Laura and Domenico were probably right – the best combination was to appreciate soccer with Aldo and Adriano in the bar, or with local kids in the *piazza*, or in the comfort of our living room watching it on television, while sharing American baseball talent with new friends in Malnate. Italian baseball lacked the competitive profile of Matthew's Little League Red Sox versus the Astros, but it gave the kids an opportunity to shine in a way that they might not have at home, playing against other talented and experienced American boys.

"Who would have thought?" Matthew said that evening. "We found baseball fans in a land of soccer *tifosi*."

"That's fine," Alex told him. "But you still need to work on your curve ball."

Speak Milk. Drink Wine.

CHAPTER TWELVE

Life is Meant to be Lived Slowly, With Pauses in Between Each Moment

AKA Not Living the Take-Out Life

For the sword outwears its sheath,
And the soul wears out the breast,
And the heart must pause for breath,
And love itself have rest.
-Lord Byron

I cannot point to a discrete moment when I started to feel a part of the society we were visiting. Little by little, though, I did begin to feel more "Italian." We had settled into our home and the kids were managing their transition to school. Gradually, the whole family's pace was slowing down. After-school sports and activities didn't start until November 1 so that children and families had a chance to adjust to the post-summer routine. What a great idea. And none of the moms I met signed their kids up for more than one organized after-school activity, so I didn't either, and I felt absolutely guiltless.

I was speaking slower, at first to be sure I was being understood, and later because I realized that a slow, sweet tone of voice seemed to put people more in the mood to be patient with me as I referred to *suore* (nuns) as *suocere* (mothers-in-law) or mistook the word *esprimere* (to express oneself) with *spremere* (slang for ejaculation). I was walking slower, initially because there wasn't much maneuvering room on the narrow sidewalks and passing someone could easily lead to nudging a baby carriage into the gutter, but ultimately because I was less focused on getting to where I had to go and more focused on the sights along the way. I wasn't rushing around from one activity to another, so I had more time to observe the world around me – and it suited me. I was noticing all the little details. The geraniums in the flower box on the wrought iron balcony above the *alimentari* were still blooming late in the fall. The teenager down the street must have turned 18 because he was driving a brand new blue and yellow *motocicletta*, fashioned after Valentino Rossi, one of Italy's most revered *Moto Gran Prix* stars. The managers of the shops under the *portici* were out scrubbing the mosaic on the sidewalks much earlier on Saturday mornings than other mornings because they were especially dirty after the Friday night pedestrian traffic and resulting increase in melting ice cream cones.

I was finding that most things about Italy suited me. Something as simple as going to the bar every morning with Buster and the kids, after Bruce caught the train to Milan, put me in the right frame of mind for the day. Being recognized as a "regular" gave me a sense of belonging, certainly, but it was also the way Aldo teased Matthew about becoming a *Milanista* after his first live game at San Siro, and Adriano teasing Alex that he became a *Juventino* just to spite Matthew. It was the way Adriano tussled Matthew's hair when he asked him if he'd have a *succo di albicocca* (apricot juice) or a creamy *cioccolata calda* (hot chocolate) now that it was autumn, and the way he brought me my *cappuccino* without *cacao* sprinkled on top, my *brioche con crema*, and a small glass of water to cut the sweetness, without me having to remind him. At the bar, I had something 'extra' to look forward to, right after I brushed my teeth and threw on my clothes.

I got up even earlier in Italy than I did in the States, since school started earlier, but I didn't seem to have trouble getting out of bed the way I used to in New York. Initially I thought that living in a city might be stressful, but it turned out that there was a lot to be gained by embracing city life. I was walking or biking to restaurants, to grocery stores, to rent a video, to the movies and kid activities, so even on the worst *pazienza* day, grandmothers with slow reflexes were safe from being rousted from their stop-light slumber by my penchant to lean on the horn. But I was also feeding off the energy of my environment, instead of feeding my face, the *Varese* version of the Scarsdale Diet. The dynamic atmosphere and human interaction provided by my environment gave me a sense of belonging that I felt from the moment I walked out the front door of the apartment. I reasoned at first that it was because everything was so new that we were bonding as a family because we needed each other so much.

But in time I realized that my sense of community was coming from my general state of satisfaction with my surroundings. It started when the first church bells rang – the feeling that everyone around me knew that it was 7 p.m. or 6:45 or 7:45 – that we all knew by the wedding bell rhythm that someone just got married, or by the funeral bell rhythm that someone in the community had passed. I felt connected with every familiar face at the bar, and that feeling continued when I walked down the street and the lady from the *edicola* asked me how the kids were getting along at school or the owner of the *carteloria*, stopped counting her inventory to help me pick out a birthday card. That 'extra' – that way of interacting – was contagious. If I cashed a check at the bank and "my" bank teller was occupied, but the others were free, I waited in line, rather than get the job done as quickly and efficiently as possible. I needed to find out if her husband was discharged from the hospital since the last time we spoke, despite the fact that I didn't understand if the malady described was gall stones or hemorrhoids. The baker was "my" baker, the butcher was "my" butcher, and the toy store guy was "my" toy store guy. I felt connected, supported, and at times, even loved by relative strangers.

Connection is so important to the Italians that the boundary is somewhat amorphous. When a telephone conversation ends, it doesn't sound like the end of a conversation I have with Americans – the kind that ends, "OK, bye now." It lingers like this, *"Va bene, ciao, allora. Ciao, ciao, un bacio, ciao amore, ciao, ciao-ciao.* (OK, bye then. Bye, bye, a kiss, bye love, bye, bye-bye.)" In person, the connection, and thus the act of severing the connection, is even more intense. Conservatively, you need to calculate at least an extra 45 minutes from the time you want to leave someone's house to the time you actually get out the door.

Your departure usually starts in the living room with a statement like, "We really should be going," but no one moves and the conversation continues. Ten minutes later, someone might stand to leave, but the rest present stay seated. The conversation continues for at least another 10 minutes. Finally a second person stands. The first person heads toward the door. The remaining members of your party and your host remain seated.

You could write a novella in the time that everyone eventually congregates in the foyer near the door. Someone then puts their hand on the door knob. The door opens and those departing slowly trickle out. Guests kiss their hosts on both cheeks, a third kiss on the original cheek if the kisser is young or cool. Absent severely inclement weather along the lines of a hurricane or severe hail storm, there is more chit chat outside. Eventually, the guests make their way to the external *cancello* (home security gate).

As you get into your car or walk down the street, your hosts stand and wave until you are out of sight in the remote case that you should feel deserted or unloved. The connection is not broken until you can't see them anymore and even then, you have the eerie sense that they are still with you.

I'm convinced that whoever designed the first Italian cities centuries ago, had the concept of "connection" at the forefront of their minds. American cities seem to be comprised of a main street, with other streets that run parallel and perpendicular to it and the very nature of it seems to assume that people will be passing through without stopping. But almost every Italian city has a central *piazza*, which remains a pedestrian-only area. The surrounding streets of the pedestrian area feed into the *piazza* as if the *piazza* is the magnetized hub of the spokes of a wheel, drawing people to its center – you couldn't avoid connection even if it were your main objective in life. There are people sitting on stone benches in front of fountains gushing water from the mouth of a fish in *Liguria* or the bucket of a fair maiden in *Trentino* or cascading over Apollo's shoulders in *Lazio*. I have never seen so many different ways for water to spew from an orifice. People are sitting in outdoor cafés. Toddlers give pigeons a run for their lives. Kids play soccer with whoever shows up. Old men dodge soccer balls and lament about kids making such a ruckus so near the church. Dogs are barking. Moms are pushing baby carriages, stopped every 30 seconds by passersby performing the Italian version of 'goo-goo' which goes something like, "What a perfect *angioletto* (little angel). How could God create such a perfect *piccolino* (little one)? He looks just like you and probably identical to his grandfather as well. And when was he born and how much does he weigh? And you must be the happiest creature on earth. May you have 100 years of good luck," and on and on.

There was a consistency and routine to things that was comforting to me. I liked passing the fruit and vegetable guy on the corner and knowing that he was cutting the bottoms off the broccoli at about the same time every day in the same way his father and his grandfather had for the better part of the century. Even the doors of all the stores in town opened inwards rather than outwards, as if to invite the patron in, in the same direction they had opened for probably all of recorded time. It gave things a sense of historical relevance and permanence, if for no other reason, based on the sheer length of time that his store, the bar and most of the homes, churches and buildings surrounding us remained. I felt every day as if I were part of something greater, something that was here before me and would be there long after I left.

Every morning when I got up, Bruce was there. The kids awoke to the kisses of both parents instead of my kisses and Bruce's call from Dallas or Chicago or wherever he was on business. It was unrealistic to think that life would be like this always, but I soaked up the warm feeling of having my entire family around me first thing in the morning. It gave me a settling feeling that saw me through most of the day.

I continued to write voraciously about our Italian experiences for our local newspaper back at home and began exploring how I could turn my love of writing, travel and culture into something that might actually lead to an income. At lunch time, on Tuesdays, Thursdays and Fridays, school let out at 1 p.m. I picked up the kids while Bruce made lunch. In New York there were no "short days" during the week, but even on the weekends back in the States, my greatest lunchtime opus was a peanut butter and jelly sandwich. In Italy, Bruce wasn't in peanut-butter-and-jelly mode. On the days when he wasn't at the photography studio, he was in *spaghetti, gnocchi* and *risotto* mode, and by the time we got home from school for lunch, the table was set in our little garden now covered with thick, lush grass, and we all ate a meal together that probably rivaled *Signor* and *Signora Gian Angelo della Porta's* 15th century midday meal at *Villa della Porta Bozzolo*.

Our Italian friends worked full time, but their rhythm was not all that different. Susanna and Giampiero walked home arm in arm daily to meet Vanni who walked home from high school. Depending on Tommaso's schedule, he might be there after attending the University in Milan that morning. At 3 p.m., they returned to the office or to school after they took a pause from their hectic day, respecting their need to relax, to nurture themselves, and connect with their loved ones. The fruit and vegetable guy on the corner went home for lunch with his wife. Tiziana from the *pasticceria* and her husband picked up their kids and they ate together. Her husband always napped after lunch since he had the earlier shift at the bakery. My toy store guy, bank-teller, card store guy, and thousands of families I didn't know did the same. You can't even get a parking ticket during the *pausa;* parking is free during the hours from 1 to 3 p.m. How could you be expected to get the required hourly *tessera* (paid parking pass) from the *edicola* if you were at home eating a two-course meal? And who could give you the ticket when the local *parcheggiatore* (equivalent of meter maid) was having her daily lunch date with the tall, dark and handsome officer at the *questura*?

Simply said, Italian life is not a "take-out" life. I have yet to see the coffee bar that sells take-out coffee or that even has take-out cups, apart from the single cup fabricated for me by Adriano on our first morning in *Varese*. While it's possible to get a "take-away" *panino* or *trancio di pizza* (slice of pizza), most people I knew didn't. Why would they? It is the *pausa*. It is time to PAUSE from the day, eat, relax and connect.

Booksellers have been plying books from India to Southern California related to pausing, breathing and living life consciously. We could all save the $19.95 for the "relax" manual with matching workbook and spend it on some *pasta fagioli* and a glass of *Vernaccia* between the hours of 12:30 and 3:30 p.m.

The term *pausa*, the word that initially signaled to me only those hours in the middle of the day when all shops were closed, making life inconvenient, was taking on a new meaning for me. I was beginning to think that this concept of pause and connection was a key difference that separated my life in New York from my life in *Varese*. In New York I decided that running around was the thing to do and I did it as well or better than anyone else. In *Varese*, that mentality just didn't cut it. It wasn't done. It wasn't even normal. And so, I had permission to slow down.

The *pausa* was a gift from Italy that I could take with me when I went home. Maybe Bruce wouldn't always be there to cook us a hot lunch and maybe the kids won't be getting out of school at 1 p.m. on Tuesdays, Thursdays and Fridays, but I could pause, eat with dignity, and flip the switch to the off position for an hour or two during the day, whether stores were open between 12:30 and 3:30 p.m. or not.

The slow pace of my life was partially Italy's cultural influence, but it also had to do with the fact that our *Varese* life was a simpler one. It wasn't just that the kids had fewer activities. I no longer had a big house to take care of. I had a 110 square meter apartment with a few sticks of furniture, the most elaborate of which was a desk with a piece of electrical tape down the middle. I was finally profoundly aware that my happiness (or lack of happiness) was based on the choices I made in my life. No one had forced me to buy the big house, register the kids for multiple activities, or otherwise fill every moment of every day. Surprise, surprise – wake up and smell the *espresso.*

One morning I was speaking to Giovanni, my fruit and vegetable guy, on the way to the bar. I said to him, "I feel so much less stressed here in Italy than I used to in the States." I struggled with the word 'stress' because I didn't know the translation.

"I don't understand what you're saying," he told me politely.

So, I asked Adriano, "Stress ... you know ..." I said gritting my teeth for emphasis and simultaneously shaking a bit like I was in need of an exorcist.

"I'm not sure what you mean," he said, sheepishly grinning at my perplexing pantomime.

That afternoon, I looked up the word 'stress' in my Italian-American pocket dictionary. Nothing. I went to my hefty office dictionary that has all those nasty technical words that no one uses on a daily basis. Nothing.

I called Susanna. Since she and Giampiero were the principles in an advertising agency and spoke English with international clients, surely she could help me. "What is the translation for the word 'stress'?"" I asked.

"The word 'stress' does not exist in the Italian language," she answered.

"Yes, yes, I get it, metaphorically speaking – but what's the translation of the word?"

"In the past few years, people here have begun to use the Anglo-Saxon term, 'stress,' but it is a term we have borrowed and I'd be happy to give it back," she said, "... metaphorically or otherwise."

On and off, from that day forward, my ears tuned in, I heard, "*Che stress* (What stress)!" and "*È stato stressante* (It was stressful)!" The "ante" ending was a way of taking the foreign word and turning it into an adjective.

How could it be that the level of stress in American society, which is so often the topic of conversation in the States, was so insignificant here that the Italians managed for centuries without even the necessity of the word 'stress' in their vocabulary? Was there really so little stress, or was it offset by the '*pazienza* syndrome' – the simple acceptance of things that don't go their way. There have got to be a thousand American sociologists who have studied the phenomenon and could explain it better than I. I could just imagine the headline of the article: "PhD Stress Specialist Finds Stress Cure: Discovers link between *Pazienza* Syndrome and the *Pausa*. Unique tannins found in Italian red wine when combined with the starch from pasta water considered contributing factors ..."

I called my friend Julene, a native North Dakotan living in Boulder. I told her about the rhythm of our day, about the *pausa*, about the feeling of connection and about slowing down.

"When I get back, even if the people around me are moving at a frantic pace, I don't have to, do I?" I asked her.

"You already HAVE friends living at a more leisurely and relaxed pace — us!" she told me. "I remember when we tried to make dinner plans with you in Boulder, you seemed to be the busiest people we ever met. 'Can't on Saturday ... have a brunch thing and a dinner thing ... can't on Sunday have a ski thing and a dinner thing after that ...' I was often exhausted just HEARING about it!! I always thought it was part of your New York upbringing."

"I never thought of it as just a New York thing," I told her, "or even just an East Coast thing or a big city thing. I just assumed all Americans moved at that pace."

"I don't think it's a New York thing per se," she told me, "but I do think you can bring this sense of pause to all aspects of your life, regardless of where you decide to live. You could 'learn to smell the coffee' so to speak, while you go about the business of getting it and drinking it."

It was true that certain countries, like America, were more prone to encouraging a frantic pace that led people like me to move through life so fast that they had difficulty experiencing each moment one by one without turning every day into a marathon of lists and expectations. By coming to Italy, I lucked out. I put myself in a situation where I could now see that there was another way to live. But we live in a world of globalization where borders and oceans are easy to cross, a world where we are sharing everything from technology to language, to traditions, and every day we become more homogeneous across cultures. Which is going to win-out: the *pausa* or optimum levels of productivity? I wasn't in a position to answer that question, but I could grasp the freedom and power in my own life by slowing down, staying awake, and taking responsibility for the pace of my daily life. With enough "practice," I might learn to be in control of the quality of my life wherever I found myself and under whatever circumstances. It was only October, a fraction of our year away from home had passed and I was beginning to get it. I needed to figure out how to make it last.

As I got ready for bed, I looked at the vial of sleeping pills on my nightstand. They were a staple in my New York life but I hadn't taken one since the first few weeks of living in *Varese*.

Maybe it was the *ritmo lento* (slow pace) I was living. Or maybe it was the tranquility of all of us always sleeping under the same roof and the warmth of Bruce holding me before I went to sleep. I still hadn't ruled out the possibility that Adriano was slipping something into my cappuccino in the morning, but whatever it was, it beat the pharmacological haze of a drug-induced slumber. As I drifted off to sleep I started to dream about what my new life could be like when I returned home. It might include pausing in the middle of the day, however briefly. It could include being held by Bruce at night more often than having him away. There would definitely be pizza involved ... and not the takeout kind.

CHAPTER THIRTEEN

No Option Equals No Stress

There is only one way to happiness,
and that is to cease worrying about things
which are beyond the power of our will.
Epictetus

In October we miraculously crossed the threshold of surviving
the first quarter of our one-year experience. With that milestone,
we became aware that we had established a network of friends, an
entire community if you will, of people who saw us at a minimum
as a continuous source of entertainment. I was the woman who
walked her dog in sneakers rather than stilettos and collected my
dog's 'business' in a plastic bag. Bruce was the man who jogged in
the center of town with one of those bandanas around his head that
the Italians have seen in dubbed versions of "West Side Story" as
well as a myriad of American rock music videos. I think they
evaluated the kids as fairly normal, although I could see people
glancing over at us in restaurants as the kids spoke to us in Italian
and Bruce and I answered in English, or one of us started a
sentence in English and finished it in Italian. But hey, there's
something to be said for being a novelty.

When Bruce developed a knee problem that required surgery
(all that running on cobblestones finally did him in), we were
happy to have the sound advice of our neighbors and friends.
Adriano suggested going through the public system. With our
Permesso di Soggiorno, we could pay a small annual fee and be
eligible to have the operation in the public hospital. Barbara and
Fiorenzo, who always carried private insurance in addition to
being card-carrying citizens entitled to medical care through the

public system, insisted that we should go to the private *Clinica Quiete* where they felt the practice of medicine was superior. The Stragapedes and Sorus, along with Tiziana at the *Pasticceria* felt that was ridiculous as it was well-known that the public doctors moonlighted at the private clinic. Ultimately, the decision was made for us by the system since the waiting time for the operation in the public hospital was six months, whereas the *Clinica Quiete* was prepared to do it the following day during *aperitivo* hour, or at any reasonable time thereafter.

We opted for a time slot the following week in the early morning before *cappuccino* cutoff. When we arrived, the clinic, a renovated 16th century palazzo, was already buzzing with activity. The waiting room was a grand *sala* with a gigantic marble fireplace and vaulted ceilings with ornately carved moldings. Seated in the corner was an eager receptionist who asked for our name and then motioned for us to wait in the *ristorante/bar* adjacent to the *sala*, equally ornate with large windows, overlooking a park-like setting and filled with tables covered with linen tablecloths. We were escorted to a manually operated elevator to the third floor where we entered our private room, complete with sleek sliding doors, closet, safe, *frigobar*, desk with chair, bed, lounge chair, television with remote, telephone, electrically operated *tapparelle* (window shades), bathroom and shower. More like a hotel room than a hospital room, it was a significant contrast to the generic-brand, un-air-conditioned public hospital where Laura gave birth to Chiara. A uniformed, official-looking medical person took Bruce's blood, and asked him exhaustive questions (a medical history questionnaire which included whether he was breast or bottle-fed as an infant) but did not require an MRI more recent than the one Bruce took back in the States a year ago.

An orderly came to bring Bruce to another floor for his pre-surgery EKG. I was hopeful that they just wanted to make sure his ticker wasn't going to conk out while they were operating on his knee, but part of me wondered if they mistook him for the open-heart surgery patient in the next room.

"You have to remove everything metal when you're on the floor with the MRI equipment," he said. "Your ring, your watch, even your false teeth if you have them. Do you have any? No. Good. So. Anyway, this French lady was here as a patient. She was old, so I made sure to ask her, 'Do you have any false teeth?' No, she told me; they're all mine. Every one. Ends up they were all hers, but to keep them she had them wired into her mouth with gold. That's right – gold — every one. And gold is metal, you know. She just didn't get the point, so then I asked her, 'What did you pay for that? You know, 'pay,' I said, but she didn't understand me on account of the language. So I reached into my wallet and took out a 50,000 lire note, you know we had lire at the time, and I said, 'Pay! How much did you pay?' And she said, 'That's about right' pointing to the 50,000 lire note, which as you know is no more than $50. And I thought, OK, big joke, and when her daughter came, I asked her and she said, 'I think the cost was more than 50 million lire but she didn't pay anything, she just married the dentist.' So anyway, my point is, don't wear anything metal in the operating room. Understand?"

Bruce nodded.

"You haven't married a dentist have you?" he said, winking at me.

I shook my head.

"All right then," he finished. "*In bocca al lupo.*"

"What was he saying?" Bruce asked me as he was being wheeled out the door.

"Something about a wolf," I shouted down the hall. "Oh, and take off your watch and your wedding ring, and hold on to your dental fillings." I later found out that *in bocca al lupo*, which literally means 'mouth of the wolf,' figuratively means 'good luck.' Nice sentiment and obviously we were going to need it.

When Bruce returned, the anesthesiologist showed up, handsome as ever, not a day over 35, wearing a shirt unbuttoned at the neck and a sports jacket. Our surgeon arrived practically simultaneously, also INCREDIBLY good looking in an adolescent sort of way, with a sexy, scrubby beard, jeans and a plaid shirt, appearing as if he had enjoyed a nice late night out. This is the same doctor who lists on his stationery three numbers: one that is incorrect, another which is his mother's home, and a third which is his cell phone. Earlier in the week, I called him, and his mother answered and said, "He's eating lunch right now, he'll have to call you back." I'm not kidding.

When they asked us if we had a preference between a femoral nerve block or a spinal, we asked the surgeon what he preferred.

"*Assolutamente, una spinale,*" he said.

"I don't know how you can make a different choice when a surgeon says, 'Absolutely, the spinal.'" I whispered to Bruce. Let's face it, we wanted to give him optimal working conditions.

"The spinal is the best choice," he explained in Italian. "It completely immobilizes him from the waist down but this way, if we have to make any decisions we can discuss it with your husband."

"That would be helpful," I answered. "… if Bruce spoke Italian."

"Ah, perhaps you should wait outside the door of the operating room to be available for translation," he suggested. "For now, let me just explain to both of you … *prima, dobbiamo tagliare il menisco. Poi …*" He rattled on in Italian about exactly what he intended to do to Bruce's knee during the operation. I smiled reassuringly at Bruce, but I had absolutely not one idea what he was talking about. Some technical terms with Latin derivatives floated by and that was about it. My chest was tightening as I nodded and smiled again, first at the surgeon, then towards Bruce's blank face. Then, suddenly, I felt a wave of relief. It was the strangest feeling but honestly, I realized all at once that I couldn't control what I didn't understand. I was going to have to let go and trust a guy who spoke another language, looked like he was recovering from a hangover, and just weaned from formula and pablum a decade ago.

The surgeon finished his long explanation and showed me where to sit outside the operating room. As I waited, I was reminded of Bruce's description of the environment at the photography studio and wondered if Italian photographers and surgeons insisted on the same working conditions. I pictured the surgeon starting the arthroscopy and then, after seeing something unexpected, stopping to have a coffee to discuss it. The surgeon, anesthesiologist and nurses might stop, take off their gloves, have their coffee, talk about the decision, maybe discuss a little bit about what they did last night, what they had for lunch, then re-scrub (hopefully) and resume the operation, caffeine refreshed. And indeed, when our surgeon came out from the operating room, he looked more refreshed then before the operation, thereby lending credence to my *espresso*-break theory, but Bruce insisted they worked straight through.

When Bruce was safely back in his room, I took my leave. I needed to go to a special pharmacy to rent crutches because I didn't realize they weren't going to provide them at the hospital. Alternatively, I could have taken him home by piggyback, but I was guessing the crutch-rental option was the better choice. On my way out the door, a woman at the front desk stopped me.

"*Signora*," she called after me, "*Signora*, your husband's *codice fiscale* is wrong. It needs to be corrected."

I was exhausted and in no mood to tackle a bureaucratic obstacle. "Sure, sure, OK," I said politely but I kept walking.

Luckily, Laura was picking up the kids from school and they were with her until I got Bruce home. When I went to pick them up, Laura handed me a covered bowl, still steaming. She had prepared dinner for her family and for mine. Just the 'extra' I needed that night. I kissed her on both checks and she touched my right cheek.

"How's Bruce?" she asked me quietly, while the kids remained engrossed in re-runs of the Flintstones in Italian. "*Basta, Wilma!!*" blared in the background.

"He's fine. Just tired."

"You look tired too," she told me and motioned for Francesca to turn off the television.

Matthew and Alex came over and gave me a hug. "Did they fix Dad's knee?" Matthew asked me.

"It's looking good," I told him.

"Did his bed have a remote control?" Alex wanted to know.

"Yep, and the window shades too."

"*Figo* (Cool)!"

A dad on the mend and electronic window shades; what more could one ask for?

"What do you say to Laura?" I asked them.

"Can we get Flintstones on our television?" Matthew responded.

"Actually, that's not what I was expecting you to say ..."

"*Grazie,*" Alex said, catching on.

"*Si, si ... grazie mille,*" Matthew added.

Francesca gave me a hug. Chiara was blowing saliva bubbles in her carriage parked in the living room.

It had been a full day. The warm bowl in my hands was warming my heart. The kids were happy and safe. Bruce survived his ordeal without the necessity of making any decisions in Italian or in English. It was time to go home and be thankful.

When we arrived at our apartment, the lady who called after me at the *Clinica Quiete* about the fact that Bruce's *codice fiscale* was wrong was at our front door. I gave her one of those and-what-do-you-want looks.

"Excuse me," she said in English with an Italian accent, "You forgot your X-ray at the clinic and since I live close by I thought I'd bring it by."

"Thank you," I said, utterly humiliated by my private thoughts. "I'm sorry I ran out on you today. I was a bit overwhelmed and I didn't want to hear about any bureaucratic problems."

"I can understand that," she responded. "It's just that I wanted you to know that, based on the information you gave me, the *codice fiscale* has the wrong birth date for your husband. You'll need to correct that at some point and it will be a headache, unfortunately."

Her name was Alda, and we invited her in to share Laura's dinner. We laughed as I recounted to her and to the kids the story of the orderly and his instructions about metal objects. It was the beginning of another wonderful friendship. From that day on, if there was any need to negotiate Italy's administrative circuitousness, Alda and her husband Franco were always there with a helping hand. Her help made the most daunting task seem doable. It seemed incomprehensible, but even when things were not ideal – perhaps especially when things were not ideal – we were attracting the 'extra' into our lives. It was growing exponentially with every experience. I wanted to wrap myself in it like a cloak, and wear it through the rest of autumn. And maybe as the days crept toward Christmas, the cloak would grow incrementally thicker and warmer as each day got colder, and I would be toasty all winter long.

Speak Milk. Drink Wine.

CHAPTER FOURTEEN

When in Doubt, Blame the Tax System

In this world nothing is certain but death and taxes.
-Benjamin Franklin

The leaves were changing to hues of yellows and toasty browns with a smattering of crimson here and there. The chestnuts began to fall from the trees, inviting spontaneous games which sometimes led to Matthew, or alternatively Alex, being beaned in the head during a spirited chestnut catch. One day Alex decided that there could be a more productive use for chestnuts. He began collecting them.

"What do you plan to do with those?" I asked him.

"Mom," he said, "Have you seen what they're charging for chestnuts at the *fruttivendolo*. I could make a fortune!"

"Really?" I said. "And who do you plan to sell them to?"

The next evening at dinner with the Sorus, my question was answered as I saw Susanna breaking out her purse.

"This is highway robbery," she commented as she gave Alex five euros for the plastic sack half full with chestnuts.

"These are fresh," Alex said. "They come right from the tree in our apartment complex. You don't know where those other chestnuts have been. They could have come from as far as *Liguria*." Then he wandered into the next room to see what Tommaso was doing on the computer.

"Is this a Hummel demonstration of American capitalism?" Susanna asked me.

Vanni was stirring the sauce on the stove, a simple *sugo al pomodoro*. Tommaso was measuring out the dry pasta to get it ready for boiling. He used an individual bowl and measured out eight portions. There would not be too much or too little pasta. My nose told me there was a roast with fresh *rosmarino* in the oven.

I steered the conversation toward Italian incongruities which was my usual habit. I loved talking about what I called my 'cultural observations' about Italy, and Giampiero and Susanna loved pointing out to me things about America that were equally bizarre.

"Can you please tell me what's up with the fact that women can go topless on the beach here, they can advertise with posters of half-naked women in every store window, but they can't wear shorts in the center of town?"

"I'll answer that," said Giampiero, "if you can tell me why Americans are always covering up nudity, but you can find a dozen porno shops in any major city."

I couldn't, so I finished my pasta.

The conversation turned to class action suits in the States by ex-smokers against Phillip Morris.

"It's not possible," Susanna said. "You'd have to be *un cretino* not to know that inhaling smoke into your lungs couldn't be good for you."

"But that's not the point," I told her. "The point is that the company knew definitively that smoking tobacco leads to cancer ..."

"He should be behind bars, whoever this Phillip guy is," Matthew interrupted.

"... but they kept it from the general public," I finished.

The roast came out of the oven. The scent of rosemary was intoxicating now. Giampiero began carving and sent plate by plate down to the other end of the table.

"Alex, where's your *gallina*?" asked Susanna.

"What chicken?" Alex replied, with a mouth full of bread.

"The one you need to bring next time if you don't learn to keep your crumbs on your plate and not on the floor," she told him. Alex leaned over his plate.

"What about customer service?" I asked.

"What about it?" asked Giampiero. "Tommaso, pass the salt, please."

"I'll give you an example," I said. "I bought Matthew's sneakers at Footlocker on *Corso Matteotti.* Within three weeks they were falling apart. I went back and they said there was nothing they could do – that they had already been worn. I told them, of course they've been worn. That was the point. They had a three-week life and they were already ruined. If that happened in the States, Footlocker would have apologized and handed me another pair of shoes."

"That seems like poor training to me," Giampiero responded. "The way they train their staff in the States is the way they should train them here."

"He's got a point, Mom," said Alex, between bites.

"But it's like that with everything. If you try to return something, you can't ever get your cash back. If you're lucky, and it's within a few days of the purchase, you have your receipt, and you're willing to offer up your first born child, you can get a *buono*, a credit for the next time you come. I mean, what if I don't want to shop there anymore?"

"It's the way the tax system works," Giampiero explained. "They've already paid the tax at the time you purchased the item. They won't be able to get the tax back."

I was not going to understand this discourse any more than Susanna was going to understand some cretin suing Phillip Morris.

"It's the tax system ..." Bruce mumbled, nodding his head as if he was on to something.

"You know, at home, we'd be getting ready for Halloween right about now," I said, changing the subject.

"Ah yes," Susanna responded. "It's similar to our *Carnivale,* right?"

"From what I understand, yes," I said. "Kids dress in costume and eat candy until they need their stomachs pumped. It's one of my favorite holidays. We used to have an annual party. The Halloween before we left for Italy we invited about 60 adults and 30 children."

"I cannot imagine having that many people together at one time other than maybe at the *Oratorio*," said Vanni.

"Last year we hired a djembe drummer to come and we sat outside around our fire pit drumming, while the kids bobbed for apples and toasted marshmallows. We sipped apple cider, laced with a little rum, and ate banana bread ..."

"Marshmallows?" Vanni asked, confused. I began to explain, but was interrupted. "—then the cowboys ride in and chase the Indians, right?" Giampiero said.

"*Cretino*, that's Thanksgiving," Susanna elbowed him. "Where they thank the Indians for helping them through the winter and then they herd them onto reservations."

"So, let me get this straight," said Giampiero. "You invited 60 people over to beat drums and catch apples that are floating in water and other people's saliva, with your teeth. Then you eat candy, smashed bananas in bread, and a burned, gooey white substance."

"You bet."

*   *   *

Not wanting the kids to lose out on any childhood Halloween memories, I put little notes in the mailboxes of all our neighbors in our apartment complex. Nothing elaborate, just a bit of the history of the tradition and a friendly invitation to buy our kids candy.

"In America," I wrote in Italian, "it is a tradition for the evening of Halloween, October 31, to knock on the door of our neighbors requesting a 'trick or treat' in the form of a sweet. If you'd like to participate, just leave this note with your name and apartment number in our mailbox, and we'll give you a visit at around 19.00."

"Do you think it's presumptuous to impose our traditions on others?" I asked Laura by phone.

She hesitated. "I think those who want to participate will do so, and those who don't, won't," she answered.

"Am I doing it again?" I asked her.

"Doing what?"

"Am I trying to create this little bubble around my kids to protect them from disappointment?

"You? Never…"

The following day, much to my surprise, there were several notes in our mailbox, and in the days that followed, even more. All in all, 22 families that we had not met before responded. Laura and Domenico sent over Francesca in costume, and the kids invited Enea and Gianni, as well as Alex's friend, Michele. Two rock stars, one witch and three ghosts.

At 7 p.m. on Halloween, we started our rounds. It was the perfect time to do it – late enough for people to be home for *aperitivo*, and right around the hour of preparing dinner.

"If you knock on the door and the guy who threatened to pull your pants down and spank you answers the door, run for it," were Bruce's instructions. But those who responded were the quintessential Italian children lovers. Sometimes the lady of the house answered, sometimes both husband and wife, but more often than not, the entire family came to the door to see the trick-or-treaters. Some gleefully planted kisses, on both cheeks of course, and at one home we were offered a glass of wine while the kids stopped for a moment to trade their candies with each other.

"Treeek or treeet," the kids said in unison, the Italian accent predominating over the English.

They were handed *brioche* and *biscotti*, apples and *caramelle*, and in many cases, a neatly wrapped package containing a small gift.

"*Siete bellissimi!*"

"*Bravi!*"

"What a great costume!"

"Maria, go get the camera!"

"*Fantastico!*" cried Enea.

"They give you all this for nothing," said Francesca, "it's not even my birthday!"

"Great Halloween …" said Alex, examining his loot.

"*Figo* (cool)!" said Matthew.

I was not entirely sure whether I did the right thing. It might have been better to let them experience the loss of a uniquely American tradition in order to appreciate it that much more. It might have been more appropriate not to impose ourselves or our culture on others. On the other hand, Matthew and Alex were so happy. Their Italian friends got to do something they ordinarily did not have the opportunity to do. The Italian families were, at the very least, amused by the experience and happy to meet us.

In the following days when we passed our neighbors in the complex we were stopped by people who normally passed us by. Even the old ladies who routinely accused the kids of breaking the grass had something nice to say.

"I hardly recognize you without your costume!" said one lady.

"I'm completely out of treats!" said another.

"Not to worry," I told them, "they have enough memories to last them at least until Carnivale."

In truth, the few hours that comprised our Italian Halloween were probably going to last a lifetime.

CHAPTER FIFTEEN

Beware the Unwritten Rules

You must look into other people as well as at them.
-Lord Chesterfield

One day, after waving goodbye to the kids through the glass doors at school, I was asked by a group of moms from the fourth grade if I wanted to go for coffee. For a long time I knew that they went for coffee almost every day after dropping the kids at school, and I understood why I had never been invited. My lack of fluency often changed the interaction of the group from spontaneous to something along the lines of a black and white film viewed in slow motion with subtitles. Besides, they had probably been getting together since their kids were in first grade at the very same school, maybe since they themselves were in first grade. Why then were they inviting me today? Never mind. It was something better left unanalyzed. I could just go with the moment, sip my *cappuccino*, and laugh at the appropriate moments.

When we arrived, the *barista* brought each woman their usual without inquiring, then turned and asked, "*La signora?*"

All eyes turned to me.

"*Un cappuccio,*" I responded, using the Varesino nickname for *cappuccino*. The mothers smiled contentedly. I felt really cool.

The conversation began where it probably left off the morning before in my absence. I had no idea what they were talking about, so I nodded affably, smiled appropriately, and chuckled at just the right time. Then one of the moms turned to me.

"Denise, why don't you take on the role of *rappresentante?*" she asked me.

Representative? What is she talking about? Is she wanting me to run for some local political position? Doesn't she know I'm not a citizen? Didn't she realize that I can't execute the pronunciation that differentiates between *marrone* (the color brown) and *marone* (slang for male genitals) or between the words *anni* (years) and *ani* (the plural of anus)? These small pronunciation difficulties could get you into serious trouble in formal circles.

"Um, I'm not exactly sure what you're talking about," I told her hoping that my olive skin was masking the flushed feeling I had in my cheeks.

"Class representative," she explained. "You seem like you have a handle on things."

Though I wasn't sure how she knew, I *had* spent a lot of time pondering why Matthew's class seemed to be so dysfunctional. If we were back in New York, the principal of the school would probably have assembled a team of learning specialists. There would have been scheduled observations by the principal and others. The district supervisor may have been informed. A meeting would have been held with parents and specialists. Ultimately, President Bush himself, along with some sort of State of the Nation Educational Task Force would be advised of the travesty. In *Varese*, we were on our own. There was no principal resident at the school. There was one principal responsible for several schools and his office was at the *Scuola Parini,* two kilometers away. He was apparently far too busy organizing the next parent-teacher *tarantella* night to involve himself in what appeared to be a simple disciplinary issue at *Ugo Foscolo.*

Further complicating things, in the Italian elementary public school system, the same teacher normally stays with the class from kindergarten through fifth grade. Theoretically, this continuity for elementary age children had significant advantages over the American system where children adapted to a different teacher from one year to the next. In the case of Alex's class, it turned out to be a substantial benefit for Francesca and many of the children. But in Matthew's class, no one teacher remained for more than one academic year before coincidentally being transferred (more likely having begged a transfer) to another province. Let's face it – what teacher would want to stay with a group of children who didn't give a damn when you had a damn toothache?

I had spoken haltingly, but passionately, at a previous class meeting about the chaos in Matthew's class, but that in no way qualified me to represent Italian families. I was unsure what to make of their suggestion. Were they pulling my leg, or worse, were they making fun of me? Or could it be that they really liked the idea of an external perspective, new blood coming in to mobilize things? In any case, I had never been one to back away from a challenge. If my new coffee crew of fourth grade moms had the faith or stupidity to have me take on this dilemma, I was not going to let them down. Besides, if I handled my new role well, this could be an important right of passage for me. If I fixed this problem, I might become one of the girls.

"Sure," I told them. "I'll give it a try."

"I'll help you when you have to write any notices," one mom offered. I hadn't thought about the fact that I'd have to write in Italian from time to time.

The other moms were smiling and nodding in agreement. How hard could it be?

Days later, invigorated by my new position of prestige, I scheduled a meeting between the moms and the fourth grade teachers: *Maestras* Marta, Lella and Roberta. I painstakingly set down some suggestions for how to change the atmosphere of the class and I made copies of my plan to share with everyone. True to her word, one of the moms helped me with the translation. We all found seats in the more spacious first-grade classroom, parents in the smaller children's seats, teachers in normal-sized adult seats. I was already feeling a bit small before I sat down. After sitting, I felt like I was ready for a pacifier and a nap. The teachers smiled and the parents fidgeted nervously in their chairs. All eyes were on me. After a few moments of silence, I realized that I was probably the one who was supposed to start speaking. I cleared my throat.

I began. "Some of the parents, including myself, feel that the issue of discipline in the fourth grade needs to be addressed by alternative solutions than those that have already been tried."

"What discipline problems?" asked *Maestra* Roberta.

Was she serious? This was going to be harder than I thought. "Well ... ummm ..." I said with great eloquence, "in my limited observations, I notice ... for example ... that the children all speak at the same time, whenever they want to, without being called upon, and that you teachers scream to get control of the classroom (very diplomatic of me) and that ultimately, that method doesn't seem to have any significant long term effect on changing the children's behavior."

I looked around to see if there were any nods or anyone dying to chime in with their opinion or some other words of reinforcement. The silence was deafening.

"*Signora* Hummel," said *Maestra* Lella, "I know you mean well, but we have tried everything. If you have some thoughts on a new system we haven't tried, let us know," she said chuckling.

"Well, as a matter of fact, I do," I said. We Type-A, take-no-prisoners Americans know quite a bit about dissecting a problem, getting to the root of it and culling it out. I got up and handed out the first official-looking document I had drafted since my days as a New York lawyer. They had to be impressed.

POSSIBLE SOLUTION TO DISCIPLINARY PROBLEM

Define the Problem:
There is too much noise in the classroom. This noise causes interference with the teachers' ability to teach and the students' ability to learn and to concentrate on the materials presented.

Define the Cause:
a.   Children speak in loud voices.
b.   Children speak all at the same time.
c.   Teacher yells to regain control of the classroom.

Define the Solution:
a.   Retrain children to use "school voices" rather than their "home" or "playing" voices. Demonstrate tone of voice that is acceptable.

---

b. Institute a policy that children must raise their hand and be recognized by a teacher before they speak and that only one person speaks at a time.

c. Introduce alternate methods for teacher discipline other than yelling.

d. Change the acoustics of the room by adding a rug to the floor (I will donate it) and fabric or other decoration on the walls.

e. Ask parents to be partners in solving this serious problem.

Step One: A Letter to Parents

a. Send a letter home to parents explaining that this class is having a problem because the sound level in the classroom is too loud. Discuss the acoustics of the room and the fact that some children are more sensitive to this problem than others.

b. Explain the changes in policy that will take place for regarding expectations for the children's behavior.

c. Explain the consequences that will occur to children who do not follow the rules.

d. Request that parents give their teachers support and become partners in solving the problem.

Step Two: Modifying Children's Behavior: An Alternative to Yelling

a. Establish what the rules are for the classroom.
   i. No loud voices.
   ii. Must raise hand and be recognized by teacher before speaking.
   iii. No talking when another child or teacher is talking.
   iv. No talking when a teacher is involved with another child, another teacher or a classroom guest.

b. Ask the children if they think there should be any more rules to make the classroom better. If they are appropriate suggestions, add them to the classroom rules.

c. Get each child to agree by signing the list. Post the list on the chalkboard.

d. Make a list of consequences for breaking the rules:
   i. First offense: "Yellow Card" (like in soccer).
   ii. Second offense: "Red Card" (game over: like in video games or "penalty box" like in hockey).

> e. A child who gets a red card gets a punishment. For example, the child misses recess or gym.
>
> f. A child who gets a red card must write this information in his diary for his/her parent to see.
>
> g. After five (six? seven?) red cards, a letter must go home to the parent stating the problem and that the parent must come in to speak to the teacher. It would be helpful if the principal were present (or another teacher).
>
> **Conclusion**: Problem solved. Plan celebratory luncheon!!!

"You see," I explained cheerfully, while parents and teachers stared at me in utter bewilderment, "I think that it's possible that in the past, you may have been reactive to the problem, rather than proactive. Perhaps if we approach the situation more systematically ..."

They continued to stare; some jaws were visibly descending.

"... analyzing the problem, and reviewing possible alternatives to the current method of discipline we might get better results," I continued.

Taking a quick breath, I quickly scanned the room to evaluate the likelihood of fleeing the scene unnoticed.

"*Signora* Hummel," interrupted *Maestra* Roberta. She had an odd grin on her face and was twisting around in a way that lead me to believe that she was suffering from either a collar bone dislocation or a severe intestinal tract disturbance. "We appreciate all your effort. Really, we do, but I have to say that I think you are concerned over something that does not exist." *Maestra* Roberta was the matriarch of the teacher team. She had been teaching since before God invented dirt.

"It's true that some children need more supervision than others," she continued, "but this is something that each teacher can handle individually on a case by case basis. In my opinion, this is not a problem worthy of this kind of attention. Wouldn't you agree?" she said glancing toward her colleagues, *Maestra* Marta and *Maestra* Lella, who nodded pleasantly.

"Is there any parent who feels differently?" *Maestra* Roberta asked.

The only sound was that of my irregular heartbeat.

"Good," she said, still smiling. "Then I thank you for your time and I wish you all a pleasant afternoon." She stood, and the other teachers followed suit. Parents began filing out the door, some stopping to shake *Maestra* Roberta's hand, others nodding, looking down, car keys in hand. The mom who translated my disciplinary opus patted me warmly on the back. I said a nervous "*grazie*" in the general vicinity of those present and headed for the door.

As I drove away it began to rain, but it was my own tears that made negotiating the tiny alleys between *Ugo Foscolo* and the apartment difficult to manage. At the turn beside the *Chiesa* San Michele Arcangelo, I pulled over abruptly into the tiny piazza screeching the tires in a way that brought more dramatic attention by passerbys than I had intended. I waved on the two elderly women sharing an umbrella who peered through the window at me to determine whether I was having some sort of trouble or was merely an erratic driver. My lips were upturned as if to say that everything was OK, a fact contradicted by the mascara stains on my cheeks, but they moved on nevertheless. What had I been trying to prove by taking on this crusade? What did it say about me as a person that I came waltzing into a classroom in a foreign country as if I were in a New York courtroom? I was so focused on fitting in that I had put myself in a situation that made me stand out even more.

To say that I felt like a total idiot does not quite capture the moment. I knew instantaneously, maybe even as I was handing out my multiple-paged analysis, maybe even as the brief words of my presentation were being uttered, that my 'observe the situation, analyze the problem given the facts, and propose active solutions,' had no greater chance of success at *Ugo Foscolo* than it had at the tax code office. This class needed someone with the diplomacy of a Roman diplomat. A person like Susanna who could wrangle a *codice fiscale* from a clerk with a single well-placed compliment. A parent who understood the delicate balance of power between parent and teacher in the Italian school system, and who knew the unwritten rule that parents were in charge at home and teachers where in charge at school. They needed a representative who knew that for decades, maybe centuries, parents blamed teachers for their lack of ability to control the classroom and teachers blamed parents for raising children without adequate manners.

The other moms knew that there was nothing they could do to change the situation. Perhaps they hoped that because I was an outsider, more allowances would be made or different boundaries would operate.

At home in the following days, while I relived over and over again my folly, I pondered what next steps to take on Matthew's behalf. Given that there was only one fourth grade classroom at *Ugo Foscolo*, I felt that we needed to explore the possibility that we might have to transfer Matthew to another school. How much longer could he hold out in that classroom? And if I made it worse by being the one to actively confront the situation, maybe I had turned a bad situation into one that was irreparable. There was a public school just across the street from us, next to the practice prison. We had not chosen to go there because we had wanted the kids to be in the same school as Francesca, but now it began to look like the better choice, at least for Matthew. I decided to speak to the *direttore* of that school to explore the possibility of transferring Matthew.

"Are you certain you want to open this door?" Bruce asked me, but I was determined.

On the day of my appointment, I took pains to explain the classroom environment at *Ugo Foscolo*. I was the epitome of diplomacy this time. I described to the *direttore* as tactfully as possible the general environment, and how difficult it was to learn in such a *casino*. *Casino* was a word I heard my father use when we were little. It meant chaos. But for some reason, the director's eyes widened and eyebrows lifted in apparent alarm.

"I don't know in this type of setting if you want to use the term *casino*," he explained. "It is a term that does describe confusion, but it is derived from the brusqueness and impolite atmosphere of the brothel."

"*Oh Madonna*," I said, and then cupped my hand over my mouth. "Oh no. I did it again, didn't I?!"

"Yes, well, I think it's just because you Americans have that pop star 'Madonna,' that you all use that expression, but here, in formal settings, Madonna is the Holy Virgin Mary and we tend to use that phrase in prayer and on holidays."

I made a grand impression. He invited us to think about our decision to transfer Matthew and to let him know after the Christmas holidays.

When I got home, I discussed with Matthew the fact that we didn't think his classroom situation at *Ugo Foscolo* was likely to change. Then I explained that I had visited the *Scuola Morandi* and that it seemed like a nice place. No screaming, all the students still had their watches, and as far as I could tell, none of the teachers had any problems with their teeth (or at least seemed to be the sort who wouldn't publicly complain in profane stereophonic tones about it). Bruce smiled.

"Do you want to transfer?" I asked him. I knew, ultimately, the decision had to be left to him. He had already been through so much – adjusting to a new society, a new school, new friends, a new language.

"No Mom," he told me with a little smirk and a sideways glance. "I'm fine."

"Matthew, it's not fine," I said. "Your classroom is a disaster."

"It is *un disastro*," he told me, gesturing with great emotion, "but I'M fine. I learned Italian, I know the whole *storia* of the Estruscans. I have Enea and Gianni so I know just the right time to pluck *pomodori* in the garden. I'm learning *geometria* and *tutti i angoli*."

"But ..."

"There's a big difference between how my classroom is doing and how I'm doing, *mamma*." He never spoke to me that way before. He was so grown-up, mature. Really sharp. He wasn't afraid.

Bruce sat back contentedly in his chair, not in a smug way, but in a knowing peaceful way, a manner that let me know I could have saved myself the trip to *Scuola Morandi* had I been a little more awake to what Matthew was actually experiencing.

My dad's favorite quotation came to mind, the one about not seeing the forest for the trees. I really had missed the big picture. I was analyzing a dysfunctional situation without regard to the fact that my child was doing fine. Actually, not fine. Great. I was running around trying to fix something that wasn't broken. I was so used to analyzing, trying to control variables, trying to fix things, that I hadn't been able to see that something that looked wrong from the outside was actually right for my child.

"You're right," I answered him. Don't cry, I was telling myself. "I didn't see you. I was only seeing the kids climbing on the window sill and talking out of turn."

"It's OK, Mom," he told me. "Can I go out on my scooter?"

Before I could answer him, he was off. "Taz, let's go," he yelled, the last word trailing behind him as he made his way out the apartment door and down the corridor to the paths that winded their way through the complex. Right before the door slammed I heard, "Move the world forward, Mom!!!" I hadn't used that expression since the day I arrived home to our new apartment with only one chocolate *brioche*.

CHAPTER SIXTEEN

Due to the Possibility of Diverse Cultural Norms, It's Always Best to Ask if a Turkey has Hooves

Dear Lord, I've been asked, nay commanded,
to thank Thee for the turkey before us ...
a turkey which was no doubt a lively, intelligent bird ... a social being ...
capable of actual affection ... nuzzling its young with almost human-like
compassion.
Anyway, it's dead and we're gonna eat it.
Please give our respects to its family ...
-Buy Berkley Breathed, Bloom County Babylon

Thanksgiving arrived. It was just another day in Europe; No fanfare and worse – it was a school day. Bruce and I, however, set about the business of preparing a traditional Thanksgiving dinner. A week before, I had ordered a *"tacchino grosso, abbastanza per sette persone* (a big turkey, enough for seven people)," from our butcher, *Signo*r Ripoli. I still wasn't very good at converting pounds to *kilos* and I was concerned that the butcher's estimate would be too conservative. The Italians typically did not prepare a whole turkey; it would have to be special ordered. And the dainty pieces of sliced turkey breast they do eat from time to time are consumed in reasonable portions without the contemplation of overeating to bursting and days of leftovers, so traditional of Thanksgiving. Our friend, Marc, was coming into town from the United States and was used to the usual Thanksgiving excess. We had also invited Barbara and Fiorenzo to join us. They had invited us to many parties filled with guests from her native Germany, Fiorenzo's Italian friends, along with English-speaking friends to round out the evening. Thanksgiving represented an invaluable opportunity to share with them our version of an international *festa.*

"It's got to be big," I said, gesturing nervously.

"It will be big enough," *Signor* Ripoli told me when he saw the tentative expression on my face.

The day before, I stopped by to confirm my order. "Don't worry," said *Signor* Ripoli, "it will be here tomorrow by 11 a.m."

My friend, Judy, forwarded to me an email from New York, one of those anonymous ones that make their way around the Internet. I read it to the kids in the hopes of focusing them on something other than the fact that Thanksgiving in Italy didn't involve a four-day weekend.

One day a father of a very wealthy family took his son on a trip to the country with the firm purpose of showing his son how poor people live. They spent a couple of days and nights on the farm of what would be considered a very poor family.

On their return from their trip, the father asked his son, "How was the trip?" "It was great, Dad." "Did you see how poor people live?" the father asked. "Oh yeah," said the son. "So, tell me, what did you learn from the trip?" asked the father.

The son answered: "I saw that we have one dog and they had four. We have a pool that reaches to the middle of our garden and they have a creek that has no end. We have imported lanterns in our garden and they have the stars at night. Our patio reaches to the front yard and they have the whole horizon. We have a small piece of land to live on and they have fields that go beyond our sight. We have servants who serve us, but they serve others. We buy our food, but they grow theirs. We have walls around our property to protect us; they have friends to protect them."

The boy's father was speechless. Then his son added, "Thanks, Dad, for showing me how poor we are."

"Isn't perspective a wonderful thing? Makes you wonder what would happen if we all gave thanks for everything we have, instead of worrying about what we don't have," I said as they put on their backpacks.

"Right, Mom," said Alex. "Did you pack my snack?"

I looked expectedly at Matthew but he was already walking out the door.

After sending them off to school, I passed by the butcher on my way to yoga.

"I'll see you at 11," I waved and smiled.

"It's already here," he responded. "I suggest you bring the car. It's not going to be that easy to get home."

Italians are always underestimating women, I thought.

"Don't worry. My husband will come get it," I said.

"*Prenda la macchina lo stesso* (Bring the car, all the same)," he said.

I was beginning to wonder whether I was supposed to have specified a *dead* turkey and whether I should have warned Bruce to bring a leash.

When Bruce and Marc went to pick up the turkey, they called me from the butcher.

"I don't think this turkey is going to fit into the oven," Bruce said. I could hear Marc chortling in agreement in the background.

"Sure it will," I said with my telepathic/cellular-powered vision. Silently, I congratulated myself that I adequately conveyed to the butcher a truly *large* turkey.

"I hope you're right," Bruce answered. "It weighs 15 kilos (approximately 38 pounds)."

When I got home, Bruce and Marc were leaning against the oven door trying to contain the poultry beast.

"Let me see it," I said.

"Stand back!" Marc exclaimed. "If I let go of this door, the oven is going to explode."

"That's hilarious, Marc," I said, shoving him aside.

I opened the oven gingerly all the same. The sight left me speechless. The turkey was the size of a small horse and what's more, the ends of the legs were so large they resembled hooves much more than turkey leg nubs. Even without a rack, and the pan placed directly on the bottom of the oven, there was barely an inch between the breast and the top of the oven. The legs, a few feathers clinging to them, were plastered firmly against the door and rear wall.

"I couldn't understand why the butcher was beating the top of the turkey before he threw it in this box," said Bruce, pointing to what appeared to be a well-used fruit box. "But now I understand it was so that it would clear the top of the oven."

"We'll be eating at midnight," I moaned.

Marc was an American friend we've known for years and I knew he would cope, but what would Barbara and Fiorenzo have to say about eating dessert first and turkey last? And how was I going to convince them that whole turkeys are normally not served charred black on the outside and raw on the inside.

"Denise, I don't want to further alarm you," Bruce said slowly and calmly, "but there appears to be something wrong with the electricity."

"What are you talking about?"

"Well, I realize we can't have multiple appliances on at the same time, but now we can't even have a light on the living room when the oven is on."

"Are you kidding?"

He wasn't.

I called Susanna. "It's possible that ENEL (the nation's electric company) has reduced your current," she told me.

"Reduced my current? How? Why?"

"Have you paid all your bills?"

"Yes."

"Electronically?"

"Yes, that's how you do it, right?"

"Yes, but Denise, let me explain to you the definition of 'electronically.' 'Electronically' means that you have a 75 percent chance that the money got there, not a 100 percent chance."

"Ah."

"You'll have to go to the ENEL office on *Via Milano*."

"Why can't I call?"

"Because that's not how it's done."

Sure enough, ENEL did not receive our July payment. "But I paid it at the post office, electronically months ago," I told the clerk.

"May I see your receipt, *signora*?"

"Uh, I don't keep my receipts for more than about a month or two."

"*Signora*, in Italy, you are required to keep your receipts for five years."

I paid the bill again and gave her an additional deposit required of people who don't pay their bills on time. All the Italian apartments I saw were so small. Where, in God's name, did they put all that paper?

"Your current should be back up to its original level *proprio adesso*."

"Thank you *signora*."

I already knew that *adesso* didn't really mean 'now,' it actually meant some time in the future. I was also familiar with the other Italian terms such as *fra qualche giorno* (in a few days) which really means in a week, two weeks perhaps, and/or never. The term *fra un po'* (in a bit) means forget it. So I was really thankful she didn't say *fra un po'*. Come on, it was Thanksgiving! If the beast was cooked before 9 p.m., I was OK with turkey by candlelight.

By the grace of the patron saint of *Varese*, and for reasons unknown to me, the turkey took a mere six and a half hours to cook. It looked strange when it came out, the legs singed by their proximity to the side of the oven and the top tilted to one side. The meat under the apricot and herb-glazed skin was bruised from its post- rigor mortis beating, which gave it the appearance of having been in a drunken brawl. It was tender though, and we had a Thanksgiving story under our belts funny enough to reminisce about over the next several decades of Thanksgiving dinners. Barbara and Fiorenzo were very complimentary about the odd mish-mash known as "Bruce's stuffing." The sweet potatoes sold here as "American potatoes" were also a big hit.

Before dinner, we each wrote on separate index cards one thing we were grateful for in each of the people present. Each card was folded and labeled "to" and "from" and placed in the slot, a cardboard painted turkey with a trap door in the back that Alex made out of shoe boxes. During a welcome break between dinner and dessert, we each received a pile of cards with our name on them and one by one, we read them aloud.

"I'm grateful that Dad's knee healed," read one.

"I'm grateful that Barbara likes to bake more than she likes conjugating verbs," read another.

"I'm grateful for new friends and old ones."

"I'm grateful that we didn't need a leash."

When it was time for dessert, we invited our new neighbors from the adjacent apartment for a "quick taste of American pie." They were having two of their friends over for dinner and they joined us too. As these guests spoke no English, Bruce, who still spoke limited Italian, and Marc, who spoke none, politely nodded now and then in an effort to stay engaged, despite their fatigue and the sudden flow of Italian words streaming in non-stop, overlapping bursts across the table. I struggled for two hours translating sporadically and by midnight our neighbors and their friends looked more comfortable in their chairs than when they arrived. I began to wonder despite my spiritual state of gratitude when I would have the opportunity to *thank* our neighbors for coming.

"I need to go to sleep," I whispered to Bruce and Marc.

Marc turned to Bruce, "Is she kidding? She's not going to leave us, is she?"

Then Fiorenzo, bless him, said, "Wow, look at the time!" and the crowd began moving in the direction of the door for the Italian departure sequence. Our neighbors lingered in the foyer for another half hour after Barbara and Fiorenzo left. When I finally closed the door behind them, Marc dove onto the couch, having shown the most incredible restraint by not unbuttoning his trousers an hour before.

The kids went to bed exhausted but glowing, telling us that yet a second American holiday, although not on American soil, was "the best we ever had." It just goes to show you that a family tradition is transported in the hearts of those who carry it forth, and that you don't have to have the day off from school to have a good Thanksgiving.

Speak Milk. Drink Wine.

CHAPTER SEVENTEEN

Less is More

The ability to simplify means to eliminate the unnecessary
so that the necessary may speak.
-Hans Hoffman

Just before Christmas, our tenants from New York called. From the very start they wanted to stay an extra year, and we had been very clear that the house was only available for one year. However, when they called to re-state their preference, it forced us to examine whether we should stay in Italy longer.

"I miss my family and my friends," I told Bruce. "But I don't miss the frenetic life I was leading." Even more than that, I was falling in love with my everyday Italy. Adriano's coffee, Tiziana's opinions about just about everything, Bruce's cooking, the smile on his face each time he told me about his day at the studio, the kids laughing and fighting with Italian words thrown in. And we were growing here in a way we hadn't at home – a way that I still couldn't put into words.

"Then let's stay," he responded. "There's no perfect job waiting at home. We can visit friends and family this summer and then come back to *Varese* for another school year. We still have the rental income from New York, I could keep interning at the studio, and you could keep writing about cultural differences and travel."

"School ..." I muttered. "Not another year of *Maestras* Roberta, Lella and Marta ..."

"Matthew's fine," Bruce said. "Can't you see he's really fine?"

"But Pound Ridge Elementary School is so much better," I said. "How can we consciously choose *Ugo Foscolo* for another year? It's one thing to say we're having a one-year, cross-cultural experience, that we survived the Italian dress code and learned how to pay bills electronically. It's another thing to ignore the clearly better choice for their education."

"They're still young," Bruce said. "They're not going to be writing college applications next year."

"What about you?" I asked. "You've been having a hard time with this language now for months. Don't you feel isolated?"

"Sometimes," he said. "So what?"

"So, it's not healthy."

"It's not going to kill me either."

"Look, I want to stay. I love it here. I don't want it to end, but there are some very good reasons to go back."

"We can transfer Matthew if you really think a second year at *Ugo Foscolo* will be a mistake," he added.

"After my last demonstration of linguistic skill and cultural savvy, I think the *direttore* of the *Scuola Morandi* will probably decide that I'm too socially inept to register him. Besides, we have no guarantee it won't be a repeat of *Ugo Foscolo*. I mean, in general, the public school doesn't leave a whole lot of room for cooperative problem solving. I don't think I want to spend another year feeling like the hunchback of the Italian school system."

"Why don't we ask the kids whether they have a preference?"

"We can, but I know what they'll say."

In the following days, we broached the topic.

"Let's stay," Alex said.

"Let's what?" I asked, finding a seat. Bruce's face communicated no sign of surprise.

"I think we should stay," Matthew echoed, matter-of-factly.

How did we get from books being thrown across the room, run-ins with *Padre* Filippo in the piazza, and kids climbing on window sills, to "let's stay."

"What about your friends, your house in Pound Ridge?"

"I miss them," Matthew answered.

"Then why do you want to stay?"

"It relaxes me," he told me. It relaxes him?

"The food's way better here," Alex noted as if he had been a gourmand his whole life. "I'd about had it with peanut butter and jelly and macaroni and cheese, anyway."

There were so many reasons to stay, some of them considerably more significant than the difference between peanut butter and *gnocchi*. We were thriving here, each of us in our own way. But there were some very important realities, too. Neither Bruce nor I were any closer to figuring out how to make a living that would be satisfying, pay our bills, and still perpetuate the pace of life we had established here. The rental of the New York house helped, but we were continuing to dip into savings every month. It wasn't prudent to stay another year.

And if we stayed, the mechanics of staying would fall to me. I was the one who would have to find an educational environment for Matthew that didn't resemble a circus with an errant ringmaster. I was the one who experienced every social engagement and bureaucratic snafu as an exercise in simultaneous translation. I didn't think I could stand another year in an apartment with sock balls sailing over my head in the living room and playing the elbow game with Bruce across the electrical tape line on our desk. That meant another move, and I'd be the one to have to deal with the next set of pathological landlords.

"You're right," Bruce said. "The burden of pulling this off is going to rest mostly with you. You're going to have to be the deciding vote."

There was only one thing to do – a pro and con list. I whipped one off to some close friends in the States with a plea for assistance in making the decision.

The responses trickled in ...

Dear Den,

I noticed that most of your pros are written in the first person, while the cons are mainly worries about Bruce and the kids. What are they saying about all of this? For example, regarding the kids, it's true that they have had difficulties adjusting and perhaps they'll have difficulties readjusting to American life, but I imagine there have been many payoffs as well, right? Regarding your comments about Matthew's graduation from elementary school next year, have you asked him if it's important to him if he graduates with his class or are you just projecting what you think is important to him? How's he doing, anyway?

Love, Alexa

I made a mental note to rid myself of all insightful friends who knew me just a bit too well.

Hi Denise,

I think the big question is, "does this cost us anything?" By cost, of course I am not talking about money. What does it cost all of you socially, emotionally, spiritually, etc. Only you can answer that – you know that. It's easy for anyone to sit halfway across the world and marvel at your situation. But we don't struggle with the day-to-day stuff that you are talking about. I dunno – it's not "easy" anywhere. Life is for living – you are definitely living it. Too many questions can spoil the experience.

Much love, Judy

See what I mean? Come on, who needs friends who highlight your neuroses?

I was asking the question 100 times a day. I ruminated over it at the food market on Sunday, at *aperitivo* hour at *Biffis* with friends, at times when I should have just been enjoying the moment, especially if there were precious few left in the months to come.

"I'm so grateful for what we experienced here," I told Laura, "but I feel we need to get back to reality. Every day we prolong it, is just going to make it more difficult to leave."

"The kids seem to be in a good place with school," she offered.

"They are, but they'll ultimately have to get back to the American school system. I have no idea how extensive it might be for them to catch up."

"Don't worry, American history isn't very long."

"That's hilarious, Laura."

"Sorry," she said, sheepishly. "Just trying to lighten up the moment. Whatever you decide, it'll be fine."

Well, I'm not sure if "fine" is a word I would have used. The term, disappointed, comes to mind. I think I had a lot of people, even our own kids, convinced that I was the adventurous one in the family, but my role as an Adventurer-Neurotic-Type A kicked in. I wanted to go home. I was tired of being challenged and of making mistakes and of being a cross-cultural misfit. I wanted things to be easy again – to live in a place where I understood the words and all the nuances behind the words and where I could take for granted that most of the time, everything from my phone bill to the kids' schooling would go according to plan.

Fortunately, Christmas was approaching and there was no time to obsess about anything else. Back in the States, I had slowly but surely become a Scrooge. The stores were so crowded. Do they increase the prices just for the month of December? Have they already sold out of Super Mario for Game Cube? Should I bother with our Christmas cookies this year; do the kids really appreciate the tradition? Will I ever get my Christmas cards postmarked before Christmas? Scratch this person off my card list; they haven't sent me a card in three years. Why do I always put the fragile ornaments in the farthest corner of the attic? If my Aunt Veronica gives me another reversible polyester scarf with matching rain hat or motion-activated Santa with glow-in-the-dark Rudolf, I'm going to scream.

This Christmas, we lived in a small apartment. There wasn't room for a lot of extra things. And we had a limited budget; I couldn't buy gifts for every relative and friend from here to New

York. Besides, it wasn't appropriate; it wasn't the Italian style to make things so complicated. Most people had no credit card debt in Italy because credit cards here generally had to be paid in full 'electronically' every month. There were no Christmas lights on the houses in *Varese*; electricity was much too expensive and, besides, lights were hung in the piazzas by the municipality. It was the same theory as reading the newspaper at the bar – why buy it if you can get it for free? The drive to buy a lot of gifts at great expense was also not a part of the Italian scene. I had to go with the flow, and everyone else, including the kids, had to understand. I wanted this to be our first simple Christmas but I braced myself for resistance.

"Guys, I wanted you to know that in some regions of Italy, like *Varese*, *Babbo Natale* brings only one gift for each child and in some families, the parents buy a few more gifts. But you should understand that this is a small apartment, and we don't have room for a lot of things."

"Duh, Mom ..." Alex responded.

"*Ma, mamma, non siamo mica scemi* ... (But, Mom, we're not fools ...)" Matthew added.

"You're right, Matthew," I said. "Sometimes kids are smarter than their parents."

> "*Cari* Denise and Bruce," Susanna wrote by email later that day, "It's time to think about the Christmas menu. To avoid to be imprisoned in kitchen the day before Christmas, we thought a menu easy to do. We'll start with hors d'oeuvre: salad with shrimps and tuna mousse, and then the first course of *tagliatelle* with salmon (alternative for children, *tagliatelle al sugo di pomodoro*). For vegetables we can have *patate al forno* and fresh salad.
>
> Italian tradition wants on the Christmas table: Fruits – white grapes (auspicious), pineapple, citrus, dates. Cakes – *panettone o pandoro* with *mascarpone* or

without. Everyone has their opinion. I already brought the ingredients for hors d'oeuvre and first dishes, potatoes and salad. I buy panettone, dates and pineapple. Then, if you agree I thought Bruce can make the second course. He had mentioned an *ossobuco* or roast, as you prefer. Maybe if you have an American specialty we are happy to taste it.

If you want to prepare a typical American cake (as Denise told me) we agree. Otherwise you can buy a *pandoro* - please without any cream inside that we can eat it with *mascarpone* and (for adults only) mixed with some cognac. Tell me if you agree. If the children don't like fish, it is enough buy some *prosciutto* or *salame* or cheese pieces. As I told Denise, after lunch we can reach your house for the cakes so the children can play more comfortable. I'm looking forward your answer. In the afternoon I send you the Italian translation so - finally - we improve your Italian!

Un abbraccio. Susi"

Easy enough. We went to the *macelleria* to order the meat. We specified *kilos* this time, rather than number of people. Then to Tiziana's for *panettone* and *pandoro*, the traditional Christmas sweet breads. We chose the *Motta* brand, because the packages were emblazoned with a photo Bruce and his colleagues took in the studio months earlier. When we went to friends' houses, we brought our brand then we came home with another one. It was like being a part of a massive recycling program. Along with the traditional gifts, I needed to buy a little something to be delivered by the *Befana*, the kindly witch who comes on January 6 and brings sweets to all children who left their shoes outside the door the night before. Matthew and Alex were planning to put their snow boots out to maximize the square-centimeter capacity available to her.

On Christmas Eve, the communal pageantry and show took place. First, the surrounding streets of *Piazza San Vittore* were converted into a mini town of Bethlehem. The local kids dressed up as shepherds and townspeople in burlap sacks, spinning make-believe wool and tooling make-believe leather. The littlest ones were dressed as chubby angels in their moms' old bed sheets covering their snowsuits and crowned by tinfoil halos. When the church bells rang, they walked in procession to the steps of the *Chiesa di San Vittore* and stood on and around a stage made for the occasion.

Hundreds of us, packed in the piazza, had waited an hour to pounce upon the few rows of seats. The rest hovered behind us, hopping from foot to foot to stay warm in the freezing chill. We sat transfixed as a ballerina, dressed as a more professional-looking angel, performed an ode to Maria and Giuseppe who struggled toward the church with their donkey. A shepherd took the donkey as Maria and Giuseppe entered the church by foot through a side door while a hundred children or so broke into song about baby *Gesu*. Once the holy family disappeared into the church, the huge 10-meter doors of *San Vittore* opened. Alex stood up as dry-ice smoke rose from the back-lit church. The light bursting through the smoke was almost blinding.

"I can't see," he lamented.

Vaguely we could see the silhouette of a man and a woman carrying a baby. The baby was crying.

"It's Maria and Giuseppe holding baby *Gesu*," Matthew explained, but all else was silent. Then the crowd let out a collective sigh. From the center aisle of the *piazza*, adults dressed as shepherds entered with camels and horses to pay homage to the new baby. Even if you weren't religious you couldn't help but get caught up in the moment. The majesty...the sheer joy of the moment. The crowd started singing an Italian carol in unison, but Bruce and I didn't know the words. It didn't matter; we were two sentimental saps, too choked up to sing anyway.

That night, we arrived for midnight mass at 11:30. At the stroke of midnight, from inside the church, we heard cheers rising up outside the basilica from the *Piazza San Vittore*. Non-church-goers were apparently celebrating in their own way. At the end of the mass, a statue of baby Jesus was laid gently in the manger on the altar and the parishioners filed out into the *piazza*. The sight that greeted us outside the church resembled a New York New Year's Eve celebration. There were bottles of champagne everywhere, people talking and laughing in groups. They weren't drunk or obnoxious, just happy.

"It's a party," said Alex.

"It's a birthday party," Matthew responded.

On Christmas morning, snow fell magically on cue as in a Renaissance play. The church bells in *Piazza San Vittore, Piazza della Brunella* and *Piazza Giovane Italia* competed to be heard. They were tuned to traditional Lombardian carols for the day. Despite all the differences in Christmas this year, the remainder of the day was very familiar. Christmas morning, the kids got up too early and were ordered to go back to sleep until sunrise. The tiny remote-control car we got them didn't work, an unexpected disappointment. On the other hand, the kids showed amazing appreciation for the care we took to wrap each present uniquely, an unexpected joy. Our family gifts were a little homespun and didn't take up much space. I gave the kids boxes I decoupaged with images of the latest Moto GP motorcycles. Alex gave Matthew a T-shirt he designed. Matthew gave Alex a gift certificate to see the *Varese* professional basketball team play Pesaro. Bruce presented me with a mere 572 of his "recent" photographs. The new and the familiar melded together like the lovely blend of spices in the *ossobuco* that simmered in the kitchen. We shared some of the chocolate brought by *Babbo Natale*, the only gift requested of him.

"He's great, that *Babbo* guy," Alex said.

"Yeah, but it's weird that his workshop makes chocolate from Switzerland," Matthew murmured suspiciously.

"Matthew, Switzerland is only a few kilometers away," Alex responded.

"I suppose, but just the same ..." Matthew's voice trailed away as he munched the next bite.

The rest of Christmas day was filled with simple pleasures as we prepared the second course of Christmas dinner to carry over to the Sorus.

"Mom, do me a favor, don't discuss Footlocker or pornography, OK?"

"Very funny," I said. "You're hilarious."

We sat around the table lit with flickering candles, the familiar perfume of enticing odors emanating from the oven, all of us squeezed elbow to elbow in the Soru's kitchen, laughing and talking at the same time. I was reminded of one of the first dinners I had at the Soru house. Laura was pregnant at the time with Chiara. Now we had two Stragapedes for the price of one. Chiara was a real entity of her own, sitting up in her own special seat at the table when she wasn't on my lap pulling Francesca's hair in the seat beside me. There was so much love at that time, and that love had deepened over these past few months as the table had grown more crowded.

Francesca reminded me of one of the Christmas gifts I had sent from New York years ago. It was a Disney carousel with various removable Disney characters. She had treasured it so, the movement, the song it made as it turned, that it was still in pristine condition for Chiara. I watched the action at the table as if in slow motion. Susanna's laugh pulled her chair backwards precariously on two legs. Vanni's pushed him forward almost into the plate of *osso bucco.* Giampiero's eyes singing the color blue. Laura's eyes, wet as she watched Chiara eating with two hands … Francesca horrified by the spectacle.

I missed extended family in New York, yet I was home just the same. Christmas marked the halfway point of our trip. It was going to be very hard from this point on, not to see every precious moment as a last one before returning home.

*   *   *

Days after the festivities, we were settled into post-Christmas vacation when Alex asked to use the phone. He wanted to call a friend to clarify the Christmas break homework.

"That's fine," I said. "Don't forget to say Merry Christmas."

I hadn't exactly been cherishing the thought of spending our Christmas break in our usual posture at the kitchen table, laboring over history or geography or even math, having to stop every sentence or two to look up a word in our fat, ever-present Italian-English dictionary. The situation had improved steadily over the months, but we still weren't at the point of memorizing for the *interrogazione* until we finished whatever translation we had to do.

Blanching at the thought of it, I overheard Alex talking into the phone in the far corner of the living room. He wasn't struggling cryptically to get his point across. He was speaking fluent Italian, as if he had spoken it all his life. "*Ma dobbiamo memorizzare tutto, o è sufficiente leggere* (But, do we have to memorize it all or is it adequate to read it)?" he was asking his friend.

I looked at Bruce, dumbfounded. The teachers had asked me to wait until Christmas, and almost as if they scripted it with a higher power, my Christmas miracle arrived. By letting go of my fear, not out of choice but because I completely lost the ability to control their day-to-day environment, I gave my children a gift without price. Sometimes *Babbo Natale* leaves more than chocolate.

Speak Milk. Drink Wine.

CHAPTER EIGHTEEN

Don't Take Yourself So Seriously

You must learn from the mistakes of others.
You can't possibly live long enough to make them all yourself.
-Sam Levenson

Happy birthday!!! I hope you are finding a nice Italian way to celebrate. Perhaps with strolling musicians? A *piazza* rented out in your honor? A small parade of the local villagers reenacting important moments from your life? Bruce reciting love poems from beloved Italian romantics from the 17th century? I'm not sure what the general custom is there in Italy. In case you've forgotten the ways of your native culture, or at least as it's practiced here in my small (WASPy) corner of the world, birthdays (adult birthdays) are usually acknowledged several hours after awakening by a hurried phone call to the person at work. Later, the children are cajoled, coerced, reprimanded and threatened into making birthday cards (accompanied by surprised announcements, "I didn't know it was Daddy's birthday today"). Then there are guilty attempts to make dinner slightly special (a candle in the taco, an umbrella in the Diet Coke, etc.). Finally there is the relief the next day that the terrible pressure is off (although in my small WASPy corner of the world the next day is our anniversary and the nightmare gets played out all over again).

OK, gotta go. Happy birthday again.

Love, Alexa

So apparently some of my friends were under the impression that I tended to make a big deal out of things. Not true. We were simply going to the beautiful Italian island of *Sardegnia* for the weekend – the very place where the seeds for our current adventure were sown a decade and a half ago. Winter was far from the optimum time to go, but we found a cheap off-season deal and, at a minimum, it was an opportunity to reminisce about meeting the Sorus and Stragapedes, the *agriturismo*, the evenings under the stars, devouring watermelons from our host's garden, talking and drinking *grappa* into the wee hours of the morning. Our *Varese* babysitter, a local graduate student, agreed to take the kids for the night and on Saturday we were off for a romantic weekend, our first time alone in months. It would be short but sweet.

On arriving, it was immediately apparent why most people take their *Sardinia* break in the warmer months. The air was cool and crisp, and thoroughly unsuitable for swimming. But *Sardinia's* beauty transcends temperature. There is an austere roughness to the island that defines its character – craggy rock outcroppings that tumble into the sea and white sand bleached by the sun paint the coastline. With the exception of the *Costa Smeralda*, visited by yacht-faring foreigners, many towns and villages, particularly in the interior of the island, retain the ambience of their simple past.

The sea is so transparent here, and the blue sky reflects in it in a way that makes you stare to examine where the sky ends and the sea begins. Bruce and I walked, hand in hand, our toes squishing in the cool sand, picking up the odd pebble or piece of sea glass to take back to the kids. New York seemed a long way away, as did *Varese*, and in the waves I could practically see the images of Vanni and Tommaso galloping around, with Susanna and Giampiero in hot pursuit. GP pretending to be a wild sea creature on the attack, and the kids retaliating with a handful of sand.

Dinner accentuated the memory. The taste of a robust *Sardinian cannonau vino*, or crispy, paper-thin *Sardinian* bread drizzled with the purest of the island's virgin olive oil. *Agnello con finocchi selvatici* (lamb with wild fennel) accompanied by *carciofi alla sarda* (artichokes prepared *Sardinian* style) stuffed with ricotta, garlic, lemon and oregano. Lastly, a candle-lit *crema allo zafferano* (saffron cream) with almond *biscotti* for dessert. Much to my relief, the waiter did not sing, "*Tanti Auguri a te ...*" in honor of my birthday, and so the night was pretty perfect. By the time the last few drops of *cannonau* were consumed, we probably should have rolled into bed. However, how often do you get to go away with your husband for your birthday, and to a hotel that has after-dinner entertainment no less?

The show on this particular night included *Il Gioco delle Coppie*, an imitation of a popular Italian television show which roughly resembles the "Newlywed Game." The emcee, Riccardo, asked for couples to volunteer for the competition. The husbands were isolated while he asked the wives questions. The wives had to guess how their husbands would respond when they returned from being sequestered. It was good for a laugh.

Riccardo, try as he might to coax contestants from the audience, was having difficulty. It seemed like the whole plan for the evening show might be crumbling.

"Let's volunteer," I said. "It could be fun."

"Are you kidding? I don't understand enough Italian to get involved in this."

"Come on. I'll translate for you. Besides, it could be a way to meet people."

How trusting men can be.

Up to the stage we went, with two other hesitant, but at least Italian-speaking, contestants. With emcee-like velocity, Riccardo began speaking in Italian colloquialisms as I tried valiantly to keep up with the translation.

Leaning toward Bruce, I whispered, "He just said ... this lovely woman to my right is the scorekeeper. She's 23 years old and wants to marry a hunter (*cacciatore*)."

"A hunter?" said Bruce, looking somewhat surprised.

"Oh, I'm sorry," I said, realizing my mistake, "I meant a soccer player (*calciatore*)." Now it began to occur to Bruce that he might really be in trouble relying on me as a translator. It's amazing what messing up one little "L" can do in the Italian language.

The game continued with Riccardo asking the wives questions, while the husbands were absented from the outdoor theater by the able-bodied young woman who wanted to marry either a hunter or a soccer player.

"Where was your first kiss?" he asked us.

"What is his nickname for you?"

"What will he say is your worst personality trait?"

All the wives answered and then the men were invited to return. The audience was in stitches as we all made fools of ourselves. Bruce and I actually fared better than most. Then onto a second game which had as its objective some task that needed to be performed by the husbands.

Riccardo lapsed into a long and serious explanation of what the men had to do, interrupted by some splendidly humorous remarks that again left the audience in stitches and us laughing in nervous bursts of imitation, so as not to feel left out.

"OK?" asked Riccardo after the long explanation.

Bruce leaned over toward me.

"What did he say?" he asked me.

"I have absolutely no idea," I answered, apologetically.

"*Vai!*" shouted Riccardo.

"That means 'go.'" I said.

"I know that!" Bruce replied in a slightly panicked voice. "But go where?"

Meanwhile, the other male contestants were rushing into the audience and taking young women by the elbow, one by one, and urging them to go on stage. Bruce caught on immediately to what he was supposed to do, even if he had no idea why. At the end, he managed to persuade three women to follow him to the stage. A fourth one, a woman of about 65 years old, hit him with her handbag. Two of the three women looked to be five or six months pregnant. This got a good laugh, as ultimately we learned that the task was a competition to see how many women each man could "seduce" to join him.

Divine retribution for my failure as translator was not long in coming, however. The next game seemed to involve a task to be performed by the women, but I couldn't make out anything further. I had the advantage and rude awakening of not being the first female contestant to have to perform the task. I watched, horrified, while the first female contestant, wearing a smart outfit of perfectly pressed white pants and a floral blouse stood patiently while Riccardo tied a string around her tiny waist, which hung down her back like a tail. The "tail" had attached to it a pencil.

Aghast, I watched as she stood with her back to the audience and squatted lower and lower trying to get the hanging pencil into the neck of an empty wine bottle.

I mumbled, "no, no, please God, no" as Riccardo made farting noises into the microphone each time she squatted further.

"This is not happening," I said under my breath.

The entire audience was hysterical, Bruce more so than anyone else.

I had picked *this night* to wear a dress, something I don't often do. A short dress, and yes, a fairly tight dress. I prayed it was just a bad dream, but I felt far too awake. My turn. He tied the string. I squatted. He farted into the microphone.

Santa Maria, if you are listening, please bring me a power failure. Not a huge outage, I prayed. *Not even the whole island. Maybe just the stage. Just trip a breaker. Please.*

More farting noises interrupted my prayers. Santa Maria was apparently busy with other more pressing problems and I soon gracefully bowed out of this portion of the competition. The next woman, wearing an even shorter and tighter dress, got up, squatted once, endured one farting noise, and bingo, with maximum precision, her pilates-like thighs helped her execute the task with a minimum amount of embarrassment.

We definitely did not leave as champions, nor were we a monument to American wit or lower body strength. On the other hand, we were the only ones to know each others nicknames and the location of our first kiss. What's more, we were given a dose of humility, which is more than I can say for our competitors who were looking pretty pleased with themselves.

"*Sei stata buffissima* (You were hilarious)," A young woman said as we exited the theater.

I turned to Bruce smiling, "I told you we might meet people."

The next day, still a little loopy from our evening escapades, we pulled over near a small store on the way to the airport, to see if we could pick up a souvenir for the kids. Since there were no parking spaces available, we parked with our right front and back wheels on the sidewalk so as not to block traffic, and collapsed the driver's side-view mirror (so as not to lose it!) in a manner we have seen hundreds of times in the short span we have lived in Italy. Bruce remained behind the wheel and I jumped out. Two minutes later, I returned to find a policeman talking to Bruce in Italian at the rate of 120 kilometers an hour, gesturing wildly. I could hear him saying roughly,

"What do you think you are doing? You are on the sidewalk! You can't do that!" And best of all, "This is a very serious offense in Italy."

Now, up to this point, I was making my way quickly to the car to act as a translator for a very confused and somewhat alarmed Bruce, but when I heard that last phrase, it was all that I could do not to laugh out loud. I managed to control myself and explained to him that my husband didn't speak Italian very well, that we were foreigners, and that we were only doing what we saw many other Italians do.

"That's no excuse," he replied taking out his ticket book "Others breaking the law does not make it right."

"He's got a point," I mused.

On cue, another car pulled up directly in front of us, pulling its right front and rear wheel onto the sidewalk. Now Bruce and I both had to contain ourselves, as a very relaxed Italian vacationer sauntered up to the officer.

"I'm just going to leave the car here for a moment," he said in Italian. "Is that a problem?"

"No," answered the officer, not appearing to be cognizant of the inconsistency in his reaction. "Just be quick about it."

I was pretty much figuring it was time to try out my quasi-fluent Italian and give this guy a straight talking-to about double standards and ethnocentricity, but thought the better of it as he put his ticket book away and began to ease up on the finger pointing and other miscellaneous gesticulating. Soon his barrage of instructions regarding our transgressions muddied into mumbling as he continued down the street, casting his comments over his shoulder as he walked away.

One last stop at the ocean on the way to the airport. We sat on a dune and watched the sun stream through the clouds, casting splashes of sun and shade on the waves below. I closed my eyes periodically, trying to remember the summer days so long ago that lead to our present day experience here. Giampiero and Bruce both had a full head of hair. I was more svelte in a bathing suit. Susanna, Domenico, Laura, we all had fewer wrinkles and perhaps less wisdom as well.

Watching Vanni and Tommaso chase each other, wrestling, tumbling, an occasional tear from a spill in the sand was the first inkling we had that we might want to have a Matthew and Alex one day. I remembered Susanna's touch on my sun-drenched back, the coolness of sunscreen, unsolicited. Laura's *panini* and the carbonated *acqua frizzante* that tickled my nose. Bruce and Domenico had missed going to the beach that day, stuck at the repair shop that was fixing our car. They had come back sweaty and tired, but laughing at the make-shift repair made by the son of the brother of the mechanic who was away on vacation for *Ferragosto.*

It was a good birthday. No, actually, a great birthday.

Speak Milk. Drink Wine.

CHAPTER NINETEEN

Italian Women Don't Get Fat

Excess on occasion is exhilarating.
It prevents moderation from acquiring the deadening effect of a habit.
-W. Somerset Maugham

"You have such a magnificent bosom and such a splendid face, if you just did a little more *sport*, you would look incredible!" That's what Giampiero told me when he saw me one weekend. Was I insulted? No. How could I be? I could never be insulted by GP He meant it as just some kind of helpful suggestion that one good friend gave another. No big deal. To the Italians, the state or condition of one's body is just what it is, a simple fact, requiring no special parentheses, especially between friends.

Having said that, another simple issue was that despite the fact that I was slowly losing weight from the time we arrived in Italy, compared to my Italian friends and neighbors, I was – how shall I say this – fat. At size 14, I might as well been size 22, because I have never been in a store in *Varese* that sold pants that I could get past one of my thighs. They say that French women don't get fat, and maybe that's true. But, Italian women aren't getting fat either.

We've all seen film images, the 70-year-old Sicilian widow, dressed in black, with the enormous bosom and ample hips. But on the streets of *Varese*, the women are hot, lean and lovely. It is my personal suspicion that Italian women do so much housework they don't have time to eat. Statistically, they do seven times the housework of American women (I personally think it's all the ironing). Be that as it may, I have never met women so obsessed with fashion as the women of northern Italy. It's scary. The hair, outfit, shoes and accessories have to be just so. And as the *moda* (fashion) of the moment changes, so must the Italian female. God knows how they do it on the meager salaries that seem to be a mere fraction of American earning capacity for the same job, but they do. Their waistlines are tiny, their legs are long, and given the amount of pasta per capita that is consumed in this country, I really needed to understand why. The Slow Food Movement began in Italy and was the first time that anyone tried to label the concept of eating *alla Italiania*, slowly, with fresh ingredients. To use the words of the organization, it was founded to "counteract fast food and fast life, the disappearance of local food traditions and people's dwindling interest in the food they eat, where it comes from, how it tastes and how our food choices affect the rest of the world."

Lyn, a very close friend from England and somewhat of a health guru, was always telling me that Americans had the worst diet of any living humans. When I emailed her my thoughts on the subject of Italian women and their luscious figures, she jumped at the opportunity to email me a jibe.

Dear Denise,

Haven't you ever heard of the Pasta Diet? You walka pasta da bakery. You walka pasta da candy store. You walka pasta da ice cream shop. You walka pasta da table and fridge. Get it?

Here are some little known facts: The Japanese eat very little fat and suffer fewer heart attacks than Americans. The Mexicans eat a lot of fat and suffer fewer heart attacks than Americans. The Chinese drink very little red wine and suffer fewer heart attacks than Americans. The Italians drink excessive amounts of red wine and suffer fewer heart attacks than Americans. The Germans drink a lot of beers and eat lots of sausages and fats and suffer fewer heart attacks than Americans.

What's the moral of the story? Eat and drink what you like. Speaking English is apparently what kills you.

Love, Lyn

So, I suppose, theoretically, since these days I was speaking far more Italian than English, I had increased my life expectancy by quite a bit, not to mention I would out live Lyn despite the fact that she ate a far better diet than 99 percent of the population of the Western world.

Lyn was obsessed with organic food, organic medicine and clean water, and she was just getting started when she sent me the "Italian Pasta Diet." She was determined that I see the serious side of the pun. Her next email pulled no punches:

Hi D,

One other thing to add related to your query about Italian women being so thin and trim. The average Italian drinks water rather than soda. Current research shows that many people think they are hungry, when in fact, they are thirsty. Eighty percent of Westerners suffer from clinical dehydration - scary stuff! If you drink two liters of water a day, you do not want to snack. Italians have been drinking bottled water (without chlorine) forever. Americans still think bottled water is a fashion accessory. (Sorry.)

Most Americans eat at least one meal on the run, in the car or at the computer. Food is an art, not a science. The Italians know this, whereas the Americans spend most of their time trying to outdo nature in the laboratory. Chemicals, whatever they are, have no place in the human body. Preservatives merely allow what would be condemned food to survive longer on the supermarket shelves.

Anyway, it's just food for thought (smile).

Love, Lyn

It has a ring of truth to it, doesn't it? More water, less preservatives, more "real food" eaten as a ritualistic experience rather than something to cram down while doing something else. Roll this together with the more active daily lifestyle of walking to the market, walking to the tailor, walking pasta the *pasticcieria* and I had the makings of a "dieting secret." Maybe it's just living life the way it's meant to be lived, but if I had started marketing it back in the States, I might have figured out how to have some actual income beyond that of our New York rental. We could have called it the 'Denise Pirrotti Hummel Italian Dieting Secret.' Then, I could put together some kind of a diet book ... you know with pasta recipes and *gelato* ... then ... OK, the reality was that the only one in our family who was sought after for any kind of advice associated with food was Bruce. In the entire time we were in Italy, the only advancement I made with regard to culinary knowledge was the fact that *gnocchi* consisted of a dough made with potatoes. Bruce, on the other hand, was constantly experimenting with new ingredients and products and was already being solicited by our female friends for intensive culinary consultation. Not so much for advice as to how to maintain their Northern Italian figures, but how to keep their Northern Italian husbands' stomachs happy.

Caro Chef,
Thank you for the recipe (finally). Everything is clear. However, yesterday I tried the potatoes but they didn't come out like yours. When you have time and wish, can you please explain also this recipe? Thank you also in behalf of Domenico.
Kisses, Laura

Cara buongustaia (Dear Gourmand)*,*
Copy to: My wife, the expert taster

I heard from sources within my "Customer Support" team, that my trouble-shooting services are too slow (i.e., I do not respond to emails very quickly). Yes, this is true. My apologies.

Per le patate: I always use *patate gialle* (they have more starch) and pre-cook before placing in the oven. I boil the potatoes until almost cooked (not completely soft) – about 10 minutes. I then drain, cool slightly and mix with olive oil, rosemary and 1-2 teaspoons of course salt (for about 1,5Kg patate). Then roast in oven about 30 mins. @ 200C. If I am cooking a roast, I place the potatoes in the same pan as the meat (which adds more flavor).

Molto semplice!

You take your cooking responsibilities very seriously. If Denise was that crazy about those potatoes, and I didn't give a repeat performance soon enough, she would have been out looking for a restaurant that could replicate them. Fortunately, she has many other exceptional qualities. It's just that cooking is not one of them.

Ciao,
Bruce

Just wait and see my response when they try to get my grandmother's chocolate-chip cookie recipe. Apparently, Bruce has a short memory. When I first met him in college, the extent of his culinary expertise included emptying a box of macaroni and cheese into a pot of boiling water. Nevertheless, it was undeniable that without the constraints of either being away from home on business trips or commuting three hours a day to and from work when he was home, Bruce acquired his own 'extra.' In the early *Varese* days, his menus had been limited to a variety of pastas, often followed by a salad, but as time went on, inspired by the fresh produce, spices, meats and wines, the variety of plates grew exponentially.

Food preparation, serving, and eating became more of a ritual. He set the mood for culinary creativity by playing various opera CDs, lighting a few candles, and singing very loudly and off key (thereby assuring complete privacy to express his culinary creativity). He was serving meals in courses rather than the traditional American one-plate trio of meat, starch and vegetable. The first course consisted of a *pasta* or *risotto,* followed by a second of meat or fish with fresh vegetables. The portions were smaller, and the pace of the meal slower with plenty of time to talk about the day's events and to savor each bite. After dinner, Matthew usually sat on his dad's lap and continued chatting, rather than jumping up from the table after the last morsel of food was consumed. And Alex's eating experience expanded beyond the sole goal of finishing enough of his vegetables to earn dessert.

I also began to notice a change with regard to my "relationship" with food. Yes, I know it sounds a little over analyzed to talk about a human relationship with an inanimate object. And I certainly don't mean to imply that I suddenly became a Northern Italian fashion plate, nor did I expect to ever have the figure to support the ambition, should I be so inclined. But something had changed. In the States, food was my best friend when I was down and my party companion when I was up. Then I felt guilty when I knew I ate more than I should and looked to food to console me. In Italy, food became for me what it was probably intended to be, fun to be with in small doses. I ate when I was hungry and I stopped when I was full. There were no emotions involved other than appreciation for the taste and the time we had all together at the table.

Every morning I had a *brioche* and *cappuccino*, a breakfast that no reasonable person would describe as dietetic. I had pasta for lunch, also a serious no-no in most dieting books. For dinner, I ate both courses; they just weren't super-sized. I even ate *gelato* now and then. So, was it that my pattern of eating was following the trend of my lifestyle and simply amounted to less frenetic consumption? Was the quality of the food that much better? Were the trips to the dry cleaner and the post office, by foot, adding up to some great expenditure of calories? I couldn't be sure. I needed to keep my eyes and ears open for the answers and enjoy the results of the change. In the meantime, I planned to rely on the best dieting secret I've seen. It's hidden between the lines in the menu of *Bella Napoli* pizzeria, one of our favorite pizzerias in town, and here it is free of charge, even if I never get rich:

Le cose migliori della vita sono le più semplici.
Un buon bicchiere di vino,
una fetta di prosciutto,
del pane, una goccia d'olio d'oliva e una pizza fumante.
Una chiacchierata con gli amici.
In fondo non occorre nulla
di più per essere felice.

The best things in life are the simplest.
A good glass of wine,
a slice of prosciutto,
of bread, a drop of olive oil and a steaming hot pizza.
A discussion with friends.
What else could we possibly need
to be happy.

Speak Milk. Drink Wine.

CHAPTER TWENTY

Sometimes the Greatest Gift is When You Don't Have to Think About Certain Stuff Anymore

Innately, children seem to have little true realistic anxiety.
They will run along the brink of water, climb on the window sill,
play with sharp objects and with fire, in short,
do everything that is bound to damage them and to worry
those in charge of them,
that is wholly the result of education;
for they cannot be allowed to make the instructive experiences themselves.
-Sigmund Freud

By the time February chill set in, the children's ability to speak Italian increased so dramatically, that when they were confused in class, their teachers were not sure if Matthew and Alex were not understanding a particular *word in Italian*, or they were having actual academic difficulty with a *concept* that was being taught. Matthew thought this frequent misunderstanding was quite funny.

"For example," he laughed, "our teacher said, '*Il lago si forma dai ghiacciaio delle Alpi* (The lake is formed from the Alpine glacier).' And I said, '*Non ho capito* (I don't understand).' And she said, '*Vuol dire che ... il ghiacciaio delle Alpi ... per esempio ... forma il lago* (It means that ... the Alpine glacier ... for example ... forms the lake).' And I could tell just by the expression on her face that she wasn't sure if I didn't understand how Alpine lakes are formed or I didn't understand the word for 'glacier'! Isn't that hilarious?"

"Hilarious," I said.

Alex preferred to recount the crises of other children in the class, which he found equally amusing. One afternoon, in response to my typical after-school question, "Did you have a good day?" – which I was now allowed to ask – Alex responded, "Yes, but Lucca didn't."

"Oh really? What happened?" I asked.

"Well," said Alex, "he was drawing something in his diary and the teacher screamed, 'Luca, what are you doing?' and Luca started crying. I mean, what is he kidding? This is Italy; they have to yell!"

And thus a stereotype is born, although contrary to the more diffuse abuse of the generalization, the volume of his environment was a cultural phenomenon that Alex now understood and accepted. Both Matthew and Alex grew in such a way that enabled them to laugh with ease at themselves, and in a way that gave them the right to laugh at others as well. The important thing was that events which in former months caused anything from confusion to rage, now gave them fodder for laughter. I was really happy for them. They seemed so grown up, so sure of themselves.

With every month that passed and our time to return to the United States grew nearer, I consulted my mental checklist to make sure we exposed them to everything we could abroad – to give them the opportunity to grow and expand in every way possible. *Carnivale* was approaching and I discussed with Giampiero what the event was like in *Varese*.

"Sometimes *Carnivale* makes me sad," he said.

"Why is that?" I puzzled.

"Because it's the last opportunity for celebration before the serious business of Lent begins. We eat *chiacchiere* with powdered sugar and special *caramelle* (candies) before sweets are put away and things become more serious and reflective. *Capisci?*"

I tried to picture GP, the *malifico baciatore* in 'serious-reflective' mode.

"How is it celebrated?"

"Every Italian village celebrates *Carnivale* differently. In *Varese*, there is a parade with floats; children and adults in costume, ranging from the traditional to the ridiculous, march for hours through the center of town. Silly string, confetti and even shaving cream are fair game if you are out and about that day."

"Susanna once explained to me that it's celebrated like our Halloween ..."

"Yes, similarly, but if you want to experience a real extravaganza, you must go to Venice. Not only is it a world-famous *Carnivale* celebration, it is one with great historical relevance. It will be touristy and crowded, but it won't be something you'll forget any time soon."

So, we booked a *pensione* and I asked the kids to join me for some research so they'd have an idea of what they were going to experience. Through various Internet sites we learned that, for centuries, *Carnivale* was a celebration that enveloped the entire city. Venetians donned mask and costume as a means to transgress against regulations imposed by the Republic against gambling and other forms of merriment.

I read out loud, "Gentlemen used them to court ladies other than their wives. Noble women used them to attend parties in the palaces of the Venetian aristocracy while remaining anonymous. Common people wore them so that they could mingle and be part of a more noble crowd. The mask, in fact, transcended the classes rendering everyone the same: tumblers, noblemen, prostitutes, and charlatans." Alex got up and left the room.

"Where are you off to?" I asked.

"I'm going to make my mask."

Internet images depicted the recreation of ancient times, palaces hosting sumptuous feasts, people dancing and gambling, and nobility flaunting extremely costly costumes made for the celebration.

"It says here that with the crisis and decline of the Republic during the 18th century, the celebration of *Carnivale* also took a dive and was, for all intents and purposes, annulled. Then in the 1970s when tourism started to peak, it was revitalized."

"In other words, *Carnivale* could bring in the big bucks," said Matthew. Both kids were now really good at synthesizing historical information.

Truthfully, Bruce and I were skeptical that the event might be too touristy or commercial, but on the other hand, even if the modern day celebration was one-tenth as exciting as the ancient one appeared to have been, it would be worth the trip.

Alex's mask was a combination of paper, paint and paper cups. It resembled more a projection of Venice's science-fiction future than its past.

"Come on Matthew, make a mask!" Alex cajoled his brother, but Matthew, like Bruce and me, decided to take a back seat and "watch" *Carnivale* rather than immersing ourselves in it. We were curious, of course, but not quite certain how all the pomp and circumstance would play out.

On the day of our departure, we walked to the *Varese* train station, our small overnight bags rolling behind us like a pedestrian caravan. We took the train to *Milano Cadorna* and then transferred to the *Stazione Centrale.* From there, we caught a *Euro-Star* Express to Venice. We had successfully avoided taking one of the worst, most heavily trafficked highways in Italy, and even better, been lucky enough to avoid the spontaneous train strikes for which Italy is so famous.

"Can we eat lunch in the restaurant car?" Alex asked.

"I see no reason why not," Bruce answered him.

After a cheer from the boys, we traipsed down two cars and sat at a table covered with a white linen table cloth. We chose between *tagliatelle al pomodoro* and *lasagna verde* for the first course and *pollo con funghi* or *manzo alla griglia* for the second. Sipping a glass of *vino bianco* and swaying gently to the motion of the train, I was in heaven. Some day someone is going to have to explain to me why a country whose citizens can't even pay a utility bill by check can produce a multi-course meal on a train that rivals the average high-end restaurant in the States, while the most "advanced" nation in the world continues to serve hub-cap hamburgers and cardboard pizza as the only consistently available source of nutrition to the average traveler between destinations.

On arrival, the magic of Venice consumed us. Of course, Susanna was right, the crowds were tremendous but Venice was so surreal, it constituted an out-of-body experience under almost any conditions. An ancient city built on stilts, carless, surrounded by canals, and spanned by ancient stone bridges. Matthew was smiling serenely.

"Are you thinking about how beautiful it is?" I asked him.

"I'm thinking I'm glad we got there before it sank," he said, thoughtfully.

Ornate *palazzi* lined the Grand Canal, handsome (and not so handsome) gondoliers rowed their craft through the watery labyrinth, long boats motored fresh fruits and vegetables from the mainland, and there was even a hearse-like boat heading out toward the burial island of San Michele.

My first thought, as we hopped off our water taxi, was that this experience was likely to be a significant departure from all that I had heard about its counterpart in Rio. From a practical point of view, costumes appropriate for winter's high water in Venice's *Piazza San Marco* probably differed significantly from Brazil's tropical costumes where the key accessory is a spangled thong. The afternoon we arrived, the wind was blowing fiercely and huge puddles of water made wandering the narrow warrens a fierce athletic odyssey that was better weathered with a snow parka than a bathing suit. I found myself wishing I was wearing one of the long gowns, heavy wigs or embroidered jackets I saw swishing around the pier, if not to be part of the atmosphere, at least to be warmer.

Everywhere on the tiny streets, on the bridges overlooking the canals, in every *piazza*, wandered men, women and children wearing the traditional costumes and hand-made masks fashioned after those of the 17th century. Women wore wigs that soared three feet above their heads and were gowned in embroidered satin and golden cloaks. Men with painted faces wore velvet coat, tails and buckled shoes. A mysterious figure in a black cloak and white mask slipped in and out of the crowd.

"That guy's a charlatan," Matthew told Alex.

A woman passed by dressed in light green silk, her arms covered with pink gauze that resembled butterfly wings.

"That one's an insect," Alex added.

I couldn't figure out if they were Venetians or wealthy tourists, but not knowing added to the mystique of the experience.

In the famous *Cafè Florian* in *Piazza San Marco*, those of us who weren't spectacularly adorned enough to gain entrance stared through the window at the spectacle of these elegant figures sipping their drinks, some through masks, as if it were an every day event taking place centuries ago.

Bruce, Matthew and I had come to *Carnivale* as observers. But the Taz was here to party! Without any fear of reproach, Alex proudly donned his paper-cup mask and inserted himself between costumed Venetians posing for tourists in Piazza San Marco, and was photographed along with the best. He even collected a total of 30 *centesimi* worth of tips for his efforts.

"Mom, why are there so many winged lions here?" he asked me after his modeling debut was finished.

"Aha, so you weren't listening carefully when we were doing all that research," I said in mock accusation. "Don't you remember that the Venetians were totally enamored with lions? Citizens kept live lions in their gardens, and for a time a state lion lived in a golden cage in the *piazza*. So as a tribute, they carved him on their doors, their bridges ... They're everywhere."

"How many are there?" Matthew asked.

"No idea," I answered. "Why don't you count them?"

That day, the boys stopped counting at 353 winged lions. It was like a life-sized game of I-Spy. They found some on huge, elaborate statues and fountains, and smaller ones on door knockers. They were everywhere.

"Look, there's one up on that flag pole," Alex said, pointing.

"I'm not looking up. These pigeons fly the way the Italians drive," Matthew said.

I was going to instruct Matthew not to generalize, but as I watched the pigeons circling overhead, flying in miscellaneous patterns, sometimes head-to-head, missing each other at the last moment, I realized he had a point.

Instead I said, "There's a really famous *gelateria* near here, but I can't remember the name of it."

Matthew casually strolled off in the direction of a man selling packages of corn kernels to tourists who wanted to feed the pigeons. "I'll find out," he said casually. The boy, who back in the

States was too shy to even make eye contact with an adult, was asking a stranger for directions in perfect Italian.

We followed Matthew, our newly appointed tour guide, over a few streets away from St. Marks square to find the *gelateria*. Alex ordered his second favorite ice cream, *crema*, and Matthew, his *stracciatella*. Bruce sat on the curb next to Alex, coveting his cone, and I sat next to Matthew, coveting his. Both adults needed to heed the 'walka pasta the gelateria' diet after the Christmas season.

"Mom," Matthew said to me softly between licks, "did I ever tell you that from the time I ate that first *stracciatella* ice cream the first week we came to Italy, I knew everything would be all right?"

I sat quietly, quite stunned. I looked around at the glitz of the Venetian stores. In the reflecting colors of Murano glass in every window, I saw flashes of Matthew's anxious face that first day of school, Alex's meltdowns, Bruce 'speaking milk,' my anxiety wondering if I was guiding my family down a courageous, but foolish path in coming here ...

"No," I answered him. "You never told me that, but I thank you for telling me now."

"Why's that?" he asked me, looking much more interested in each isolated chocolate chip than the actual conversation.

"Because," I said, "in a way you've given me a very special gift."

"How's that?" he asked.

"Sometimes parents try to do the right thing for their kids, giving them experiences they think will be fun or useful or will help them grow. Often they never know until their kids are grown if it worked out. When the kids become adults, sometimes they say to their parents, 'This was the worst thing that ever happened to me,' and the parent had no idea it was a bad thing for all that time."

"So, the gift is that you don't have to think about all that stuff, right?" he asked.

"Yeah," I said, "I guess I don't have to think about that stuff anymore."

Matthew was quiet for a moment. Then he offered me his cone. "Want a lick?"

"No, thanks," I said, and hugged him in a way I knew he would be resisting as adolescence creeps in. "I'm already full."

CHAPTER TWENTY-ONE

What Doesn't Kill You Makes You Stronger

You gain strength, courage and confidence by every experience in which you
really stop to look fear in the face. You are able to say to yourself, 'I have lived
through this 'horror.' I can take the next thing that comes along.'
You must do the thing you think you cannot do.
-Eleanor Roosevelt

"I don't know if I want to do gym," Jonathan said as he kissed his mom goodbye. "Play it by ear sweetie," Kathy replied.

Kylee and Jonathan Hansan and their parents were visiting us from our hometown in New York. Brave and curious souls that they are, they decided that if they were permitted, they wanted to spend a day in school with Matthew and Alex.

In the car, Matthew explained the essentials. "If anyone uses the word '*fidanzato*' or '*fidanzata*' in any context," he advised, "just answer, 'no.'"

"Why?" asked Kylee.

"Italian kids are obsessed with knowing if you have a boyfriend or girlfriend," answered Matthew. "I think it's safer. When in doubt, just say no."

Kylee and Jonathan arrived at school to the shouts of cheers from the third and fourth graders.

"*Adesso state zitti sennò li spaventate e se ne tornano subito in America* (Quiet or you'll scare them and they'll want to turn around and go back to America)!" shouted *Maestra* Marta.

Miraculously, the kids quieted down and charged up the stairs to put their backpacks away and take their seats. Kylee brought photos of the school in New York with her and proceeded to explain them.

"This is my school," she said.

"*Questa è' la mia scuola,*" Matthew translated, as calmly and matter-of-factly as if he were on assignment at the United Nations.

"And this is our new library," she continued.

"*Questa è la nostra nuova biblioteca,*" Matthew went on.

Slowly, the Kylee-Matthew team explained who Mrs. Cunningham was, the name of each fourth grade student, and all about the recent construction changes to their school, to a classroom full of children so quiet I wondered if *Maestra* Marta was hiding the real children in the coat closet and replaced them with wax figures. They were so excited; I expected them to be completely out of control.

"This boy looks like you," Kylee said, referring to a boy in the photo and then pointing to Davide, a child in the Italian classroom.

"*Questo ragazzo ti somiglia,*" Matthew translated.

I popped my head into Alex's classroom to see how Jonathan was doing. An Italian student was performing long-division at the blackboard and Jonathan was watching intensely as the boy explained what he was doing in Italian.

"At least the numbers look the same," Jonathan whispered to Alex.

I wondered if Jonathan was getting overwhelmed. "Want me to stay awhile?" I asked him.

"Oh no," he said. "I'm fine." With that, I snapped a few photos and took my leave.

When we picked the kids up at dismissal, a few children in the third grade were just finishing up their cards for Jonathan.

"How do you spell 'Jon-o-ton'?" asked Federico.

"Are they staying here for a year too?" asked Riccardo.

Kylee and Jonathan recapped the day for us in rapid succession.

"It was freaky; I had no idea what everybody was saying," said Kylee. "Everybody came up to me and started to ask me questions in Italian, so I asked Matthew to translate for me. They wanted to know my favorite color, my birthday, my brother's name and lots of other stuff."

"In math, they're learning about grams," Jonathan told me. "They spell 'grams' the same way we do."

"They don't have rugs or pillows or anything. And they don't have a library center in their classroom."

"They don't have an overhead or a white board and they have no projects on the wall."

"They barely ever get up out of their seats except for lunch and recess. It's hard to sit in one place for a long time."

That was an understatement. They were used to a New York classroom where the room was divided into a section for reading on a rug in the corner, a section with math manipulatives in a cubby at the back of the room, and another area overflowing with supplies for art projects to a classroom. Their classroom had an overhead projector, tape recorders and computers. There were maps on the walls, art projects the kids created, and a mock-up of the solar system. The *Varese* classroom followed the minimalist genre of classroom decoration: bare cinderblocks. And whether it was lack of funds, or not wanting to overstimulate the kids, the adjunct accoutrements of the educational environment included desks, chairs, and a blackboard.

"They gave me a lot of presents, like balloons, cards. And the other nice thing is that some of them tried to speak English just for me," said Jonathan. "But I like my school better because I know more people and because at home there's only one thing going on at a time."

Jonathan's comments brought me back to a conversation I had with one of Matthew's teachers. Despite Laura's suggestion that I might want to let the ADD issue slide, rather than bringing it to his teacher's attention, I had, at some point, briefly mentioned it to *Maestra* Marta.

"*Signora* Hummel, don't worry. The Americans invented ADD, but it really doesn't exist."

"Excuse me?"

"It's a matter of convenience, just like the hamburger."

"Like a hamburger ..."

"Yes, you see, with the hamburger, the Americans have taken one simple ingredient, smashed it up into a ball, and they eat it for the speed and convenience of ingestion ..."

"Uh huh ..."

"And in the case of ADD, they took multiple symptoms, lumped them all together and labeled it for similar motives."

"I see."

"Attention 'deficit' is not a 'disorder'. It is a description of a child who doesn't pay attention."

"I ..."

"Children here are not coddled the way they are in America. Italian children have no option but to pay attention. It is the rule."

Our experience in Italy thus far demonstrated that there were some things about the American culture that the Italians adored, like our music, our films, and our more casual and free lifestyle. There were some things they didn't accept or appreciate at all, like our gun control policy or hamburgers. And there were some things that they genuinely believed that the Americans made up. Until that moment, the only subject I knew of that fit into this latter category was the 1969 lunar landing – something that several Italians told us they suspected was staged by the Americans in Hollywood. Now, I knew of a second subject for that category: ADD.

But long story short, as Jonathan's comment demonstrated, the *Varese* classroom environment never changed. But as it turns out, Matthew did. He somehow figured out a way to adapt to his environment. Either he was shielding out the noise and confusion, or he figured out another coping mechanism to deal with it. Either way, his language acquisition increased gradually, he was understanding his studies, and to use his words, he did seem "OK" In fact, the child labeled "ADD" was having in depth conversations with Giampiero and Tommaso about the differences and similarities between President Bush and Prime Minister Berlusconi, IN ITALIAN !!!

"*Ma, io non lo so,*" Matthew said. "*Secondo me, sono tutti e due uguali* (In my opinion, they're both the same)."

"*In che senso* (In what sense)?"

"*Nel senso che pensano più a se stessi che al popolo* (In the sense that they think more about themselves than about the people)."

"*Eh si, noi siamo abituati ai politici ricchi che pensano solo ai propri suoi interessi* (Ah, yes, we're accustomed to rich politicians who care only about their own interests)."

"*Mi sono proprio stufato* (I'm really sick of it)."

Based on his voiced political views, Susanna dubbed him "*il piccolo Michael Moore,*" the little Michael Moore.

In November, despite the crazy environment he was dealing with, we had decided to do a trial of no medication. And he still seemed fine. Christmas came and went and still no regression. He became more and more fluent and seemed to be absorbing his school material. By *Carnivale*, he had grown from a timid, insecure little boy into a social, confident young man — almost before our eyes. As time moved on, we began to see that Matthew's self-proclaimed OKness was an objective reality. Not only was he coping, he was thriving. He could recite complicated issues in Italian about the history he was learning. He was absorbing advanced concepts of Italian grammar, some of which his Italian classmates were not absorbing. He was performing mathematical calculations under the metric system without difficulty, something he had not yet been exposed to in the States. He was having no trouble with concentration. His teachers were thrilled with his progress.

During the winter, Matthew took a makeup test. When I arrived to help with a scheduled class project, he was still hard at work. He was sitting at his desk. His teacher was speaking to another teacher. Some of the children were talking to each other, one was sitting on the windowsill, another crawled under Matthew's desk to retrieve a small ball he was rolling on the floor with a classmate. It was noisy. Very noisy. And distractions were everywhere. Matthew was examining the test questions on the pre-printed form and then calmly writing the answers. His eyes moved slowly and methodically from the test form to his paper. He worked consistently and quietly, without even noticing the turmoil around him. The scene left me speechless. That afternoon, in *Varese*, Matthew's teacher walked by to look at the creative writing portion of his test. She read it, smiled, and handed me the page:

I Pensieri Che Rimbalzano
Di Matthew Hummel

Erano le sei di mattina
Nel Grand Canyon.
Il tempo freddo mi lasciava da solo
Con I miei pensieri,
Senza turisti.
Potevo sentire
Il rumore del mio respiro.

Tutto quello che pensavo o dicevo
Sembrava rimbalzare
Sui muri meravigliosi
Mentre il sole si saliva
Nel cielo.

Thoughts that Bounce
By Matthew Hummel

It was six in the morning
in the Grand Canyon.
The cold weather left me alone
with my thoughts
without tourists.
I could hear
the sound of my breath.
All that I have thought and said
seemed to be bouncing
off these marvelous walls
as the sun rose in the sky.

Matthew had never been to the Grand Canyon.

What is ADD, anyway? And how did Matthew's symptoms disappear in an environment which, by all logical reasoning, should have augmented the symptoms? Why was he focusing, concentrating, and thriving in a way that he did not in an American classroom that was clearly more functional and where the modalities of teaching were more diverse than anything he was experiencing in the Italian school system? It's impossible to know, but for Matthew, it seemed that his symptoms were relieved by having to survive the intensity of his transition. He was so highly challenged, perhaps almost to a saturation point, with learning a new language, trying to understand his surroundings in terms of verbal and non-verbal cues, and adapting to a new culture, that it is almost as if he didn't have time for ADD.

Jonathan was spot on; it was easier when one thing *was* going on at a time. But for Matthew, leaving his friends behind and entering a new school without speaking the language, was undoubtedly the most difficult thing he had ever done in his 10 years of life. The fact that he survived the transition, maintained his New York friendships through email and telephone, made new friends in Italy, and learned to speak Italian fluently simply by "showing up" every day, gave him a confidence that he had never known. One night before bed, a few weeks before we left America, he told me, "I would give up everything I have, including video games, to have confidence." In effect he had. He gave up everything familiar, everything known to him, and because I was powerless to micromanage the situation, he faced something on his own that was stupendously difficult for him. In surviving, he "bought" himself confidence. At home, he couldn't write the simplest creative school writing assignment. In Italy, he asked for more paper and continued to write way beyond what anyone requested of him. In New York, it was agony to get him to read 10 minutes a night. In Italy, it was difficult to get him to turn off the light at night when reading time was over. For Matthew, the act of surviving what seemed insurmountable made the rest of life seem easy. His success in something so difficult gave him confidence regarding other aspects of his life that seemed more commonplace, and it had a self fulfilling effect. As each day went by that he survived, he had more evidence of his worth. That feeling of self-worth grew and grew and turned itself into another success and then another, day after day.

I don't know what happened to the ADD symptoms. Are they gone? Did they just go underground? Will they return when we go back to the States and Matthew isn't the unwitting participant of a survival-of-the-fittest experiment? I didn't have a crystal ball. I wasn't prepared to agree with *Maestra* Marta that ADD was a hamburger, but I was prepared to keep my mind open to the possibility that in the same way our fast food days disappeared, maybe Matthew's ADD had too.

CHAPTER TWENTY-TWO

It is Only a Matter of Time Before the Student Becomes the Teacher

When the student is ready ... the lesson appears.
-Gene Oliver

Easter was right around the corner and Chiara started to crawl on Good Friday, just in time to show off in front of Laura's brother who was coming in for the holidays from Rome. Bruce and I wanted to use the time off from school to travel, but Alex wanted to be home for the Easter Bunny. As far as I knew there was no Italian Easter Bunny, mouse, or even a chicken that was supposed to bring a basket of treats to kids in Italy, so we decided to spend the holiday in the region of *Campania*. We heard that this part of Italy, *Napoli* and environs, was an especially traditional place to spend Easter, and Bruce and I were eager to experience it. Before leaving we tried to color eggs as is our usual practice, but by the time we remembered that only brown eggs were sold in *Lombardia*, we didn't have time to cross the border into Switzerland, where both varieties were sold.

"What's Easter without coloring eggs?" Alex lamented.

"Take it easy crying-baby-whiner," Matthew said. "By this time next year we'll be saying, 'What's Christmas without *panettone*?' Let's just try something new."

I described for the kids the famous Amalfi drive and distracted them with a story of my stupidity when I was young. An old boyfriend and I had traveled all the way from Rome to Amalfi by *autostrada* (highway) without helmets or jackets in the pouring rain and continued our journey the entire length of the Amalfi drive, one of the most dangerous roads in the world.

"Why is it so dangerous?" asked Alex, his eyes widening.

"Because there are tremendous curves, and it's high on a cliff, with a dazzling, distracting view of the sea," I said dramatically, holding my hands in front of me as if I were steering the motorcycle and turning the imaginary wheel drastically from side to side.

"Vrrooooom!" said Alex, mimicking me. "Matthew, let's play the motorcycle game," he added, and they were off, Matthew taking the role of the motorcycle, Alex behind him as the driver, steering him around the living room.

"Don't EVER let me see you on a motorcycle without a helmet," I called after them.

Our first stop was *Napoli* (Naples) and I had heard a lot about the *Napolitani*. I was told that they had the more laid-back attitude of southern Italians, yet they were also apparently famous for the 'extra.' They gave it freely, gushing to every passing baby carriage, offering tastes of local cheeses to strolling tourists, pinching your cheek to say hello, even inviting perfect strangers for dinner. But they also evidently took a lot of extra too. By that I mean that I was told that *Napoli* was as full of thieves as it was of generous, open-hearted souls, and we should plan accordingly. As I lived the greater part of my life relatively close to a metropolitan area, I was confident that I was adequately street savvy.

We took a commuter flight to *Napoli* and rented a car. The drive from the airport to the historic center was a *pazienza* odyssey. Every street corkscrewed and every other street was one way, although that seemed to be relevant to only a certain percentage of the drivers. Traffic lights were of absolutely no assistance because they were all but ignored by the locals. We edged out at every corner, accelerated, braked, prayed for our front bumper, and proceeded with white knuckles.

"Everyone has their seatbelt on, right?" I shouted to the back seat.

"Yes, Mom, for the FOURTH time," Matthew yelled back.

At that moment, a Vespa driven by an adult, loaded with three children behind, whisked by us on the sidewalk.

"Holy *merda*!"

"Mom! Watch your language!"

By the grace of the patron saint of *Napoli* (whoever he or she was) we found a pay-parking lot near the center. We were told to choose that kind of lot and to tip the attendant generously. As I shelled out euros to the attendant, he put his index finger to the corner of his eye,

"*Occhio* ..." he said. "Pay attention, particularly on the bus."

"Right, OK, thank you," I told him. I heard that too, before leaving *Varese*. The buses were notoriously crowded, a perfect feeding ground for pick pockets.

We needed to ask several times to find the bus stop that took us to the *Piazza Museo Nazionale* to see the *Museo Archeologico Nazionale.* We had only a few hours before we needed to move on to *Ravello*, our ultimate base for Easter week.

"Be careful on the *autobus*," said the lady who gave us our third set of directions.

"We really need to pay attention on the bus," I told Bruce.

"I understood," he answered.

At the bus stop, I asked an elderly woman which bus went to the *Piazza Museo Nazionale.*

"That's my bus," she told us. "You get on when I get on."

When her bus arrived, we followed her.

"Take this seat, *signora*," I told her, gesturing to an empty seat in front of me.

"No," she told me, gesturing to Bruce with her cane. "You tell your husband to take off his back pack and have him sit here."

I shrugged and Bruce sat. As the bus lumbered through the narrow alleys of the ancient city, swaying precariously around the corners and blasting through intersections no wider, it seemed, than an arm's length, all we could glimpse was flash after flash of laundry hanging in the warm breeze. The staccato of light, motion and rocketing velocity was a dizzying swirl. To the left of the bus, a Vespa was trying to squeeze past, alternately avoiding oncoming traffic, roaming pedestrians and parked cars. When it couldn't, it simply rode on the sidewalk and passed to the right amidst passengers embarking and exiting the bus, oblivious to the wild hand gesturing and cursing of the bus driver and passengers.

At our stop, the *signora* gestured for us to leave.

"*Attenta,*" she said.

"*Si, grazie e arrivederla,*" I responded.

There was a tremendous amount of pushing toward the exit. I held Matthew by one hand and Alex by the other. Bruce held his backpack in front of him. We had been adequately warned. Once we debarked, we tried to get our bearings. I could see an edifice in the distance that resembled the photo of the museum I saw in a guide book. Then I felt a tap on my shoulder.

"*Signora,*" a young woman said. "Have your husband check his pockets. Someone had their hands in them as you were exiting."

Sure enough, she was right. Bruce's wallet had been zippered in the breast pocket of his jacket, but his loose change went the way of the *Napolitani* pickpocket.

"What?!" I cried. "But we were being so vigilant!"

"I didn't feel anything ..." Bruce mumbled.

"Thank you *signora*," I said, kissing both her cheeks.

She smiled. "Be careful," she said, "*e Buona Pasqua.*"

"Can we stop somewhere and just regroup?" I asked Bruce. I was already exhausted by the drive and bus ride alone.

"Let's stop for a pizza," he suggested, motioning to one on the corner. "Everyone keeps saying it's the best in the world here."

"It's the best in the world because that's where pizza was invented, Dad," Alex added then turning to Matthew said, "*Maestra* Alma taught me that."

Maestra Alma was not exaggerating one bit. We sat a few meters away from the pizzeria's wood stove. The chef was moving at about 100 kilometers an hour. A pizza in, a pizza out, a pizza turned, a pizza checked, all in front of an oven whose flame was as hot as Hades. Four *pizze margherite*. We were told by Giampiero to keep it simple in order to savor the delicacy of the crust. We asked him what made the pizza so different.

"Everything," he told us. "It's the temperature of the oven, even the difference in the water, the technique of making crust without yeast."

"How do they do that?"

"I have no idea."

Whatever magical process took place, it was the most incredible pizza we had ever tasted.

Rested and full, we headed off to the museum. It was filled with artifacts of Pompeii and Herculeum.

"Are we going to see any of these 'brokens' in Pompeii?" Alex asked me.

"They're not called 'brokens,'" I said. "They're called 'fallen down rocks.' And, yes, we are ..."

The one hall we wanted to see, one that we heard contained the most precious artifacts, was closed. There was a guard standing at the entrance, a rope closing off the area.

"I was wondering ..." I said tentatively. "The sign in the entrance said this gallery was open."

"*Ormai è chiuso* (At this point, it's closed)," he told me.

We were disappointed but without significant regret. It was wonderful to get such a nice overview of Pompeii before going there later in the week

By the time we finished our walking tour we were exhausted, so we hailed a taxi to return us to our own car. The results of the *Moto Gran Premio*, a motorcycle race, were blaring on the radio.

"Rossi again," Matthew lamented, gesturing as if he himself had been born in *Napoli*.

"I'll bet Gibernau came in second," said Alex. "He always comes in second in Germany. He loves that track, but he always gets nervous around the last turn."

"You're quite the experts," the taxi driver marveled.

"*E cosa avete visto nella nostra bella città* (And what have you seen of our beautiful city)?" he then asked, turning to Bruce and me. "The *Museo Archeologico Nazionale*," I told him, "but one of the principle galleries was closed."

"Was there a guard standing outside?" he asked.

"Yes, there was ..."

"You needed to tip him," he informed me.

"Aha ..."

"It's a beautiful city," he continued, waving the one hand that had been holding the steering wheel. "But it's a punishment to live here at the same time. Nothing functions as it should."

I nodded, wishing he'd use his free hand to talk.

"Furthermore," he said as we careened through a red light for the third time in six minutes, "no one stops at the red lights. It drives me crazy."

Bruce gripped the door handle as we skidded through a screeching left turn.

"I'll tell you another big problem," he added in an accent so strong I could barely understand him. "The *Camorra*. You probably have read about them. You know, like the *Mafia*. You can't do anything without their say-so. For example, you know the health care here is included in our taxes, right? Wrong. Not in *Napoli*. In *Napoli*, when a woman gives birth to a baby in a hospital, she has to pay the *Camorra* doctor, the *Camorra* nurse, and the *Camorra* hospital. You don't have money? You better not get sick in *Napoli*. Everybody has some kind of clever thing going. I remember one day I bought a box of nuts and when I got home I realized they were full of rocks. Can you believe that? Rocks!!! *Che furbi* (What sneaks)!"

"But I'll tell you something else," he said, "Being *furbo* also means being able to think on your feet. When I applied once for a job in Rome, the man who interviewed me asked me where I was from. I said, 'I come from *Napoli*, city of great soccer players and great prostitutes' and he said, 'My wife is from *Napoli*.' And I said, 'Oh really, what position does she play?' Not bad, huh? Thinking on your feet. We're famous for it."

As he turned into the parking lot, we thanked him and gave him a generous tip for the entertainment.

Having determined that our car and the possessions inside, were still intact, I tipped the parking attendant again and we were off.

"How long will it take us to get down to the Amalfi Coast."

"*Beh,*" he said, holding his hand diagonally in front of his body and moving it up and down horizontally in a motion that I later recognized was the gesture that indicates that it was anyone's guess. "*Diciamo un oretta* (Let's say about an hour)," he said.

We made the one hour drive in a mere two and a half hours. As we winded around the *Costiera Amalfitana* (the Amalfi Coast) I reminisced about the last time I was there more than two decades ago. The fog-silhouetted hills and terraced crops of lemon trees came back to me, as did the famous drive that, without your total attention, had you plunging off the cliff and into the sea below.

"Mom, I want to suggest keeping over as far to the right as possible," Matthew said after the third car out of 10 came around the corner taking more than its share of the road.

"I am in perfect agreement," I answered, and slowed down a bit which irritated the driver behind me, to the point that he passed me around the next curve, narrowly missing the oncoming car.

We arrived at the cusp of the spring season, so we were a bit too early to appreciate the colorful explosion of blossoms I remembered from years ago. But in doing so, we also bypassed the intense crowds and traffic that bloom along with the flowers beginning right after Easter. This fortuitous timing also coincided with the *Settimana Santa*, the holy week preceding Easter. It was the most reverent week of the Roman Catholic holidays and we were excited to have the opportunity to experience the pageantry of *Giovedi Santo* (Holy Thursday), including *Lavanda dei piedi* (the washing of feet), symbolic of the day and the procession that followed.

We chose as our base *Ravello*, a village in the hills above the *Amalfi* drive, which we knew to be less hurried than the coastal cities of *Amalfi* and *Positano*, and more accessible to other destinations, such as Pompeii and *Napoli*s. By the time we settled into our hotel, it was the hour of *aperitivo.* We decided to take in the ambience of the central *piazza* which included the church, *La Chiesa dell'Annunziata*, renowned for its immense bronze doors dating from 1179 that depict scenes of Christ's death and resurrection. There, in the *piazza*, beyond the signs warning of "no ball playing, no bicycling, no rollerblading and no scootering," we sat outside at the local bar and watched Matthew and Alex join 10-

year-old resident Enrico and his friends, playing ball, bicycle riding, rollerblading and scootering.

Through the happy din, I could already hear the Taz screaming plaintively for the group to pass him the ball. "*Passami!*"

As the children got to know each other, we began to talk to the owner of the bar, Enrico's Uncle Luigi. "It's such a beautiful, tranquil setting," I said to him as he brought us a glass of *pinot grigio*. "All the kids seem to get along so well."

"We're practically all related," he told me. "See that shop over there? The one that sells ceramics. She's my cousin. The travel agent around the corner? That's her husband. Then there's Vincenzo ..."

What followed was an explanation of their extended family, as well as another glass of *pinot grigio*. It turned out that Mario, Luigi's cousin, owned a tour company specializing in planning weddings on the *Amalfi* coast, but also organized just about any other kind of tour you can imagine. Mario's wife is Paola. She's the one who owns the ceramics store next to the bar. Vincenzo, Mario's brother-in-law, teaches cooking classes out of his private home, situated on a cliff top 350 meters above sea level. After many years as a chef and owner of a restaurant in *Ravello*, Vincenzo developed a cooking school where, he says, people can cook and eat "with the heart and not just the mouth." Luigi's description of his brother-in-law's classes sounded so enticing. First, he takes his students to some of the little food shops located in the historic alleys of *Ravello*. Speaking Italian and English, he introduces his students to the shop owners, an explanation of how the locals choose their wine and vegetables follows. Together, they decide the menu, according to the season and tastes of all gathered. Finally, they proceed with the hands-on preparation of the meal, from *aperitivo* and wine, past il *primo* and *il secondo,* and finally to dessert and *espresso*. If the weather cooperates, as it so often does in *Ravello*, his students will eat on the terrace, their culinary experience enhanced by the spectacular view of the Mediterranean.

All of our days in *Ravello* were memorable, but the most memorable, by far was the night of *Giovedì Santo* (Holy Thursday). At 9:30 p.m., after the 8 p.m. mass, the town assembled in the main *piazza* in front of *La Chiesa dell'Annunziata*. The principle figures in the procession were men dressed in long white hooded robes. During holy week, the statue of Christ's body on the crucifix was covered by a cloth indicating that he had been sacrificed. The Friday before Easter his image was laid to rest. For now, the townspeople followed the official mourners through the streets, up to the hills, stopping at each church in *Ravello*, and periodically in the cobblestoned alleys, to chant mournfully, and with dissidence, their soulful lament.

"These guys look like the KKK," Matthew whispered.

"Maybe that's where they got the idea," Alex answered, and I laughed nervously in spite of myself, having mentally made a similar observation.

The mourners continued their lament. It was as if they were grieving for one of their own friends or relatives that recently passed away.

"Wow, they really miss him," Alex told me.

"Miss who?" I asked.

"Jesus," he said.

I nodded and we followed the townspeople into the night.

On Saturday, while local families prepared for the festivities of Easter, we visited Pompeii. Even as early as spring, the air was uncomfortably dry and hot. I was immediately transported back to my childhood holidays spent wandering around the ruins of Rome and Sicily and Pompeii, too, with my dad. If it was this hot in April, it must really have been as stifling as I remembered it in August.

The kids had a reasonable attention span, given the conditions. They were stunned, in particular, by the images of people who had been overcome by the toxic plumes of gas, and then lava and volcanic ash as they slept in their beds. Some remained in the fetal position of what was to be an eternal slumber. The boys were less impressed with the fact that an entire buried city had been discovered, parts of which were still intact.

"You can call it what you want, Mom," said Alex. "It's still broken."

Some things never change ...

Easter morning arrived and the kids were relieved that the Easter Bunny somehow was able to make his journey over the Atlantic and managed to find the two little American boys living in *Varese* and vacationing in *Ravello*. He was a smart little bunny; no one could question that.

We had our Easter dinner at an *agriturismo*, a farm in a hillside community. It wasn't by any means the same thing as having Easter dinner at home with grandparents, aunts and uncles, nor were there any painted eggs, but it was a cozy family environment and we enjoyed watching the other families who gathered at tables in the courtyard in order to be together in large numbers. The *agriturismo* seemed to be an extension of their own dining room, just as the *oratorio* was an extension of the Italian living room.

The Italians have an expression, "*Natale con i tuoi; Pasqua con chi vuoi* (Christmas at home; Easter with whomever you wish)." Susanna explained that it wasn't an expression that had any religious significance, it was just demonstrative of the fact that families spent Christmas close to the hearth, but with the advent of spring and the will to spread one's wings, one could decide where, how and with whom to celebrate Easter. So I guess we were in tune with cultural custom.

Our dinner was served outside on the terrace, under a *pergola*. There was a poem in *Napolitano* dialect on each table:

La Pasqua Napoletana

Pasca vo' 'a menestrella maretata
cu 'a gallenella, 'a 'nnoglia e 'e saciccielle,
'll'ainiello a 'o furno, 'o ppoco 'e spezzatiello.
'a felluccia 'e ricotta e e' supressata.
Quatt'ova toste na cimm' 'e nzalata,
Na carcioffola e 'o fiasco 'e marainiello;
Po', se sape, 'a pastiera, 'o casatiello,
'a pres 'e roce e na pres arraggiata.

G. Fico

Easter cries for a soup in which wedded are
Pork, and sausage;
roast lamb and a bit of stew;
A slice of ricotta and one of *soprassata*;
Four hard-boiled eggs and a head of salad;
An artichoke and a flask of Maraniello wine;
And, of course, *pastiera* and *casatiello*;
A shot of liqueur sweet and a shot fiery.

Apparently Easter was "crying" loud and clear in *Ravello*, because the food just kept arriving. First served was an antipasto of roasted artichokes and cheeses we never before tasted. This was followed by *lasagna verde*. Roast lamb followed that, and then *insalata* with hard-boiled eggs. The *vino del luogo* flowed freely, and the desserts were plentiful. I chose a pie with a ricotta cream, an obscene delight which I was quite certain hadn't made the pages of any diet recipe book anywhere in the world.

The following day we made our way back to the airport in *Napoli*. When we returned the car, the clerk informed us that they could not honor the original price.

"Why is that?" I asked.

"Well, *signora*, for some reason, your credit card company cancelled the original reservation. Therefore, when you picked up the car, we calculated the price based on updated prices."

"My credit card company wouldn't do that," I said, bewildered.

"I don't know what to tell you, *signora*. I can only tell you what's in the computer."

"I'm sorry you're having difficulty," I said calmly. "We'll wait while you figure it out."

She looked at me, and then at her keyboard, and then began clicking away.

"What about 420 euro? *Va bene?*" she asked.

"*No, non va bene*," I answered. "That's 80 euros more than the guaranteed price in my contract."

More clicking.

"*380 euro, va bene?*"

"*No, non va bene,*" I said again, even more calmly this time.

"*Va bene signora allora devi aspettare un po* (OK *signora,* then you'll have to wait a bit)," she mumbled. Finally, after about 1,000 key strokes on her computer, she came up with the price originally written on my contract. I left, shaking my head.

"Amazing," I said. "It's just like everyone says, they really are *furbi!*"

"Mom, I'm really surprised at you," Matthew said.

"Why's that?"

"What about the guy where we parked the car near the center of *Napoli* when we first got here? He was nice," said Alex.

"And the old lady on the bus," Matthew said.

"And the young one at the bus stop."

"And the ..."

"OK, OK, I get it!" I said.

"You're always telling us, 'you can't judge a whole group of people by the actions of a few,'" Alex said, wagging his finger at me and mimicking the tone of my voice.

"I guess it was only a matter of time before the student becomes the teacher," I told them.

"Is that going to be another one of your expressions?" Matthew asked.

"I think it just might be ..." I looked at Bruce. By his smile I knew he was enjoying the moment as much as I was.

If they went back to the States having learned another language, as well as the message of not generalizing about any one population, the journey was well worth the trip.

CHAPTER TWENTY-THREE

Talk the Talk. Walk the Walk

And since you know you cannot see yourself,
so well as by reflection, I, your glass,
will modestly discover to yourself,
that of yourself which you yet know not of.
-William Shakespeare

There was sadness in the air. The news channels were buzzing with the fact that the Pope was gravely ill. His presence and fame as a "pope of the people" was obvious to us from our first few weeks of Italian life. We knew that the thought of his passing was difficult for a majority of the Italian population, but we had no idea just how significantly his steadily declining health would affect everyday life. Laura and Francesca stopped by the *Chiesa San Vittore* at least once a day to say a short prayer. Adriano's bar wasn't buzzing with the usual soccer scandal, erroneous referee call or stolen tournament. The tone of Tiziana's greeting at the *pasticieria* which always started with "*Ciao gioia* (Hello, joyous one)" did not match the communicated words.

In the *Piazza San Pietro* in Rome, more than 100,000 people gathered on Friday, periodically clapping in a slow, methodical fashion to let him know they were with him, standing vigil, imploring *Dio* for his salvation. In *Varese* and throughout Italy, thousands were glued to their television sets. The beep on my cell phone, an SMS indicating the receipt of a text message, sounded fairly continuously throughout the day from Friday morning through Saturday night. Messages of weekend plans cancelled and vigil messages passing from friends. On Friday my phone contained a message passed on from Laura's brother: "*Questo SMS parte da Roma. Lasciate la luce accesa fuori della porta, come segno d'amore e preghiera per il Papa. Manda questo SMS a un altra persona. Non fermarlo.* (This SMS started in Rome. Leave the light on outside your door as a symbol of love and prayer for the Pope. Send this SMS to another person. Don't stop it.)" This was not a joke; a blatant waste of electricity. The Stragapedes and most Italians we knew lived in relative darkness except for the most minimal use of light necessary in the room they occupied at any given moment, and here they were leaving a light on outside in broad daylight.

On the Friday prior to the Pope's death, the Vatican announced that Giovanni Paolo II's respirations were shallow. From that point on, although the *fruttivendolo, pasticciera*, Adriano's bar, and most shops in the *centro* remained open, each of them could probably have given you an up to the minute account of the Pope's pulse rate at any given time of the day. The differentiation between the word *Papa* (Pope) and the word *papà* (father) in Italian is an accent over the last letter "a" and apparently, for many Italians, this difference was only a technical distinction. Churches in every *piazza* of *Varese* were opened around the clock to give worshippers the opportunity to pray.

O Dio, nostro Padre, che nel tuo Figlio Ci hai riaperto la porta della salvezza, infondi in noi la sapienza dello Spirito, Perché fra le insidie del mondo sappiamo riconoscere la voce di Cristo, Buon Pastore, che ci dona l'abbondanza della vita. Egli è Dio, e vive e regna ... Amen

Oh God, our father, who, in your Son, opened for us again the door of salvation, do give unto us the knowledge of the Holy Spirit so that we can, amidst all the pitfalls in this world, recognize the voice of Christ, Good Shepherd, who gives us the abundance of life. He is God, and lives and reigns ... Amen

On Saturday, Laura called to tell us he had died.

"When did it happen?" I asked her.

" 9:37 p.m." she said with the utmost precision.

I snapped on the television. The cameras showed an aerial view of *San Pietro* at the Vatican where thousands had been gathering shoulder to shoulder for days. The sounds had progressed from the methodical clapping used to show their solidarity with him each day that his health declined, to the sobs and chanting that signified his passing. The Pope could no longer hear the earthly sounds of his parishioners.

"I'll bet you tomorrow's game is going to be cancelled," Matthew offered.

Sure enough, within minutes, the SMS on my telephone read, *Domani tutto sospeso in segno di lutto* (Tomorrow everything will be suspended as a symbol of grief).

"I'm really sorry and all, but I don't see why we can't play baseball," Matthew told us.

"Yea," Alex echoed, "I mean if he's really as nice as everyone says he is, he'd probably want us to play baseball. I mean, I bet he even liked baseball. He's not the kind of guy to say, 'go be sad and cancel your game.'"

"Actually, you might not be that far off in your assessment," I told them. "This Pope, maybe more than any other in history, had a reputation for promoting children's needs."

In the contagious spirit of concern during the days prior to his death, I had read quite a bit about what this "guy" represented. I explained to the kids that he was the first non-Italian Pope to be elected since 1523. I told them that he was kind of like them in that he wasn't afraid to cross geographic boundaries to make friends with other people. I explained that he was credited by the Italian people as having had a major role in the collapse of communism in Eastern Europe, and that he spoke openly about social and economic problems. They did listen quietly for awhile before grabbing their mitts and going off to practice for the next big game; I guess that "guy" would have wanted it that way.

The intensity of the atmosphere surrounding the decline of the Pope's health led me to examine my own religious beliefs. I was raised Catholic, but other than attending Sunday school for a year or two, our family never attended church regularly. One day at Sunday school a nun had asked me why I hadn't been to class for several weeks and I explained that my mother was in the hospital and wouldn't let us cross the busy street from school to church. "That's no excuse," she told me. I stormed out with a flippant, "I thought you said to honor thy mother and father, you ... you ..." and that was the end of my church-going days.

Over the years, and especially in my teens and 20s, I had difficulties expressing exactly what I "believed." I was OK with the fact that a guy with long hair and sandals by the name of Jesus existed, and that he was a teacher of all that was good and kind, but I wasn't overly enamored with what I read about the politics of the Catholic church over the centuries, or for that matter, any organized religion, really. And I didn't believe Jesus had any miraculous powers, other than that of love.

I often prayed as a young person but not really to any particular entity. My prayers were to some higher and more powerful force that in some way governed our collective universe, and often involved hoping that a particular boy would pay more attention to me. Later in life, the lack of a traditional belief system made it difficult to find spiritual community. I didn't want to "belong" to any one religious institute; I did, however, want to "belong." I wanted to belong to other people where I lived and I wanted them to belong to me.

In actuality, I found the Catholic church in Italy to be more in line with my thinking. I was being stupefied when Alex came home from school one day and showed me that he was studying the evolution of man. I thought that this theory was in direct contradiction with the teachings of the church. One day when I picked up the kids from a birthday party at the *oratorio*, I asked Father Paolo how that teaching could be permitted in a school that was so connected with the church.

"Meaning what?" he asked me.

"Meaning that teaching the theory of evolution is in direct contradiction with the fact that God created man in his image and that the whole process took seven days."

He looked at me with a perplexed expression while composing his response. "*Signora*, that was a metaphor," he told me, his lips curled in a soft smile.

My thinking during this somber experience of the death of a great religious leader, focused on whether I was creating a spiritual, or at least, a soulful life for the kids at home. Was I modeling for them the teachings of Jesus, of Buddha, of other great spiritual leaders? Did my words and actions demonstrate compassion, caring and understanding? I vowed to be more introspective and observant of my own behavior, and not let this moment of reflection become nothing more than a passing thought.

In the next few weeks, conversation in the bar shifted from grief to the complicated process of the election of a new Pope. Aldo, with a surprising depth of knowledge beyond the confines of his role as barber, explained how the cardinal electors would enter the conclave to choose the next holy Roman pontiff.

As Matthew ate his brioche, adding chocolate fingerprints to the coveted *Gazzetta dello Sport*, Aldo competed with the soccer scores for Matthew's attention, in an attempt to explain to him the formality and significance of the process.

"They can't have any contact with the outside world: no mobile phones, no newspapers or television, no messages or letters or signals to observers. They will be visible to the public twice daily when they walked from the *Domus Sanctae Marthae* to the Sistine Chapel and back again. You can watch it on television," Then he winked at me. "After the *Juventus* match, of course."

Aldo was right, the media was buzzing with Vatican "experts" who interpreted the facial expressions and demeanor of the electors as they moved to and from the chapel. But it took no special expertise to understand the sentiments of the Italian people. Giovanni Paolo II was their *Papa*, he was gone, and he would be sorely missed.

That evening, we were checking email while the kids were getting ready for bed. The nightly call from Alex came. "*Mamma, papà, devi* snoogolare!" – we had invented our own Italian verb for snuggling.

Hurrying to finish at the computer, we could hear Alex and Matthew talking.

"*Mi sembrava veramente una buona persona,*" Alex said. He was telling Matthew that someone, I didn't know whom, seemed like a really good person.

"*É proprio vero,*" Matthew responded, "*Si vede dagli occhi.*" Matthew agreed and said that you could see it in that person's eyes.

"*Ci sono le persone come il Papa che vivono la loro vita in modo giusto, e ci sono quelli che parlano, parlano, parlano, e vivono in modo completamente diverso da quello che stanno dicendo,*" said Alex. He felt that there were people like the Pope that lived their lives in a just way, and those that just talked and talked and talked and lived in a way completely different from all that they talk about.

What will these little hearts say about us when they are grown? I had no confirmation through eavesdropping.

"Mom, Dad, snuggle!!!" Alex said in a raised voice.

But I was glad to know they were contemplating the issue.

"Say a prayer for the Pope, Mom," Matthew said when I entered the room.

So I did ...

CHAPTER TWENTY-FOUR

There Are Always Several Ways to See the Same Set of Facts

Do not follow where the path may lead.
Go instead where there is no path and leave a trail.
-Harold R. McAlindon

"Your children have won the *Premio*," *Maestra* Alma told us.

"Excuse me?"

"The *Premio*," she repeated. "It's the award the mayor of *Varese* gives every April 25 at a public ceremony, in celebration of the *Festa della Liberazione.*"

"And that would be for ..." I hesitated, wondering if it were, perhaps, for the children of foreign families that create the most trouble that year.

"It is given to one child in each of the third, fourth and fifth grades who demonstrates an exceptional academic record, class participation and an extraordinary will to learn."

"This is a practical joke, right?" Bruce spurted.

"The children voted and we teachers approved," she responded calmly. "They literally went from zero to 100. They had no language skills whatsoever when they came, and now are excelling in every subject. It happened because they are intelligent boys, of course, but just as importantly, because their minds were so open. They absorbed knowledge like a sponge absorbs water."

Quietly, I reminisced about all the difficulty and challenges the academic year brought. All the conversations and frustrations of adapting to an educational system and a way of interacting between parent and educator that I hadn't understood.

"It's your victory too," I sniffled.

At home later that day it was like a Hummel family crying *festa*. Bruce and I hugged and kissed them, sobbed and stuffed them full of *gelato*.

"Forget about homework; we're going out to celebrate. How about another ice cream?"

"Dad, I'm gonna puke," Alex said.

I marveled at my academically 'superior' son, "Good thing you haven't forgotten how to speak English," I smirked.

"What exactly is this celebration about?" I asked Laura the following day.

"It's about the day the *partigiani* (partisans) liberated the north of Italy from the *fasciste* (fascists)" she told me. "Our family will always remember that day because my father, who was 18 years old at the time, repeatedly told me about the generosity of the American soldiers when they liberated this region. They gave the children chewing gum and chocolate, which for some of them was the very first thing they had eaten in days, and they tasted that sweetness in their mouths decades later, as if they were tasting it for the first time."

Her explanation took me back to my conversation with the old man at the *edicola* that first morning in *Varese*, where he told me not to make excuses for my nationality and declared that the Americans had liberated the Italians from fascism. For days after the announcement, parents stopped us at school.

"You should be so proud," said a woman who I recognized as a teacher in the second grade.

"What an honor," said another, pinching Alex's cheek.

"*Incredibile!*" Enea raved.

"*Fantastico,*" from a parent I had never met.

Domenico and Laura stood around the boys, expanded chests, straightened posture, glowing as if they themselves were their parents. I wondered if Francesca might be jealous or put off, but she seemed to be just as pleased.

Giampiero, our resident historian, helped us to understand the significance of the day and the irony that two little Americans had won the award.

"Historically, the process of liberation began in the south and crept slowly northward until the Nazis finally were expelled. *Varese* was among the last cities to be liberated. Many of the *Varesini* who lived through the experience were grateful to the Americans for working with the Italian *partigiani* – they were partisans – to liberate their country."

Having no discernable response from Matthew and Alex, he moved into Giampiero animation mode. "The battles were fierce. Machine gun fire echoed off the stone buildings. Ra-ta-ta-ta! Boom! See those indentations there?" he said, pointing to chunks of stone missing from the campanile, "They are permanent reminders of the pain of that era."

Now he had their attention.

"On April 25, 1945, in the wee hours of the morning, the *partigiani* received news from Radio London that liberation was imminent," he continued. "The *Varesini* braced for the worse and prayed for the best. Seven days earlier, their countrymen in Milano programmed a *sciopero* (a strike), which completely shut down the factories, transportation, stores, everything, demonstrating to the fascists that if they did not retreat, they would be met with complete and total insurrection. Street by street, the Milanese *partigiani*, inspired by the success of the nearby American troops, expelled the Germans."

Matthew and Alex were transfixed.

"You are now part of that moment. When you receive that award, you will become a part of *Varese* history."

Bruce and I listened, immobilized, and caught up in the energy of the moment as if one of the Nazis could come bolting out from behind the *chiesa*.

"On that famous day, Mussolini called from Milan at 10 a.m. asking what the situation was in nearby *Busto Arsizio*. When he was told that it appeared the city was being liberated, he was furious, ranting and raving at the border patrol. He wanted to send his family to *Varese*, just a few kilometers from the Swiss border, to attempt their escape."

"He didn't make it, did he?" Alex said with a knowing air.

"No, he didn't," Giampiero answered tweaking his nose, "and that's why today we're still speaking Italian, instead of German."

Adriano's parents, Ambrogio and Marisa Martinati, now in their 70s, lived through the whole experience. At first it was difficult for them to recount the happenings of those last few days of the war, but slowly the images came flooding back.

"I remember a cemetery on *Viale Belforte*," Ambrogio said. "It was in the shape of a triangle with about 100 small marble crosses with numbers on them. They were the graves of the Americans who fought in and around *Varese*. For years after the end of the war, Americans came to claim the bodies of their loved ones."

"Everything was rationed," Marisa continued. "We got meat rarely, and bread only from the black market." Then she started laughing as another memory drifted in. "Children born after the year 1935 could have *marmellata* (jam)," she said. "So, we called the kids in that grade, '*la classe della marmellata* (the jam class).'"

"We were forced to house a German colonel," she told me. "There was no choice. Every day his subordinates came to iron his uniform, clean his room and shine his shoes. On April 25, they came as usual, but behind them were the *partigiani* and they took him to prison."

"We knew from the beginning it would finish badly," said Ambrogio. "The Italian army was ill-prepared in both body and spirit. We will always be grateful to the Americans for what they did. We had the will to take back our country, but not the means to finish the job without the might of the American military."

"Not everyone remembers with equal clarity the role the Americans played in liberating Italy. Italian schools, especially in recent times, have downplayed the heroism of the American soldiers in favor of the bravery of the *partigiani*," Domenico told me later, and in the days ahead I could see that he was right.

"They only came in at the end," Aldo said one day at the bar. "They were just collecting weapons by the time they got north. The *partigiani* did all the work."

"Ridiculous," Tiziana said. "Without the Americans and the rest of the Allies, we wouldn't have had the courage for the uprising. It happened because we knew they were making their way up the coast. It was the right time to strike." Things actually began to grow heated, cappuccino cups spilling, and hands pounding on the table as more customers began expressing their views.

"I don't think the Italians could have expelled the Nazis without the Allies," I offered. Then, as Aldo poised for rebuttal, I added, "Still, the *patrigiani* had quite a pair of *ballini* to mount that kind of an insurrection."

An additional benefit of Matthew and Alex's award was the rare opportunity to see clearly how many different ways there were to look at one isolated event. And there were as many ways to look at this one moment in history as there were people to talk to about it.

On the day of the *Festa*, indifferent to all political, historical, or cultural viewpoints, we Hummels felt like self-appointed American ambassadors. Giampiero, Susanna, Tommaso, Vanni, Laura, Domenico, Chiara and Francesca all dressed in their finest, followed us to the piazza as if we were part of a U.N. entourage. The celebration started with a blessing in the *Chiesa San Vittore* and then continued outside in the *Piazza San Vittore.* Walking under the *arcomera* (archway) that leads from the *piazza* to *Corso Matteotti*, I stared at the names of the fallen engraved on the thick marble walls. Not more than 20 meters behind me was the bell tower that housed the secret radio used by the *partigiani* to communicate and collaborate with the Allies – the radio that helped bring *Varese* a breath closer to freedom. From behind the *campanile*, Enea peeked out. "Shhhh ..." he hissed, coming toward us to give the kids a hug. "I'm not supposed to be here. My parents are working. I have to go home." And then he was gone.

The marching band of the municipality of *Varese* led the procession down the street. Parents, teachers and children followed closely behind on the way to the local *teatro*, the only building large enough to seat all those who gathered. Barbara and Fiorenzo, Alda and Franco had gone straight to the *teatro* and waved from the third row, beaming. As we sat, I looked down the long row at the Sorus and the Stragapedes. Laura was dabbing at her eyes with a handkerchief, Chiara fidgeting on her lap. All other eyes were riveted to the stage as the mayor entered wearing a black suit and colorful satin sash adorned with the crest of *Varese*. Francesca pointed to a cameraman from the local station, and Domenico gently put her hand down, putting his index finger to his lips, signaling silence.

The mayor spoke about the significance of the day. Thankfully we had already heard most of the history from Giampiero and others. The emotion of the moment made most of the words jumble together, and I was not in a position to translate to Bruce who squeezed my hand knowing why I remained silent.

"Matthew Hummel, *dal Elementare Ugo Foscolo,*" the mayor called out, and Matthew rose from his seat and walked toward the stage. He took the plaque with his left hand and shook the mayor's hand with his right.

By the time Alex was called, my eyes were so blurred, I could barely make out the colors of his shirt and pants as he walked up the stairs to the stage, and I realized that whatever the absolute truth was about how much or how little we, as Americans, contributed to the liberation 60 years ago, on this day, April 25, 2005, I didn't give a flying *fascista*. My kids were the only little *partigiani* that mattered at that moment. They had every bit of the spirit and guts, with a lot less ammunition.

On this auspicious day, April 25, 2005, our two children became part of *Varese* history – the first American children in *Varese* to be honored for academic achievement at the *Festa della Liberazione*. While the mayor's wooden plaque may ultimately be more prized and remembered than the card Bruce and I gave them, scrawled on a piece of *quadretti* paper from Matthew's notebook, I hope that the sentiment of the words contained on the page will also be remembered.

25 Aprile 2005
La Festa della Liberazione

To our dear sons, Matthew and Alex,

When we first arrived in July, we had high hopes that you would find a way to insert yourself into a foreign culture, make friends, and learn a new language. We hoped that you would do it in a way that did not cause you too much stress, but rather in a way that would enrich you as individuals and give you courage to accept new challenges as you grow.

Instead, your achievements have exceeded our wildest imagination. On a day when the Americans have been credited as collaborating with the *partigiani* to free Italy from the fascists, you are being honored with a *"premio"* as the top of each of your classes.

The criteria, we are told, include excellent academic performance and a demonstration of a strong will to learn. We don't know if you can appreciate at ages 8 and 10 what an honor this is and how proud of yourselves you should be, but believe me as your parents, we do.

It is with a full heart that we congratulate you and send you our prayers that in your most difficult hours you will remember this accomplishment, and that it will reinforce your confidence in yourself and your will to achieve, whatever it is you set out to do.

With all our love,
Mom and Dad

Speak Milk. Drink Wine.

CHAPTER TWENTY-FIVE

If You Can't Say Something Nice, Don't Say Anything At All

It is better wither to be silent,
or to say things of more value than silence.
Sooner throw a pearl at hazard than an idle or useless word;
and do not say a little in many words, but a great deal in a few.
Pythagoras

The spring before we left New York for Italy, Alex and I went to the Guggenheim Museum in New York. We were winding our way down past exhibits that included a painting comprised of several thousand dead flies, a sculpture consisting of a white horizontal platform, met by a white vertical platform (which I thought was the display area, but was actually a piece of art itself), and a three-dimensional metal Star of David, Crucifix and Swastika. I stopped making comments like, "They call this art??" after the dead fly painting because I could see that Alex was engrossed in what he was seeing. By the time we got to some of the more geometric pieces, he was sketching them, rendering the three-dimensionality of them in a way that I couldn't have after two college semesters of art history and several adult education origami courses.

When we moved on to the Frick Museum, the guard asked how old Alex was. I told her that he was seven. She apologized and said that children under 10 were not admitted. I told her that we had taken a special day out of school, and Alex just stared at her with a confused, disappointed expression. "He's allowed in the gift shop," she said. So we went in, hoping to see some postcards of the works we wanted to see in person.

As the guard followed us, I could feel the heat rising in my cheeks. She was obviously supervising us to ensure that we weren't trying to sneak in. I was rehearsing the exact verbiage I intended to use to tell her off when she touched my arm and I tensely turned around.

"I can see he's serious about seeing the exhibits," she said. "If anyone asks, tell them he's 10 and keep him close to you."

"I will," I answered. "Thank you." As we wandered into the rooms of the museum, I found myself thinking that the museum was all a bit fussy for a 7-year old, when I realized that Alex appreciated the 18th century art as much as he had the modern exhibit at the Guggenheim. He was sitting on the floor in the middle of the solarium, sketching Bacchus as if there was no one else in the room. A guard approached and I thought he was going to tell Alex that he couldn't sit in the middle of the floor, but instead, he observed that I was about to make a call and asked me to put my cell phone away. Obviously everything's in your perspective.

At the end of the afternoon, we trekked back to Grand Central Station where we watched surfing on the television at the bar of Michael Jordan's restaurant while drinking lemonade. On the train on the way home, I read him a Berenstain Bears book, and minutes later we were home. A precious day came to an end. We used to call them Mommy-Alex days (yes, the ones with Matthew were called Mommy-Matthew days). They became fewer and fewer over the years. Let's face it, there's a big difference between missing a day of block building and missing the day they teach fractions.

Alex and I hadn't had a Mommy-Alex Day the whole year and I sensed he needed one. It had been a long road from New York to *Varese*. He developed from the 'Taz' who threw a fit if he were asked to eat something other than *spaghetti al burro, pizza* and *gelato al limone*, to the young man who ate every conceivable pasta and meat combination, not to mention an impressive number of ice cream flavors. From the foreign student who couldn't speak enough Italian to tell a teacher's aide that she was sending him to recess with the wrong age group, he was now the winner of the school's *Premio* award, responding to classroom interrogation in *geografia, storia* and *matematica,* and receiving all *ottimo* grades on his report card. He deserved a break.

"Matthew's going on a field trip tomorrow. Do you want to have a Mommy-Alex day?" I asked him.

His eyes lit up.

Villa Panza was having a Dan Flavin exhibit and while I am obviously not the world's most sophisticated connoisseur of art, it was the perfect opportunity to give Alex some alone time with me, and focus on his uniqueness as the artist of our family.

From a basket brimming with *parmigiano, prosciutto* and crusty bread, we ate a picnic lunch in the villa's garden under the cascading branches of a *Salice Piangente.* Alex couldn't have been happier if the meal included *gelato* as a main course. We threw our leftover crumbs to the birds and talked about our life in Italy and what we will miss. I asked him if he was excited about going back to the States, a question which during the first months of our visit would have elicited an exhilarating, "Yes!!!"

"Not really ..." he said, looking off into the distance.

I wanted to ask him what he was feeling but I could tell he wasn't ready to tell me.

He got up and offered to a bird a chunk of *parmigiano* so large, I waited to see whether we needed to call the vet paramedics before going in to see the exhibit. The villa itself had a permanent exhibit by American painter, David Simpson – square canvases of monochromatic color against the backdrop of 16th century architecture.

"I don't get it," I almost said, catching myself from finishing the end of the sentence.

At the same time as those words were falling out of my mouth, he was saying, "Mom, isn't that blue incredible? That is the most intense blue I've ever seen. And if you look at it from this angle, do you see how the color changes with the light?"

No, I hadn't seen.

The next exhibit was that of American artist, Dan Flavin. It included a series of rooms featuring florescent lights of varying color combinations and juxtapositions. Alex, of course, pointed out to me how the yellow light overwhelmed the pink one and how the red and blue lights reflected on the wall to create an unusual optical illusion. This time, I was prepared to be silent, respectfully absorbing the comments of my teacher, quietly imprinting a mental etching of the sweetness of the moment.

Things have changed quite a bit since we first arrived. I've learned a bit about listening and keeping my mouth shut. Alex, too, has come into his own. He has Italian friends, can communicate his anger reasonably, and feels comfortable in his surroundings. He's still not crazy about memorizing his homework for the next day's *interrogazione*, but he does it without the former Taz hysterics.

"*Nella regione del Fiume Giallo si alternavano periodi di siccità e periodi in cui il fiume in piena inondava la pianura circostante. Le acque venivano raccolte attraverso una fitta rete di canali d'irrigazione e la coltivazione più diffusa era il miglio, un cereale molto resistente alla siccità* (In the region of the Yellow River periods of drought alternate with periods where the river is very full due to heavy rains falling on the surrounding plains. All the water is conveyed in channels of irrigation and the most popular cultivation was millet, a cereal very resistant to drought)," he quotes with ease from his *Storia/Geografia* book.

It's almost a metaphor for our family.

"Mom, are you listening?" Alex asked me.

"I sure am," I said. "*Le acque venivano raccolte attraverso una fitta rete di canali d'irrigazione e la coltivazione più diffusa era il miglio, un cereale molto resistente alla siccità.*"

"Good job, Mom ..."

Matthew fell asleep early that night, but in the magical moments between wakefulness and sleep, there came an invaluable opportunity to glimpse what Alex had briefly alluded to during the day at the museum.

"*Mamma, quando torniamo negli Stati Uniti, fa il fotografo, Papà, o tornerà al suo lavoro?*" he asked me, wanting to know if his father would be a photographer when we returned to the United States.

"Why are you asking me that, sweetie?"

"Because he never liked his old job and now he does and you always say you have to follow your dream."

"We do say that, yes."

"So will he?"

"I hope so, honey," I said. "But now it's time to call it a day."

I rubbed his back and waited for sleep to come.

I had no idea that Alex had been sharing my hopes over the past several weeks. In the almost one year since we arrived, Bruce had taken hundreds of roles of film. Because of *Varese*'s geographic location, we saw so many Italian cities, as well as parts of Switzerland, Austria, France and Germany. Bruce memorialized each trip through his lens. During the first of these many trips, the boys and I often became impatient. A shot that took us three seconds took him 10 minutes as he composed the shot, chose the aperture, the speed and the filter, waiting for the perfect light. It used to drive Alex crazy. But after a while, we each, in our own way, realized that we were watching a work in progress — not just each individual photo, but the man. With every shot, Bruce was growing into the 16-year-old who had saved his allowance for his first 35 mm camera. The visual proof of his transformation could be found in the prints after the film was developed but it could also be seen on his face. I was convinced that the lines on his forehead were going away. Where did they go? Perhaps they were tucked away with the suits and briefcase in one of the closets in the apartment — having been brought here from America, just in case, but never used.

I think I always knew that for Bruce to be happy, he needed to be creating something — more likely than not, behind the lens of a camera. The letting go of all that made him – made all of us – secure, and allowed that need to come to the surface in a very real way. Somehow, someway, we needed to figure out how to make sure it never got buried again.

From his comments, it was now obvious to me that Bruce's ability, or alternatively lack of ability, to safeguard his dreams meant something to Alex. Maybe he just wanted his dad to be happy. Maybe it was something more.

Sitting in the dark, waiting for my son to drift into sleep, I marveled at the synchronicity of our thoughts. When at last he appeared to be asleep, I took the few steps toward the office.

"*Buona notte, mamma,*" I heard him say softly through the partially closed door.

"*Buona notte,*" I whispered back.

CHAPTER TWENTY-SIX

In Any Culture,
Body Language Speaks Louder
Than Words

Life is a foreign language; all men mispronounce it.
-Christopher Morley

By May, there was no denying spring in *Varese*. I'm speaking not of the blooming flowers, but of more practical matters. Lunapark, a traveling carnival, arrived and we were told "*quando arriva il Lunapark, arriva la pioggia* (when Lunapark arrives, the rain arrives)." Spring also meant that *cioccolata calda* (hot chocolate) stopped being served and Matthew was required to switch his daily consumption at the bar to *succo d'albicocca* (apricot juice). Lastly, it meant that Italians switched their wardrobe from the cusp season "March-April" wardrobe to the all-out spring "May-June" wardrobe, regardless of the actual climatic conditions of that particular year. Every season and subseason had its appropriate sleeve length, shade of color, and weight of cloth and if spring happened to be exceptionally warm or unusually cool, it made no difference. By May, leather and wool were placed in some out of the way closet. Cotton, linen and some blends were upgraded to a position in the central bedroom closets, reds were replaced by pinks, purples by violets. No exceptions.

Spring, too, is marked by Mother's Day, which is celebrated at the same time in Italy as it is in America. (Father's Day is relegated to the more ambiguous temperatures of March.)

My card from the kids read, "You are a great mom and thank you for bringing us here." Bruce presented me with a framed photograph he took of the kids throwing a bouquet of wild flowers up into the air in *Alto Adige* a week before. It was a moment of such joyous splendor and he managed to capture the memory for me forever, the expression of wonder on their faces reaching toward the sky, the individual petals breaking away from some of the buds, the blue sky swallowing the green stems, a blur of yellow melting into the sun.

If only the spirit of that day could have continued through Monday, but it was not to be. It poured that day, but that aside, Matthew could have told you it would be a bad day because he had to wear his unlucky sweatpants; the blue pair was in the wash. At 2 p.m., during *intervallo*, Francesca Manoni was showing off her new umbrella, the one with the cat on it. The girls were ooohing and ahhhing. The boys were making fun of it. And then one teeny tiny problem. By 2:15, the umbrella was nowhere to be seen. Francesca looked everywhere, she told the *Maestra*, but it had vanished.

"Has anyone seen Francesca's umbrella?" the teacher asked the class?

There was no response. Someone took the umbrella, either as a joke or because they coveted it, but the guilty party remained mute, and so did anyone who might have seen the culprit. These were all the ingredients of comic tragedy *alla italiana.*

Had Verdi been alive, he probably could have created a best-selling opera out of the scenario, but *Maestra* Marta, who probably was better suited to be a New York lawyer than a *Varese* teacher, interrogated the entire class for two solid hours. At some point during this time period, Enea, in utter desperation, said, "Matthew was the last person to see it; it must have been him."

Matthew was devastated. Though the umbrella was ultimately found in the jacket sleeve of a boy named Mario, there was no way to determine exactly who put the umbrella there. The intrigue continued unresolved but as far as Matthew was concerned, his reputation was forever tarnished in the annals of *Ugo Foscolo* history.

When we arrived at 4:30 p.m. to pick up the children, we were told, "*Le mamme della quarta devono andare nell'aula* (The mothers of children in the fourth grade must go up to the classroom).” We entered the classroom and were met by 14 sullen faces, several with tear-stained eyes, several quivering lips, a few expressionless, but with downcast face. Bruce reached for my hand and squeezed it; I was frozen were I stood. Matthew was sitting at his desk, his head down, his arm covering his face. I could see that he was crying. I didn’t know whether I should go to Matthew’s side to comfort him or not. He was celebrating his 11th birthday in June. Was he too old to be comforted by his mother in front of his friends?

“Cos’è successo?” I asked. (What happened?)

“Niente di grave (Nothing serious),” *Maestra* Marta said. A true statement in a certain sense. The missing item was an umbrella worth about seven euros. It was recovered and the class was instructed about the importance of honesty. The gravity, however, was evident in Matthew’s eyes. I looked down and shook my head in disbelief.

“I am never going back to this school,” Matthew said to me through his tears as we left. He oscillated back and forth randomly between English and Italian. “It would have taken three words to clear up the whole stupid situation. *La persona che l’ha fatto poteva dire, ‘l’ho fatto io! Nessuno ha avuto il coraggio di dire la verità.* (The person who did it could have said, ‘I’m the one who did it. No one had the courage to tell the truth.)”

“You will go back,” I told him gently. “You’ll go back because you need to face Enea and tell him that friends don’t do what he did. You’ll need to explain to him that he hurt you and maybe help him not to make the same mistake with another friend.”

“I don’t care,” he told me.

“You don’t care at this moment,” I told him. “But you will care eventually because you love him.”

On the way home, Matthew sat silently in the back seat wiping away the tears involuntarily escaping. I did the same in the front seat, trying desperately not to be noticed. They say that it’s important to be positive in situations like this, that your children shouldn’t be able to tell you’re rattled. You’re supposed to exude confidence that everything’s going to be all right. So, why then are we wired to feel every pain our children experience as our own?

Why was I remembering in technicolor at this moment, every betrayal I've ever experienced as if it were yesterday, making this particular incident all the more painful? I felt connected to him as if we were two marionettes sharing the same strings. I wanted to make his pain go away. I wanted to shake Enea for rocking my confidence in him, my affection.

Matthew and Alex had a baseball game to play that afternoon, one that they looked forward to for weeks. I asked Matthew if he still wanted to go. He didn't respond, but went off to his room to find his uniform and cap. Alex followed and I heard them talking quietly behind the closed door, though I could not make out what they were saying. At the game we could see their hearts weren't in it, but the team tied and the game provided some welcome distraction from the day's events. Afterward, we went out for a pizza. The earlier trauma of the day was beginning to wane a bit. Dinner conversation was focused on how many errors their third baseman made and the team's need to concentrate more on their fielding generally.

As soon as we got home, I saw the light flashing on the answering machine. We had four messages. Listening to the first one, we heard the muffled voice of a child a moment before the phone was hung up. The second one was similar to the first. The third one, we heard: "*Perchè non mi risponde* (Why isn't he answering)?" The fourth one: "*Scusa Matthew ... sono Enea.* [pause] *Non te lo volevo fare.* [pause] *Non l'ho fatto apposta. Te lo voglio spiegare domani. Ciao.* [pause]" Another littler voice in the background, Enea's baby brother: "*Chi era?*" [long pause] Enea: "*Ti voglio bene Matthew.* [long pause] *Capito ...?*"

The translation is roughly as follows: "Excuse me, Matthew. It's Enea. I didn't want to do it. I didn't do it on purpose. I want to explain it to you tomorrow. Ciao." Enea's baby brother: "Who was that?" Enea: "I love you Matthew ... Do you understand?"

The following day, he was waiting for Matthew by the entrance to the school. "I only said 'It must have been Matthew' because everyone knows you're the best behaved kid in the class," he said. "I figured that would put an end to it. *Mi sono stuffato* (I was sick of it). I said it in this really sarcastic way, and didn't you see the way my hand was moving?" Enea was using the

Napolitano gesture, 'Yea, sure, right, whatever you say' or something to that effect.

Obviously, language fluency and cultural fluency were not the same thing. Body language, tone of voice and group assumptions were nuances that took years to assimilate, not months. But these were no longer facts that needed to be analyzed or judged. Love, true love, really can heal, especially when that love is expressed directly from the heart of one 10-year-old to another, more like a transfusion than a conversation.

When Matthew explained the situation that evening, tears of disillusionment had somehow transfigured into tears of tenderness. Alex hugged Matthew tightly. Hugs were not uncommon in our family, but on this day, the boys clung to each other for a long time before they let go.

"*Non era facile,*" Alex said, a look of relief on his face. He was acknowledging to Matthew that the day hadn't been easy.

"No, it wasn't," Matthew murmured against Alex's shoulder.

It was one of those experiences a boy remembers, and I could picture Matthew telling his own child about it someday.

Bruce made the boys a cup of *cioccolata calda*, one of the last of the season, perhaps. It was a comfort food that was as appreciated here as it was at home, though here it resembled more a steaming hot, soft pudding than a drink. He put his hand on Matthew's cheek. I walked by and hugged him from behind. Alex pulled his chair closer. We were all there for him. In fact, as I looked around the table at my family, I realized how much closer we had become.

"Let's go outside and play Frisbee," Matthew said.

"Matthew, it's late and it's dark and besides, you know the *portinaia* doesn't let people play on the grass," I replied.

"Mom, what's the worst that can happen?" he said. "They can say no."

Well, nobody said "no." Maybe because our game was played under the cover of darkness, lit only by the garden lamps and no one else was around to imitate our lead and create a mass "breaking of the grass." Perhaps it was because the universe knew that Matthew just needed to play.

Speak Milk. Drink Wine.

TWENTY-SEVEN

There's No Love Without Loss

One cannot divine nor forecast
the condition that will make happiness;
One only stumbles upon them by chance,
in a lucky hour,
at the world's end somewhere,
and holds fast to the days ...
-Willa Cather

Our time to leave Italy and return home was drawing near. In a few months, we'd be back in New York. One Sunday, I met Giampiero for coffee and he looked fairly washed out.

"*Ciao Giampiero, Cos'è successo?*" I said. "*Sembri molto stanco.* (What happened? You seem very tired.)"

"*Eh, si, eh ... siamo stati fuori fino alle due di mattina ieri con Barbara e Fiorenzo* (Yeah, we were out with Barbara and Fiorenzo until 2 a.m. last night)."

We had been wondering if we affected the lives of our friends in a manner that was in any way as significant as the impact their friendship had on us. Hearing that the four of them were up until the wee hours of the morning enjoying each other's company left us with a warm feeling. Giampiero and Susanna had not known Barbara and Fiorenzo previously, despite the fact that all four of them have lived in *Varese* for about 20 years. They met because the kids organized an "art show" where all invitees were encouraged to bring something they created. Alex brought his drawings and his three-dimensional paper sculptures; Matthew, some photographs that he produced with Photoshop under Bruce's tutelage. I brought my decoupage boxes and Bruce, some of his photos. Barbara hung some of her paintings. Giampiero, an artist by education and training brought some of his sketches; Vanni his cartoons; Laura, some photo albums she covered in colorful fabrics, and so on. The kids attached price tags to their work and made a mint. Susanna went home with a 3-D paper skyscraper and a purse that was 15 euros lighter. Fiorenzo went home with Alex's *Carnivale* mask, the one made from cardboard and plastic cups, now a recognized art medium at the Guggenheim. In the meantime, we helped to build a connection between people who might otherwise never have met. Perhaps in our absence, they would gather together for an *aperitivo* at Biffis and reminisce about the crazy Americans who left their jobs and home and moved to another country where they spoke milk, for just one year. Maybe their lives will be enriched by continuing their friendship with each other long after we leave. It was a comforting thought.

Then there were Matthew and Alex's friends. I wondered if they would remember our kids years from now as they continued with the daily routine of their lives in Matthew and Alex's absence. Did they change their ideas about foreigners, Americans, or people in general by their experience of knowing us? Did they at least know that Americans were about more than cowboys, Star Trek and diet soda? Maybe the fact that our kids went to another country without being able to respond to a question about Spiderman, and ultimately were able to speak the language fluently, will give them the courage some day to do the same. With any luck, one or two might keep in touch for years or decades in the spirit of the Hummel-Stragapede-Soru bridge across the Atlantic.

We were looking forward to reuniting with old friends from New York. Matthew, in fact, had just received a message from his best N.Y. buddy, giving us an idea what re-entry will be like when we touched down at JFK.

Dear Matt,
How are you? Me, I'm feeling great!! In 'Super Smash', I figured out how to earn Sonic and Tails!! (I saw it on the Internet with my own eyes.) <u>To earn Sonic and Tails, do 20 ko's in cruel melee!!!!</u>

Congrats on the *Liberazione* award!! I'm sure your family is proud. Keep up the good work buddy! In Yugioh, I got a "Jinzo!" JINZO: ATK/2400 DEF/1500 STARS/6 effect: As long as this card remains face up on the field, your opponent cannot activate any trap cards. When summoned, all trap cards are negated. Pretty cool, eh? When you get back, will you remember English? I hope so ... Miss you, John

Talk about assimilating a foreign language.

Yes, we had a lot to look forward to, but everywhere I went, every conversation, every sound and smell was making me conscious of what we would soon be leaving behind. From the other room, the kids were calling *"Mamma!"* instead of mommy, over the sound of the church bells. It was so easy to connect with them in our tiny apartment, listening to them speak to each other in Italian before they went to sleep, or arguing *"Non è giusto!"* instead of "It's not fair!"

Adriano's perfect cappuccino seemed that much more heavenly, and sitting in the *piazza* at *Biffi's* bar that much more relaxing and entertaining. Last time we were at one of the outdoor cafés with the Sorus, Alex was eating with his usual gusto which included bread crumbs all over every conceivable surface as well as his T-shirt, and oil flying with every forkful of *aglio oglio* to the point where Giampiero was using his outstretched napkin as a vertical shield from the flying debris. It was impossible to instruct him on improving his table manners when we were in such hysterics.

Every time I walked to the market or the dry cleaners, stopping to talk to Aldo at his barber shop with both hands full, practically holding the clean shirt on a hanger between my teeth, I pictured hauling around in my car from place to place back at home. I wanted to keep sitting in front of the *Chiesa San Vittore* and feel the hot sun reflecting off the stone buildings and the pale, worn shutters outside the *Bella Napoli* pizzeria, while Matthew and Alex play soccer, deftly avoiding the teenagers with their newfound footwork.

Back at the apartment, I continued to hang my laundry and struggle to fit my groceries inside our tiny refrigerator. Even that had taken on a nostalgic quality. The idea of having a dryer or a refrigerator that could hold a gallon of milk rather than only a liter at a time, seemed wasteful and unnecessary. Outside the window, the *portinaia* was chasing the kids with a broom in her never-ending quest to keep them off the grass. Later that day, she came to me to discuss her forensic analysis for determining whose fingerprints were on the glass entrance door and who put their plastic bottles in the wrong color bag. I nodded absent-mindedly; I would miss her too.

It was probably going to feel good to be able to discuss my innermost thoughts with friends in English when I got home. Everyone told me I was speaking Italian fluently by this point, but the language would never be mine. It might be a relief to get back and not have to labor with 20 words when two would suffice.

I remember with such clarity lying on our couch in New York before we left and daydreaming about buying a Cinque Cento, that great ultra-compact car Fiat produced in the 60s and 70s. It seemed the perfect symbolic car. You know, going from a more complicated life to a simpler one. Of course, we never did buy one. It was too small for a family of four. But we did shed our SUV for a while at least, along with a lot of other baggage. Our life is lighter now, more fluid. It will not take as much gas to run it anymore. We saw ourselves from the outside in, just as I hoped we would, and it's something that many people never get to do. As Americans, many of us live so far from the nearest international border that rarely do we get the opportunity to really understand how people from other cultures perceive us. We don't get to hear firsthand what they think about the way we face problems, the pace of our day, and how we interact with others.

It will always amaze me that people from two different cultural backgrounds can experience an identical set of facts and see those facts in a completely different way. That experience alone showed us that there is good and bad, efficiency and chaos, and beauty and ugliness in every culture. It made us appreciate what is precious and sacred in our American society: our freedom to explore and express new ideas, not to mention the wonders of air-conditioning

... and to freely reject what is not: the excess, the frantic pace, and Super Mario for PlayStation, to name a few.

Every little nuance about being in a different environment had some effect on us, ranging from the minute to the profound. By not having a clothes dryer, a shower that we could turn around in, or being able to communicate complex issues to school administrators or the phone company, we learned to want what we have, and respect the futility of wanting what we do not. We understand now that what we thought we needed may have been a mere convenience, and what we really needed was to relish being together and being alive.

"We got over a lot of scary things," Alex told me one day.

"I know. Like the Italian dress code, Telecom Italia, practice prisoners ..."

"I meant school and stuff, Mom."

It was true that confronting the scary stuff also had its place, because when we stuck it out, even when we spoke milk, we gained not only the victory of what we accomplished, but the ability to confront the next scary thing, with the confidence that we would succeed. We have enormous potential to grow when we allow ourselves to experience things that are unfamiliar. Sometimes the need for security keeps us trapped in a world where too much is known to us, and we now know that giving into that need does not give the explorer in us room to move.

While we were here in Italy, we could have been anyone we wanted to be. We were not constrained to be the lawyer-turned-soccer-mom, the overworked-businessman, the-quiet-soulful-son, or the little-brother-Tasmanian-devil. Stripped of the constraints of our self-made titles, we are the same people we were when we left one year ago, yet so much the better for the ability to see ourselves for all that we are when there are no predictable patterns to rely upon.

When we left America, people asked us why we were going. The honest answer was that we weren't really sure. Now that we were preparing to return, I knew why we went. We went to re-discover who we were and what we were made of. As for me, like Matthew, I had to give up everything to leave myself enough space to let in the very thing I didn't originally have space for: a different self-concept, an alternative perception of the world, the ability to slow down and take life at a reasonable pace. Maybe that's what Bruce needed to move toward his photography and what Alex needed to move away from the 'Taz.'

As I sat writing, I knew that when I left my office, it would be one of the last thoughts I would write about our Italian experience – at least the last time I'd do so at a desk with black electrical tape running down the center. I watched Alex searching frantically under the couch for his lost Hot Wheels car and I realized that we all, each one of us, lose something every day. Sometimes those things are so insignificant we hardly notice – a sock, a marble, a pair of keys. Sometimes the losses are more lasting: an opportunity, a romance, a friendship, a special place. But when we look hard enough, we see that we're always getting something else instead. When we left the States, we lost everything that was familiar. When we arrived in Italy, we discovered new surroundings and new ideas. Now, on our return voyage, one year later, we were leaving behind countless memories. When we return to New York, we will be surrounded by the tranquil familiarity of home. One big cycle of loss and gain; we could not have had one without the other.

For us, losing our everyday Italy will be profound, but the essence of what she gave us was now part of the marrow of our existence and we were better for it.

CHAPTER TWENTY-EIGHT

Be Where You Are

Travel is fatal to prejudice, bigotry, and narrow-mindedness,
and many of our people need it sorely on these accounts.
Broad, wholesome, charitable views of men and things
cannot be acquired by vegetating
in one little corner of the earth all one's lifetime.
- Mark Twain

Every day that we edged closer to leaving, one friend or another tried to help us keep things in perspective. If it wasn't Laura reminding me that happiness was something we carried around inside us and not something that was perpetuated by where we lived, it was an email from a friend in the States telling me to focus on being present, enjoying each day for what it was worth, reveling in what we accomplished, and preparing us to re-enter our New York lives.

Dear Denise,

It is not likely that who you are and the impact your presence has had on people will be easily forgotten. Those with whom you have truly connected cannot forget you anymore than you can forget them. Therefore, your friends, new and old, will still be your friends and will appreciate your return as well as your courage and openness for newness in your life that inspired this lovely adventure of yours.

More of something, time in Italy or anything else, is not better, just more. Your commitment to live authentically, soulfully and creatively will serve you, your family, and others well and will always be the all-essential difference wherever you choose to be. 'Being' is everything, Denise! What you do and the quality of the interaction that you experience with those you elect to 'do' with, will always be influenced and effected by who you are 'being' at any given time.

I'm thinking of you,
Jeffrey

The 'being' ... the 'being' ... What I was 'being' now was stressed out. I was packing again. It seemed as if I had just unpacked yesterday, but it was a year ago and here I was packing to go home. I couldn't help but feel from every point of view, pragmatically, yes, but also deep down in my gut that it was too early to leave. How could I 'be' anything but tortured? I showed Bruce the email.

"Bruce, I was thinking ... I mean, seriously ... I know I insisted we had to go back, but ... now, again ... I mean, I'm toying with the idea ..."

"Spit it out."

I handed him Jeff's email and said, haltingly, "I was thinking that maybe we should just 'be' here. I think I've made a huge mistake. I mean, you, the kids, you all wanted to stay ... and at the time, it didn't seem sensible, or reasonable, or responsible ... but lately, I've been thinking ... we're so happy here ... And well, I think the pros of staying outweigh the cons ... so let's just 'be' like Jeff says."

"First of all, that's not my interpretation of what he's saying. I think what he's trying to say is that you can take 'you' anywhere as long you 'be' who you are. I think he's saying that everything you've experienced here, thought about, evolved into, can accompany you ... me ... the kids ... wherever we go and whatever we end up doing. *Varese*, New York, wherever ... it makes no difference."

I knew that. Really, I did know that, but Jeffrey was also saying that I should follow my heart ... that the mental gymnastics about what was right had no place, and if I was going to follow my heart, my heart was in *Varese*.

"Please, Bruce, it's not too late to change our minds."

"Denise, you'll take *Varese* with you when you go home – every G. P. Moment, every sound and scent ..."

"I can't ..." I was crying now.

"We have already put the car up for sale, along with Alex's piano and Matthew's drums. We have people scheduled to come see them this week. The tenants in New York found a new place. The Gallos have new tenants coming in on August 1. We can't turn back the clock. We made a decision. We need to stick with it. We've gone too far down the road. And besides, this is what you said you wanted."

"But I made a mistake." I was crying harder now, thankful that the kids were outside. "We could be using the fact that we're in Italy to our advantage. All my writing about cultural differences ...American companies could be really happy to have an English-speaking business strategist in Europe. American travel magazines might want me here too. We could ..."

"It's done," Bruce responded, holding me, but I couldn't hear anything but the sound of my own sobs.

Slowly, mechanically, the business of returning continued down the road I created. A road made of sensible sand and responsible stone that became more solidified with every day that passed. A road of pros and cons with no heart. I started packing a few boxes a day, just as I had over a year ago. This time, I didn't care if they made it over the Atlantic or not. They were just things, and with a few notable exceptions, I had no intention of spending a millisecond wondering where they'd end up.

Every element of preparation, it seemed, was just as difficult as the first weeks of arriving. We diligently tried to find out the new regulations for Buster to travel intercontinentally, but they were as difficult to uncover as they had been when we were leaving the

States to come to Italy. We had heard over the past year, an international regulation came into effect that required microchips to be inserted in your poor, unsuspecting animal. We didn't want to have it done unless absolutely necessary. After calling everyone from the American consulate to the Italian consulate to the vets' offices here in *Varese* and in New York, to the airlines, and getting contradictory information (again), we finally figured out that while a microchip and "doggie passport" are not required to <u>arrive</u> in the United States, they are required to <u>leave</u> Italy, a distinction similar to the difference between the permission to come (the visa) and the permission to stay (*Permesso di Soggiorno*). What can I say?

"It's the tax system," Bruce said.

"Huh?"

"Oh nothing, just something Giampiero said a while back."

Dutifully, he went to the vet, had the microchip inserted, and had the vet give Buster a required rabies shot, despite the fact that the American certificate said that Buster's rabies shot was valid for two more years. Then, I went off to the Animal Control office to get the required doggie passport.

For a change, at this bureaucratic institution, there was no line. Some higher power must have been having pity on my weary state of mind. The required paperwork was only one page! The doggie officer, Giovanni, was a whiz. He transcribed the information on the form I filled out with incredible speed. Then, "pzzzzzt."

"*Merda!*" he exclaimed.

"*Cos'è successo* (What happened)?" I asked.

"The electricity breaker," he responded. "Mario, check the breaker! Do you have all the lights on down there? I have the computer on! *Ma sei scemo* (But are you a fool)?"

"I'm sorry, *signora*, I'll have to start again," he told me. "I lost all the data."

"No problem," I answered. I was already, psychologically, about 45 minutes ahead of where I thought I would be by this time. Waiting for him to re-enter the data was no big deal. He settled down at the computer to re-enter the information and was finished in no time.

"OK, *signora*, two minutes, we'll print you the invoice, you pay *è siamo tutto a posto* (and everything will be in place)."

He pressed the print button with an air of finality. Nothing. His face scrunched up in horror.

"*Che cazzo sta facendo* (What the f–k is happening)?!" Again. Press. Nothing. By now, Mario was looking over Giovanni's shoulder.

"You have to press 'print,' then 'OK'" he said.

"You think I'm an idiot?" Giovanni replied indignantly. "I did that already." Smack! He slapped the side of the computer. Then, smack! He slapped the printer.

"Try my computer," said Mario. Giovanni moved over to Mario's desk. He started to pull up the document.

"Where the hell is it? I don't even see it?" At that point, someone named Marco in a lab uniform came in to pick up some blood samples.

"What's going on?" he asked.

"We can't get the receipt to print. *Questo pezzo di merda* (This piece of shit)."

"I don't think they're networked," Marco said.

"*Eh, si, eh,*" responded Mario. "*È vero* (Ah, yeah, he's right)." Marco walked over to the printer.

"The printer," he said, "you have to turn it on."

My 45 minute "advance" turned into a 30 minute deficit, but — *pazienza*. They offered me a *caffè macchiato* and we talked about why we were here in *Varese* and why we were going back and he suggested that we should visit Sicily before we leave. I thought about all we had done, and all we had left undone.

"Yes, yes," I told him. "There's so much to do, and so little time."

"*È vero,*" he responded. "*La vita e cosi. Pazienza. Se non la farai adesso, vuol dire che dovrete tornare ancora in Italia per forza.* (Life is like that. Patience. If you don't do it this year, it just means that you'll definitely be coming back to Italy again.)"

Speak Milk. Drink Wine.

CHAPTER TWENTY-NINE

A Change is as Good As a Rest

It is easier to be wise for others than for ourselves.
Francois De La Rochefoucauld

The impact our Italian experience had on our lives was palpable. We were counting down the days to the close of this chapter of our life, and Bruce seemed like he was well on his way to a life of creativity and fulfillment that he could build upon once he returned to an English-speaking environment. One that was likely to be more modest than the one we experienced prior to leaving the States, but that might leave him free to wrestle on the couch with the kids, cook to his heart's desire, and keep his finger on the shutter of his camera, possibly for the rest of his life. He was designing his website and perfecting his portfolio.

The kids too were soaring. Matthew evolved from a timid little boy saddled with the impression that he was not as capable as his classmates, to an outgoing kid, filled with opinions about politics and cultures, and at the top of his class in a school where he initially didn't know enough of the language to discuss cartoons, let alone academic subjects. Alex was coasting in his own world of piano, art, soccer and gelato. His only challenge was that he lost interest in reading in English, preferring instead to read in his adopted language, and sullenly accepting the fact that cursing in Italian was no more acceptable than cursing in his native tongue.

I was feeling proud of what they accomplished and my role in supporting them to reach a potential that, by any definition, was leading to a happier life for all of them, but I was feeling very insecure about my own future. What had I done to assure that my existence when we returned to the States wouldn't be a repetition of the life from which I was trying to separate? It was true that my experience in another culture augmented the business acumen I had acquired as an attorney. As an attorney back in the States, I had been taking copious notes about the ways in which culture impacted the business process. Here in Italy, many of those observations related to cultural difference came to life and I had been writing articles for our local newspaper about these differences with great consistency. That gave me some visibility as an author and credentials toward a consulting career. I even had a bit of a following. People I didn't know were writing me emails in response to the articles I wrote and telling me they couldn't wait for the next one. But I was far from determining how this translated to a career when we returned or whether I had done enough to prepare myself for a life post Italy.

A fulfilling life without the ability to pay rent or a mortgage meant trading one tense life for another. It was one thing to be scurrying around from one activity to another as I had as a stay at home mom or bouncing from one meeting to the next as a lawyer, or picking up the pieces of the family as Bruce flew from one city to the next and one client project to the next. In that scenario, life may have been a mess, but it was a mess with little green pieces of paper that got deposited at the bank, with plenty of jingling coins left over for ice cream, stereo systems and a late model car.

If we went home to a life that was as filled with the stress of scrambling to make a living in our new quality of life focused lives, without the practical biproduct of being able to put pasta on the table, our 'let's-go-to-Italy-to-gain-some-perspective' journey could be for naught. Our year in Italy wasn't reality, it was a break from the reality that was waiting for me thousands of miles to the west, and that knowledge left me with a sinking feeling of vulnerability.

It occurred to me that even though our immigration status did not allow us to take on a full-time job, relegating any earning activity to contractual work, I might still be able to make greater strides toward a fulfilling career before returning to the States. Perhaps I could contact an international law firm in Milan in the hopes of working on some sort of a cross-cultural strategy project or something related to international marketing efforts. Like it or not, the world was becoming more global every minute, and American companies and firms were always in need of consultation on how to succeed in the European market and vice versa. I had experience with multinational corporate clients, with both cultures and languages, and with the art of written expression. If I could secure even a short term international business development project, it could help me position myself for the transition when I returned.

I surfed the Internet and found a few law firms that touted international clients. Rattling off a brief cover-letter email, I suggested that although I was not licensed to practice law in Italy, I could perhaps perform an international business development function for a limited period of time. I wrote the email in Italian, asking Susanna to correct it. Then I attached my C.V. and pushed send, 99 percent sure that they would not respond and one percent curious as to whether they would. It was usually at a crossroad such as this that I was thankful for the fact that I was alternatively so courageous or so naïve that I didn't anticipate enough of the situation to be frightened. I virtually ignored the possibility that my email could lead to a train ride to Milan where I could commence the process of making a fool out of myself as I waded through an interview that by all accounts would be over my head.

The possibility of success was further diminished by the fact that I was an outsider. Our young neighbor, Beatrice, just recently was complaining to us about the general favoritism and prevailing nepotism in Italian employment. Beatrice's husband, Alessandro, a young doctor, was interested in pursuing two positions for advancement which opened up at the hospital where he worked. He immediately filled out the application, a painstaking process, and handed it to his supervisor.

"You can't apply for these positions," he told Alessandro.

"Why not?" he answered, puzzled.

"Because the son of the head of the sanitation department of *Varese* is applying and so is the son of one of the directors of the hospital. You are clearly more qualified than they are and if you apply you will take one of their positions."

Alessandro apparently nodded and torn up the application; He was all too familiar with the concept.

If this type of thing was happening to qualified Italians, it seemed unlikely that I'd land a business development position for a law firm with which I had no connection. Or so I thought. Within two weeks of my experimental email, my 1 percent curiosity landed me an interview with one of the firms I contacted. The remaining 99 percent of my emotional status could be described as outright, unadulterated fear. I hadn't practiced law for years and my Italian, while arguably intermediate at this point, was definitely not advanced enough to participate in an interview in a way that maximized an impression of intelligence.

On the day of the interview, I put on the first suit I had worn in years, borrowed a briefcase from Bruce, and marched off to the train station. I arrived in time to buy a newspaper and order a *cappuccino*. Looking around nervously, I decided that I adequately fit in with the business-commuting crowd. Dark suit, serious expression, and shoes that matched Bruce's briefcase perfectly (It's great how black accessories get you over that pesky color-coordination issue.)

My thoughts fluctuated between an "I am so nervous" mode and an "I have nothing to lose" mode, but at the core I was excited about the potential of meeting Italian colleagues, and experiencing life in a professional setting, if only for the briefest of moments. Pulling off the meeting without making a fool of myself was the primary objective.

My investigative "research" in this regard included finding the Italian words for employer, qualifications, salary, and consultant. One other important word, marketing, translated as *marketing*. Apparently the Italians had no need for the word before the globalization of businesses. Why would they if contracts, projects, jobs and other business opportunities went to their sons, brothers, cousins, and best friends in the north, and *Mafia* or *Camorra* familial connections in the south? Of course, it was likely that I would not have to use any of these words, but rather 20 other phrases for which I was unprepared, like: "No, I've never formally had a business development role." "Yes, I speak several languages including English, Italian and Milk," and the more classic, "My recent experience has included a plethora of domestic responsibilities on the highest executive level, ranging from diaper changing to the cross-cultural adjustment of two pre-adolescent boys."

When I arrived at my interview, I was ushered into a small conference room, which gave me plenty of time to consider what in God's name I was doing there. After about 40 minutes, having not come up with the answer to this conundrum, someone who I only later understood to be the senior partner of the firm, knocked on the door, and without waiting for a response, opened it.

"Do you want to eat something?"

"*Certo*," I responded, rolling my "r" a bit excessively, and along with four male attorneys and one female attorney, sauntered down the street for an early lunch.

The five men chatted amongst themselves; the female attorney was observing some sort of silent vigil, neither involved in their conversation or eager to commence one with me. I ventured a little one-sided conversation with her about today's warm weather contrasted with yesterday's rain, and then moved on to a more profound discourse about the fact that some of the stores in Milan were beginning to remain open for *l'ora di pranzo* (lunch hour), and wasn't that a certain sign of globalization. She apparently didn't think so, or maybe she just wasn't saying.

When we sat for lunch, *il capo, capo, capo* (the senior partner) said, "You have two sons who play baseball." In a feat of mental gymnastics, my labored mind concluded that he heard I had two sons, and assumed that because we were American, they play baseball.

I politely responded, "You must be a mindreader."

"No, I'm not a mindreader," he said, "but I did see you at the Malnate baseball field a while ago."

Slowly, I began the vague recall of seeing at the first game, a tanned man about his age, in sunglasses, baseball cap, shorts and sneakers, who could have roughly met the description of this very gentleman speaking to me, however paler and more formally attired. The resulting half-hour conversation was entirely about baseball, him jokingly threatening to offer Mathew and Alex a more competitive contract with his Milan team than Malnate could afford, and me offering the services of the Hummel family to give his players a bit of old-fashioned American fielding and hitting advice.

"I see from your C.V. that you have done a lot of mediation and mediation training. I love the concept of mediation. I'd love to do more of it," he told me.

"I'd love to be involved in writing the training materials. I did a good deal of mediation as a lawyer in the States," I responded.

"Yes, I'm sure," he said. "But unfortunately, there isn't much call for mediation here. Our proceedings are not as costly and protracted as yours are in the States." Then he looked down at my C.V. thoughtfully, rubbed his chin and said, "Ah, you're also interested in marketing and public relations, I notice. I love marketing. I wish we did more of that."

"I have a lot of ideas about how to market the firm's service in the United States market," I said. "Perhaps we could ..."

"No, no," he responded. "As attorneys, we have strict limitations on marketing. We've really done the maximum we are permitted to do by law."

Perhaps he called the meeting to see what an American lawyer turned mom turned international business development strategist looked like, or could it be that they needed an excuse for a leisurely expense-account lunch?

The end of the meal drew near without rendering a further clue as to why my presence had been requested. *Signor capo, capo, capo* suggested that I try a type of chocolate cake with *peperoncini* (hot pepper). I accepted, feeling that to say no was bad manners. A sumptuous looking piece of chocolate cake arrived and as the first forkful of cayenne-laced chocolate hit my tongue, I felt my face reddening and calmly reached for my almost empty glass of water. I choked through the rest of the conversion until the *espresso* arrived, whatever was left of my brain cells fried by the spicy chocolate delight.

Then *Signor capo, capo, capo* said, "So what can we offer you? Something part time?"

"Pardon?"

"Three days?" he inquired.

How could I accept a part-time job? I was packing up to go home. What I needed was a short-term assignment that I could complete before leaving Italy. Something that might smooth the transition from law to international business development when we returned to the States.

"Could we identify a specific project?" I suggested.

"*Va bene*," he said. "We will send you an offer by mail."

With that, he got up, took his jacket off the hook behind me and shook my hand. As we left the restaurant and they headed back to the office, I waved and headed off in the direction of the station.

"An offer to do what ..." I muttered under my breath, still waving, with a blank stare and a smile permanently plasticized to my face. Apparently the subject matter of my work was a minor technicality that he intended to work out over the next cayenne dessert, *caffé* or optimally, *vino bianco*.

Weeks passed with no letter and no call. I phoned and emailed them several times but got no response. Instead, I got an email from a colleague of the senior partner asking if my husband was available to have dinner to discuss baseball coaching techniques. I thought that was a good sign *il capo* felt free to pass Bruce's name on to a colleague, but a little strange that I didn't first hear back from the firm about the possibility of working for them. Bruce and the baseball guy had a nice dinner together. I, however, never heard from the law firm. I reasoned that either someone's cousin Sylvia or Sergio got the job, or the interview was a ruse to find a mole with valuable strategic insight into the Malnate baseball team, or that I made a complete fool of myself sometime between the chocolate *peperoncini* cake and the *espresso* service. All three possibilities seemed equally probable, and remain to this day a mystery. I kept my train ticket, penning, "First day in the Italian business world" on the front. Then, I flipped it over and wrote, "Last day in the Italian business world" and put it in one of my decoupage memory boxes.

In the aftermath of my anti-climactic interview, I began to step up my writing. I wrote articles memorializing every Italian town we visited and the nuances between the American and the Italian people. I sent them to editors of travel magazines throughout the

United States and England. There were articles related to Easter in *Ravello* and *Napoli*, winter in *Sardinia*, and excursions on *Lago Maggiore*. I described the topography, the architecture, my favorite restaurants and shopping secrets. They contained my fears, blunders, and hopes related to living in another culture, the kids' triumphs, and Bruce's photographs –   a bit of my soul in 1,000 word increments.

Weeks later, and no closer to anything that could resemble a hint of a career transition, Bruce called me from the studio to send me on an after-hours errand to the *Esselunga* supermarket for some sausage for a dinner he was preparing that night. Bruce had been doing all the food shopping, so my *Esselunga* experience was limited, but my instructions were clear; buy a half kilo worth. The task was simple enough until I got to the sausage case. It wasn't a choice between fat, link sausages or skinny, long sausages; there were dozens of sausages with names I never heard of. In desperation, I turned to a very knowledgeable looking fellow and, pointing to the section of sausages that seemed to differ only in circumference, length, color and name, asked, "Can you, by chance, explain to me the difference between these sausages?"

"Not really," he said in perfect Italian. "I can only tell you that the *salsiccia suino* are long, red and thin, the *salsiccia punta coltello* are red and stubby, the *salamini maiale* are stubby, fat and red, the *salsiccia saporita* are red, fat and long, the *salamella montovana* are dark and fat, the *salsiccia piccante* are red and long, and the *luganega* are pink and fat. Apart from that, since I have spent most of my life in America, I really can't help you."

From there, of course, we both began speaking English.

"I'm American – what brings you to *Varese*?"

He worked for the European division of a large American company in a nearby suburb, not more than 20 minutes from our apartment. By the time I settled on a package of sausage, he knew my life history from Brooklyn to *Varese*, as well as my career aspirations and concerns relative to our transition back to the States.

"Why don't you call Caterina Barola at our personnel department in *Azzate*? They're always looking for international business development consultation on one project or another."

Life is strange, and you never know who you're going to meet in front of a meat case or what a sausage inquiry can lead to. I silently repeated both his name and the name of the director of the personnel department over and over again, up the aisle, past the 10-meter long *parmigiano* and *asiago* cheese case, around the 20-meter long *biscotti* display, past the bar, and down the electric sidewalk to the car where I had a pen and paper to write down the information.

On the day I called Ms. Barola, I toyed with several different witty introductions and settled on the truth.

"Oh yes," she said. "I understood you had a very complex discussion about Italian sausage." I tittered amicably to fill the silence. "Unfortunately," she continued, "We have no positions available at this time."

"That's quite all right," I answered, masking my disappointment. "I'd love to meet with you anyway just briefly for coffee as colleagues, if you have a 15-minute slot in your schedule."

She very kindly agreed. I had no idea what to bring with me, but I printed off a copy of my resume, a compilation of American legal credentials that were about as useful in an Italian business environment as ketchup in an Italian kitchen. Then, I photocopied some of the articles I wrote. I had no idea if she would find them relevant and I felt silly and awkward having to prove myself after decades as an international attorney, as if I were a 20-year-old, new to the business world. It was like starting over, without the acne but with just as much trepidation.

I spoke to her about why we came to *Varese*. Without intending to, I found myself describing to her how I felt when I was writing about the cultural nuances of Italian and American societies and the business impact of those observations. I shared the intense feeling of satisfaction when someone reading my material sighed with the same understanding I breathed when I wrote the thought. In short order, my dreams of translating my life experience across cultures to concrete business utility were laid bare on her desk in an emotive display that one did not ordinarily expect at a business meeting. The seeds of hope that I could pursue a career that inspired me and leave me feeling energized to enjoy my family, were looking for roots in Caterina Barola's office. I couldn't prove to her that my experience with multinational corporate clients combined with my experience over the past year could be useful to her, but there was the ever-present possibility that she was seeing me as a real person, and someone of optimism and curiosity, or at least someone who had done more than just complain about a life that hadn't been working back at home.

When she called a week later to offer me an international business development project, it was as if a door to another dimension opened. It was just a short-term project, maybe it wouldn't amount to more than the ability to buy a few *cappucini* and *brioche*, but I was so uplifted by the experience you would have thought I was asked to analyze the impact of covert CIA activity in *Varese* on the long-term business objectives of the region of *Lombardia,* by the smug smile of satisfaction on my face.

Employees of the company seemed to enjoy the sprinkling of cross-cultural humor I tried to add to the relatively dry meetings and began to look out for me, throwing leads my way, hoping one thing would lead to another. Caterina Barola had lunch with me from time to time.

"I just hope I can take all the valuable lessons of this year, combine it with my experience in the business world, and give it some meaning when I get back home," I told her when the project ended.

"From what you tell me, you're not the same person now than you were a year ago. You're more focused on what it is you want, you've been an astute observer of human interaction all year, you speak two languages fluently and you have the experience of living in another culture to call upon. You have all the ingredients you need to make a meaningful transition when you return."

I didn't know this woman very well but at the end of lunch I kissed her on both cheeks *alla Italiana*, followed by an American hug.

"What was that for?" she asked me, smiling.

"For reminding me that it's OK to throw away the only ladder I've ever climbed and make my way up a wobbly staircase instead."

"I think I know what you mean," she said. "Be good to yourself, and let me know how you make out."

It was good advice. Being good to myself was going to be as important in the days ahead as being good to my family. I needed to be realistic with my goals and even handed with my self-assessment; things were not always as black and white as I made them seem. I needed to accept who I was. Honest and direct on good days, abrupt on bad ones. Confident and assertive in good light, arrogant in the shadow. Diligent by the Swiss clock, anal-retentive in Italian time. Caring of my children by the international standards of motherhood, micromanaging by more enlightened self-assessment. All of that was true. But deciding to pursue this new professional dream meant not perpetuating past mistakes. It meant I was being true to values I previously ignored, that fulfillment was more important than money, and time to breathe was more important than striving to be at the top of my game. I had done more than eat a lot of good food and see a lot of great sights in this past year. I learned not to be afraid or cling to a past that no longer fit me.

I thought quite frequently during this time period about the trajectory of progress over the past year. Italy's pedestrian *piazze* and ritual *aperitivo* made me appreciate the countless opportunities for spontaneous encounters and connection with friends and neighbors. Her bureaucratic ways forced patience to grow like a seed in my belly, because without *pazienza* in Italy no one could survive. My initial failure to understand the language and the culture meant that I was softer in my approach to people. I wasn't necessarily less direct, just more humble. My inability to insert myself in the educational system, no matter how hard I tried, meant that my micromanaging days came to an abrupt halt, while Matthew and Alex's independence and confidence grew from having to handle their own problems. This loss of control was not limited to the educational system ... it related to every aspect of my life. At first, I found it absolutely infuriating and didn't know how I would survive it. Dealing with ENEL and Telecom Italia made me want to ask if they included frontal lobotomy as one of their services. The teachers telling me not to ask my children about their day until Christmas made me cry like a kindergartener. But after awhile, there was a certain amount of inner peace that developed by sheer virtue of the fact that I had no way to change the outcome of the situation. What was the point of getting angry or anxious about something that wasn't going to change anyway? What was the use of lists and schedules if *adesso* actually means 'in a few days' or never? My perspective came day by day, with every *passegiata*, every GP moment, every soccer debate over coffee, and every mistake. It came with the breaths between the words.

CHAPTER THIRTY

Follow Your Dream

*Life should NOT be a journey to the grave with the intention of arriving safely in
an attractive and well preserved body,
but rather to skid in sideways, gelato in one hand, vino rosso in the other,
body thoroughly used up, totally worn out and screaming,
'MADONNA! What a ride!'
Life is not measured by the number of breaths we take, but the moments that
take our breath away.
– Taken from an Anonymous poem and "Italianized."*

The two weeks preceding our departure were miserable. Chiara
was walking now, an unmistakable sign of the passing of time. If
not for that, though, it seemed like we arrived just yesterday. Laura
and I talked about all the time we intended to spend together
during this year, and yet between her job, a new baby and our
prolonged adjustment, it seemed we barely had time for a few
coffees and a few walks together before our year came to an end.
At Chiara's birthday party, although grateful to be there on such a
momentous occasion, I looked numbly through the photo album I
had prepared for her as a memory of her first year of life,
incredulous that so much time had passed.

It took several weeks and about three kilos of paperwork to sell
our car, but we received a fair price for it. We also managed to sell
Alex's piano and Matthew's drums. We gave away or donated
most of the possessions we purchased when we first arrived, from
alarm clocks to fans, iron to telephone. We doled out to friends the
art supplies, toys and sports equipment we shipped to Italy. It was
better knowing they could enjoy them than fretting over the cost
and frustration of shipping.

On Wednesday, Alex's best friend, Michele, gave him a card with the following inscription: *"Alex per me tu sei stato un grande amico, il mio migliore amico. Alex, mi dispiace TANTISSIMO che vai in America.* (Alex, for me you have been a great friend, my best friend. Alex, I'm really, really upset that you're going to America.)" Alex, the little boy, whose range of emotions when we arrived seemed limited to the expression of euphoria or rage, was crying real tears of loss.

Enea, too, was anticipating the loss of his buddy. *"Matthew, non ho un regalo per te* (Matthew, I don't have a present for you)."

"Non fa niente," Matthew responded. *"I regali non curano le malattie* (It doesn't mean anything. Presents don't cure what ails you.)"

His feelings were clear and he was not afraid to express them. He was no longer the little boy who stood holding onto my leg in the *oratorio* when we first arrived.

On Thursday night, July 21, some of my friends, mostly mothers with children attending *Ugo Foscolo Elementare,* took me to dinner to say goodbye. Susanna, who couldn't be there, texted me: *"Non essere troppo triste. Pensa che io non ho mai conosciuto una persona o una famiglia che abbia avuto l'opportunità di fare un' esperienza come la vostra. Se pensi a quanto siete incredibilmente fortunati, forse puoi essere meno triste.* (Don't be too sad. Imagine the fact that I have never known a person or a family that has had the opportunity to have the experience you have had. If you think about how incredibly fortunate you are, maybe you will be less sad.)"

On Friday, Vanni presented us with T-shirts he made that said, *"Arrivederci Italia."*

The Italians definitely corner the market on hard-core emotional drama. One more excuse to cry and I was just going to hang out in the bathroom until the plane took off.

The following day, a response to the email I sent back at Christmas time, arrived in the midst of our *Buon Viaggio.*

Dear Denise,

I've been meaning to write about the "Pros and Cons" list you sent, and for various reasons haven't sat down to do it until now. One reason for waiting (among many ... such as preparing for the holidays ...) was that I wanted to be thoughtful in my response. Of course, here we are now, approaching the summer holidays. I expect the need to obtain the opinion of friends is now diminished, or even useless, but here goes ... You asked for my honest opinion, and I can only tell you what I would do if I were in your shoes. As I read through your list, it was my opinion that the "Pro" list contained items of charm and adventure in living the Italian way, as well as unique life experiences and the bonus of learning another language. In my opinion, this is the "fluff" of life and can be filled in over time in other ways. However, the "Con" list seemed to contain concrete concerns that would cause me to make an instant decision. I would not stay. I would be too worried about the boys, the school issue and the career issues that I would get back home to a life of stability and address these issues.

So, how's that for honesty? I was afraid to offend, so please know that I wanted to be honest without you feeling that I'm making a personal judgment if you decide otherwise. I value your friendship greatly wanted to be thoughtful and cautious in my response.

We miss you and wish you the very best!!

Love,
Janey

I printed out the email and handed it to Bruce who was in the kitchen preparing lunch. We had both been so sullen lately and I felt the email was validating and would perhaps cheer him up. I caught him in the middle of chopping garlic. He smiled and motioned to me to leave it on the counter. I kissed him, left the kitchen and went back to the computer. I heard the sizzle of the garlic hitting the oil in the pan. I associated the scent with Italy and all that the experience represented to me. Now as the strong, sweet smell filled the air, my chest tightened.

I turned to go back to the kitchen. I wanted to rush back in and tell Bruce that our experience was not the fluff of life. It was just the opposite. It was everything without the fluff. It was the giving up of everything secure that was the catalyst of growth. It was the instability, not the stability, that pushed us to examine how we lived our lives, and what we needed to change in order to be happy. But it was too late.

I picked up the placemats and set them haphazardly on the table. Then I went to the kitchen to get the four forks, knives, plates and glasses we had not yet given away.

When I returned to the kitchen, I found Bruce holding on to the sink, tears rolling down his cheeks.

"What's wrong," I said, panicking. Janey's email was still on the counter. It was covered with inky wet spots and only some of the sentences were still legible.

"I don't want to go," he sobbed.

For a long time I stood frozen and said nothing.

"It feels as if we're in the midst of a life-shaping experience and that it's just too early to cut it short, doesn't it?" I finally said.

He nodded, because he knew what he had known for a long time, that it didn't make sense to stay but it made even less sense to leave.

I held him and let him cry. His chin pressed hard against my shoulder. My shirt felt warm and damp. I gently pushed back and looked at him. I was acutely aware of every sensation in my body. There was a weakness in my legs that suggested that finding a seat might be a really good idea.

"We can stay," I offered, as if I were saying it for the first time. "We can stay because it doesn't make sense and it isn't practical."

"It's ridiculous," he sobbed. "We know we can 'be' anywhere."

"It's true," I said, wiping his tears with a dirty dish towel, "but we can also 'be' here."

The kids, by this point, came in from the living room. There were no secrets in such a small space.

"Dad, what's wrong?" Alex said, his fearful eyes giving him the appearance of a much younger child.

Bruce hesitated. He looked at me and I nodded.

"It's just that ... well, we were wondering what you guys would think if we ..."

"If we what?" Matthew asked, impatiently.

"If we changed our mind and decided to stay another year."

Their solemn faces went blank ... and then lit up.

"*Certo che vogliamo stare qua* (Of course we want to stay here)!" yelled Matthew.

"*Abbiamo pensato che siete un po' pazzi ad'andare via* (We thought you guys were a little crazy to want to leave)," said Alex.

"But, Dad," said Alex, "those tenant people aren't at our house anymore."

"*È vero* (It's true)," Bruce said. He was trying so hard to speak Italian and every phrase he managed was more significant than all of ours combined.

"Does this mean you're going to go to find a job in Milan and work all day and all night and travel like you used to in New York?" Matthew asked.

Bruce kneeled on one leg. He looked at them both in a way that I won't be forgetting for a long, long time.

"In this family we follow our dreams," he said with a steadiness that came from deep within his soul. "I may never be the most famous photographer in the world, and I have no way to predict what will happen down the road any more than you do. But I know that I will never, never settle for unhappiness again."

The boys nodded.

"Do you understand what I'm saying?" Bruce asked them.

"You're telling us that it's important to be happy," Alex said.

"And believe in yourself, right Dad?" Matthew added.

By this point, we were all sitting in the tiny space wedged between the kitchen stools and the oven. We were laughing, or was it crying? I can't remember with any degree of clarity. I just know that one week before we were supposed to board a plane to move back to New York we changed our minds.

CHAPTER THIRTY-ONE

The Secret Of the 'Extra'

The great blessings
of mankind are within us and within our reach; but we shut our eyes,
and like people in the dark, we fall foul upon the very thing we search for,
without finding it.
-Seneca
(7 B.C. - 65 A.D.)

Isn't it strange how sometimes when we follow our instinct and make a decision that on the surface does not seem logical, the universe opens up to accommodate us? On that same famous Saturday afternoon, we had planned to have a goodbye drink with Alda and Franco. Instead, when they arrived, we shared our news.

Two pairs of eyes widened in surprise. Then, without skipping a beat, Franco said to Bruce, "*Benissimo.* I just found out that the person who manages our global I.T. department is leaving the company. Do you want to interview for it?"

"I'd definitely consider it, part time," Bruce said, smiling. "I'm going to be pursuing my photography."

Franco smiled and shook his hand.

Telling the Sorus and Stragapedes was once again like being at the opera at *La Scala* – laughter and tears and a lot of kissing. Susanna sat with her hand over her mouth until her face began to turn a subtle shade of scarlet.

"*Con voi Americani c'è sempre una novità* (With you Americans, there's always something new)," Giampiero marveled.

"You'll need to find another apartment, I suppose," Laura said, after she was convinced we were not joking.

I nodded, "I'm on the look out for landlords without a doctorate in contract negotiations."

Even Chiara seemed to know the news was good, lurching with every two to three steps, joyously giggling at every tumble.

On Monday, when I spoke to Barbara and Fiorenzo, they suggested I call the *Scuola Europea*, the international school in *Varese* as a viable alternative to the public school system.

"Can't you squeeze in one small fifth grader?" I plead to the *direttore*. "He won't take up much room."

"Of course," the director responded. "One of the largest international companies in *Lombardia* just transferred 500 workers out of *Varese*. There's room in every section. Does your child speak Italian, English, German, Dutch or French?"

The day before we left to spend the month of August with our family and friends in New York, we found a small turn of the century house at the end of the *area pedonale* (pedestrian mall) behind the *Chiesa San Vittore* in the historic center of town. From the outside I could see that it had a view of the *campanile* of *San Vittore* that was illuminated at night. It had a tiny garden with a grape arbor. The rooms were small but there was space for Bruce and me to have our own offices. Lastly, there was a *taverna* (basement) where the kids could play sock ball without using Bruce's open newspaper as the goal. At 7 p.m. the night before we left, we signed a contract to rent it.

We returned to New York for the month of August. It was a bittersweet time for us. A hello to our friends and family was also a goodbye. The grandparents, in particular, were shocked and saddened by our sudden change of heart. The boys had grown so much since they last saw each other. Their faces and bodies were fuller and taller, of course, but in more ways than one, they were not the little boys their grandparents left at JFK one year ago. In thinking we were only going to be away for one year, we had not come back to visit. In the future, we needed to plan to see them more often. When they asked us how such a thing could happen, how we could have changed our minds at the last minute, Bruce never blamed me. I was, in large part, the impetus behind going to Italy in the first place, and in some respect the creator of confusion toward the end. But Bruce and I had long since stopped keeping score.

Matthew reconnected with his best friend, John. They made very little time for video games, opting instead to play baseball, swim, and talk late into the night, flashlights under the covers, expecting we wouldn't notice the hour. It was hard on both of them knowing that their time together was limited, rather than the beginning of a reunion that could have been the precursor to a new school year together.

Alex gave Enea's recipe for *spaghetti al pesto* to his Aunt Nina and suggested she use the fresh basil leaves from her garden and Nina pretended she had never made the dish before. Then she shocked him by making a homemade ice cream that rivaled his favorite *gelateria* on *Corso Matteoti*.

When Bruce and I weren't comforting our parents, we were re-connecting with friends at barbecues and happy hours, a beer in one hand, a hot dog in the other, the kids crunching corn on the cob, all of us eating one too many pieces of pie in true American style. A few of us went into downtown New York City for the day. As I took snapshots of the New York skyline, I felt a little bit like a tourist in my own country.

When we walked back into our New York home for the first time, Bruce and I went into his office. It was one of the rooms we locked up without having to pack the contents. We found everything just as he left it – papers out on the desk, an article he had been reading a year earlier opened to the page where he left off. It was as if our New York life was a video on hold waiting for us to decide what path to take. We sat there and looked at the photos on the wall, and the memorabilia thumbtacked to his corkboard. Everything about the house looked very inviting: the large rooms, the cooking friendly kitchen, the basketball hoop out front.

"It probably makes sense to sell the house," Bruce told me.

"I know," I said softly. Selling the house would give us the precious time we needed to make a go of our new professional lives. "More goodbyes ..." I added.

We had left boxes and boxes in the crawl spaces of the house and now we had to begin the process of deciding what we should ship to Italy and what we should pack for storage. This time, the packing had more of a feeling of permanence. Someone would buy our house and paint over the clouds my mother had painted on Alex's ceiling. Matthew's room was a jungle motif and I had chosen the zebra fabric for his rocking chair and every tropical animal decal on the walls. The toy chest we gave each of them for their first birthday and most everything else were all going into the dark, windowless walls of a storage unit. Maybe they'd be teenagers before we saw these things again.

I touched the paint on every wall; the colors I painstakingly chose were subtle and warm and more varied than the "Gallo-white" I chose in *Varese*. I mused at the effort with which I had purchased the wrought iron and crystal chandelier in the dining room; I had bargained for it so diligently with the former owners of our house. I had labored over the decision to buy Alex's piano as well; I didn't want it to be too expensive for a little boy who might not even continue playing or too cheap for him to enjoy.

There were kindergarten, first and second grade paintings I framed to promote the boys' self-esteem, to smile at their progress year by year. Matthew's baseball trophies and Alex's snow globes would have to be stored away indefinitely. It wasn't practical to ship all these tiny joys. Even my wonderful mattress, such a contrast with the gushy, cheap foam one that could be folded to climb the stairs of our Italian home, was calling me.

The Italians are much less mobile than we are, so why do they have so much less stuff? Where are their snow globes and kindergarten pictures? If Susanna and Giampiero were here instead of me, would they throw up their hands and say *pazienza*? These things were the only 'extra' I had ever recognized and now I was leaving them. Did I have the real 'extra' to replace it?

I thought back 17 years to the moment we first met the Sorus and the Stragapedes. As we walked along a *Sardinian* beach, I had taken Tommaso's hand in mine; it was so small it had felt like a tiny seashell. I remembered the sight of Vanni eating his watermelon on my lap at the huge farm table under the grape vines. It was nearly two decades ago that I first recognized the 'extra' I was seeking. Was it limited to certain people? Certain countries?

Every day I packed something. Every day I weighed the pros and cons of selling something versus storing it. On my 13th box, the very number I packed and shipped to Italy one year prior, my hands slowed until I was barely packing at all.

"What's wrong," Bruce asked me.

"I was pro and con-ing," I told him.

"You were what?"

"I was pro and con-ing. I was weighing the intrinsic economic value of every item we own. I was agonizing over everything in this house as if it were the 'extra.'"

"The what?"

Now he was really confused. 'Extra' was my own silent concept. I had never given it an external voice, never labeled it out loud to anyone.

"The 'extra' was always here," I said. "It was here in my friends and family before I left. It was in me and in you and in the kids."

We stopped packing and it all poured out.

"What I 'lacked' in New York and what I 'found' in *Varese*, it was always there," I struggled to explain.

With tears, mostly from happiness, I took in all the 'extra' around me. My mother, who knew I adored the theater, gave us tickets to see a musical while we were still in town. Nina's *pesto* pretense, and my sister Andrea's gift of dozens of baseball cards. The party thrown by our friends who knew it was difficult for us to connect with all our New York buddies during our short visit, and who knew we needed to be surrounded by their friendship. Bruce's mother, whose arms were laden with books in English she collected to make sure the kids kept up with their mother tongue and his father's litany of jokes and riddles to keep the kids smiling. Some of these 'things' had a monetary value of sorts, but it was the thoughtfulness and sensitivity with which they expressed their love that was the 'extra.'

On our last day before returning, my dad took me by the hand to show me the marigolds he planted in the quiet part of his garden that most people don't see. I congratulated him for making his own little piece of paradise in his yard, and we laughed about how we kids used to call ancient ruins 'fallen down rocks' while our kids called them 'brokens.'

"It just goes to show you," Dad said, "that nothing ever changes ... until it does."

The 'extra' had been there before I left for Italy but I had been unable to recognize it, so absorbed in the race. It had followed me across the Atlantic with every email and phone call. If I had more self-knowledge or a calmer life before I left New York, I might never have come to Italy. Perhaps it was fate or luck that brought me there. Whatever the impetus, it got me to a place where I was able to learn the lessons life had in store for me. I now made time for every conversation, from world politics to gallstones, always knowing that one or two of those talks were little memory nuggets to carry with me during the day. I now know it's OK to read a newspaper for an hour, simply because the sky is blue, the air is warm, and there is a gentle breeze, or for no reason at all. I never let one meal go by without kissing Bruce on the back of the neck to thank him for the pleasure of the perfume of his dishes before I even taste them. I even let the kids talk well beyond lights out, their language idly shifting from Italian to English and back again; it was infinitely more important than the lights-out rule.

In the next few days, with every item I packed, something happened to me. I was able to stop worrying about selling every little thing that had value and start thinking about the joy it might bring to someone else. Luz, our cleaning lady had never owned a formal coat and the one I was hoarding was expensive, but in the past decade I had hardly worn it. Her friend was trying desperately to furnish a house and needed couches that would have a better home in their living room than our storage facility. Our neighbor, Jimmy, could use a television for college. The custom fireplace screen cost us a bundle, but giving it to the new owners enabled them to make a fire in the beautiful stone fireplace without waiting the two months we waited to have one made when we moved in.

It was a process ... and it helped me move on ... to stop agonizing over the going and the staying, the pros and the cons. To stop analyzing the benefits and deficits of the Italian culture, versus the American one. To stop wondering who was going to remain my friend back in New York and who was going to be obscured like the clouds on Alex's ceiling.

Selling the house was the final letting go. Not just the letting go of "my" house and "my" things, but the letting go of what it represented, a security that trapped us in a life we wanted so desperately to reject but couldn't, the trappings of the image of a prestigious life that didn't fit us.

I think I can now finally focus on the things that matter: my husband's freedom from a job he hated, our finally having him really in our lives, his *spaghetti alle vongole,* and the delicate and deliberate light in all his photographs. I can cherish Matthew's Italian hand gestures that, after knowing Enea, seem to come from *Napoli*, despite the fact that we live near Milan, and Alex eating with more gusto than the average contestant in a pie-eating contest. I can relish in the simple anticipation of making *marmellata* next year from the grapes of our new arbor, the idea of walking arm in arm with Giampiero and Susanna, Laura and Domenico, and the delight of watching Chiara and the other children grow.

Just days before we were to return to Italy, I received an email from Susanna:

> *Sono sicura che il coraggio della scelta che avete fatto vi premierà. Questi passi così importanti insegnano ad essere meno attaccati alle cose ed avere sempre voglia di cominciare un nuovo capitolo. Mi sarebbe piaciuto avere avuto nella vita l'opportunità di fare altrettanto. Ti aspettiamo. Un forte abbraccio, Susi*

> I am sure that the courage of the choice that you made will win out. These rights of passage are so important and they teach us to be less attached to things and to always have the will to start a new chapter. I would have liked in my life to have the opportunity to do it as well. We're waiting for you back here. A big hug, Susi.

Speak Milk. Drink Wine.

EPILOGUE

Time is but the stream I go a-fishin in.
Henry David Thoreau

I'd like to romanticize the story a bit and tell you that we reconstructed a villa under the Lombardian sun. We didn't. But what we did do is redefine our values and reclaim our lives. We're back in *Varese* now. I'm sitting in my office on the second floor, watching it drizzle outside. The raindrops are causing the grapes to fall; we are told that this is a sign that we need to harvest them. Matthew has already started school at the *Scuola Europea* and met friends from five countries his first week there. He opted to be in the Italian section, with German as a second language. Alex was greeted by the teacher and buddies he got to know last year. Some of them knew, through conversations with Laura and Domenico, that he was coming back. Others were totally surprised.

I'm working in earnest to optimize a model of cross-cultural analysis for business and in the meantime, Fodors, a publisher of American travel guidebooks, asked me to write the Milan, Lombardia and Lakes section of their Italy book. Bruce has started working for Alda and Franco as an independent consultant and is in the process of pursuing other clients to perform similar work in addition to marketing his photography professionally.

While neither of us can definitively quantify the exact role Italy played in transforming our lives, we do know that the time we had together and the challenges we met as a team gave us a new framework in which to grow.

I do miss the creature comforts of our former life, but I now know that I do not need them. My happiness does not depend on them being there. Nor does it depend on being home – or even having a home. It does depend on the happiness of my children, on feeling safe, on feeling stimulated by my environment, and on satisfying relationships. It may ultimately be true, that in a strictly traditional sense, a cosmetic reaction to living in more than one culture may be that our children develop no real sense of home or cultural identity. But over time I've realized that we are all developing a sense of home and identity within ourselves, rather than one reliant on a specific town or country. This knowledge is very freeing to me.

We're not sure exactly what this next year will bring. I imagine it will be filled with new challenges and that we'll continue to miss our friends and family in the States. But it will also be filled with the sound of other languages, the company of the wonderful friends we have met, a *cappuccino* and a *brioche* sprinkled with magic sugar crystals at Adriano's bar in the morning, and a pizza with a robust *Sardinian cannonau* or delicate *pinot grigio* at night. We will continue to re-invent ourselves by getting more in touch with who we are without the context of our habitual and cultural surroundings.

"Trying on" this new family beyond the excitement of a one-year adventure into the world of normal, everyday life is very different from the first year. Year one was more of an experiment; year two we are focused on the practical side of our decisions and we are finding our way in the professional world one day at a time. Indeed the uniqueness of our status as Americans in Italy has been an advantage. It's useful for companies in the States to have a connection with bilingual professionals in Italy. I intend to use my knowledge of the differences in culture to help others, personally and professionally, thrive when crossing borders, both literally and figuratively. We got our perspective, and our second chance to have a life where work is play – and play is something you don't need to retire or move away from.

When my friends ask me what I do with my time when I'm not researching and writing about cross-cultural differences and expounding on some new theory of international communications that's going to "rock the business world," I tell them that my new hobby is wasting time. I love wasting time watching Buster lying in the morning sun in our garden, his eyes following the bees without moving any other aspect of his pudgy body. I love wasting time staring for the hundredth time at Bruce's photograph of the kids throwing a bouquet of yellow wildflowers into the steel blue sky of *Alto Adige*. I love wasting time at midnight listening to the over-eager conversations of young lovers in the alley below my window. And having been woken from a sound sleep, I love wasting time listening to my children breathe in the next room while they're sleeping. In. Out. In. Out. Such a lovely waste of time – all those seconds without any profound objective, other than to be.

Speak Milk. Drink Wine.

AFTERWORD

After living in Italy for three years, we returned to the United States and now live in San Diego. I am the CEO and founder of a company called Universal Consensus, a cross-cultural strategy firm that leverages the power of culture to optimize our clients' bottom line. We offer strategic solutions to businesses, universities and government agencies facing global challenges. Our work focuses on increasing operational efficiency, clarifying cross-cultural communication, optimizing cross-cultural sales, providing tools for global expansion, and eliminating lost opportunities across cultures. The analysis and assessment tools I developed had their roots in my experience as an attorney for multinational corporate clients, but they were significantly enhanced by living in another country, and have flourished over time as I travelled from continent to continent on various client projects.

I would like to tell you that Bruce and I lived happily ever after, but that wouldn't be true. Ultimately, like many couples, we grew in different directions. Though he did return to life as an executive, Bruce has promised his children that he will always make time for his passion, photography. Matthew and Alex, now teenagers and almost six feet tall, speak three languages and are attending school in San Diego. Their first love is Italy, but they seem to be adapting to the surfer lifestyle quite well. Please feel free to reach out to us at info@universalconsensus.com.

Speak Milk. Drink Wine.

ABOUT THE AUTHOR

Until her escapades in Italy, Denise Pirrotti Hummel, J.D., had been a nationally recognized litigator and mediator in the employment and international law arena. She was named one of the Top Twenty Young Attorneys in the United States by the American Bar Association in 1992. Her first position out of law school included a jurisdiction of Western Europe, Bermuda, Cuba and Iceland.

During her three-year sabbatical from American life, Denise cultivated a long-time passion that had lain dormant through much of her adult life. She started to write voraciously about her family's life in Italy and the contrast to American society, and about travel in general. Her prolific writing led to many stimulating opportunities, including the memorialization of her cross-cultural business model called the Business Model of Intercultural Analysis [BMIA] which is the core foundation of her consulting and training.

She has put her undergraduate degree from Columbia University, her studies at the University of Florence, her law degree from the Washington College of Law, and her cross-cultural experiences to good use. She is now the CEO and Founder of Universal Consensus, a company that helps clients leverage the power of culture to drive profitability, enhance communication and drive efficiency into the business process.

In addition to serving many multinational clients, Ms. Hummel has been accepted to The U.S. State Department Worldwide Speaker and Specialist Program, a program which consists of traveling and electronic events which allow American experts to engage with foreign audiences globally. She was chosen, in part, due to her BMIA model, where pain-points of an organization are evaluated through a series of six comprehension lenses and used to enhance communication and improve operating efficiency among international stakeholders.

Hummel's clients now span the business enterprise, government and university sectors worldwide. She has spoken at the Pentagon, Office of the Under Secretary of Defense for Personnel and Readiness, where she conducted a presentation called, "Beyond Multi-Lingual: The Future of DoD" to the Director, Associate Director and Deputy Director of Culture under the Obama Administration. She is also the developer of an executive certification program in Cross-Cultural Core Competence and Global Emergence Strategy for the University of San Diego. In addition to her responsibilities as Director of Universal Consensus, Hummel is the Dxecutive Director of a nonprofit organization called Global Peace Solutions where she supports and initiates projects which create cross-cultural bridges for youth worldwide.